THE CHAMBERLAIN CABINET

Stanley Baldwin, the Prime Minister, accompanied by Neville Chamberlain, Minister of Health, arriving at the House of Commons for the final sitting of Parliament, 1937

THE CHAMBERLAIN CABINET

How the Meetings in 10 Downing Street,
1937–9 led to the Second World War
told for the first time
from the Cabinet Papers

by

IAN COLVIN

LONDON
VICTOR GOLLANCZ LTD
1971

ISBN 0 575 00640 4

Printed in Great Britain by
The Camelot Press Ltd., London and Southampton

CONTENTS

LIST OF ILLUSTRATIONS

AUTHOR'S FOREWORD

A LIST OF WORKS and biographies consulted, other than the Cabinet, Committee of Imperial Defence and Foreign Office papers, is contained in the Bibliography. For brevity I have referred to official sources through the Registry filing systems of the Department concerned. Thus the papers of the Prime Minister's Office are in the Premier series; the Cabinet Minutes are referred to in the Cab. 23 sequence; and War Cabinet Minutes under Cab. 65. Cabinet Memoranda are listed Cab. 24 or with their original C.P. (Cabinet paper) number. The Foreign Policy Committee of the Cabinet is quoted from Cab. 27 references and cites memoranda and papers from the F.P. series. Various extracts from Lord Halifax and his correspondence are taken from the Foreign Office collection in the Public Record Office in the F.O. 800 series; I have also availed myself of many Foreign Office dockets of the Central Department, with the relevant comments of Foreign Office officials in their original and unpublished form, the Departmental Minutes, in the F.O. 371 series. Similarly, quotations from the Committee of Imperial Defence meetings and papers, and from Chiefs of Staff papers, are given their C.I.D. and C.O.S. references, though occasionally these also become Cabinet papers with a C.P. marking.

I have used all these Crown-copyright records in the Public Record Office by permission of the Controller of Her Majesty's Stationery Office. My thanks are due to Mr Jeffery Ede, Keeper of Public Records, and Mr Neville Williams, Deputy Keeper, for their guidance, as well as to Mr Reedham Monger, the Assistant Keeper of Public Records for his help in finding my way about the maze. I have to thank the Earl of Swinton for giving time and advice in answer to my inquiries about his differences with Neville Chamberlain. I have to thank Mr Harold Wilson for arranging access to the Cabinet Room. I am grateful to the Cabinet Office for arranging for me to see certain papers not yet on the public shelves under the Lord Chancellor's discretionary exclusion.

I am grateful to Mr Gordon Childs of the Cabinet Office for assistance in my research for a photograph of the Chamberlain

Cabinet. I am obliged to the Earl of Avon for permission to quote from his memoirs and to Lady Churchill for some references drawn from *The Gathering Storm*. I acknowledge the usefulness of Professor Keith Feiling's biography of Neville Chamberlain and am obliged to the Chamberlain Trustees and the Library of Birmingham University for permission to quote some opinions taken from the Chamberlain Diary or from letters to his sisters. Rupert Hart-Davis has kindly agreed to my drawing on the unpublished Duff Cooper Diary.

My thanks are due to Lord Hartwell for leave of occasional intellectual absence from the *Daily Telegraph*, while making this study of the latter thirties. I must thank Moira and Andrew Colvin for their assistance in reading the papers and correcting the manuscript, and Ruth Kenny for deciphering my copy hand.

I. C.

HOWBOURNE, 1970.

PREFACE

In 1967 a private member's bill was passed by the Westminster Parliament which reduced to thirty years the period after which the bulk of British official and State papers would be open to public scrutiny. The Public Records Act of 1957 had already established the responsibility of the Lord Chancellor for all State papers, most of which had until then been in the care of the Master of the Rolls. Thus for the first time what has been known as the Fifty Year Rule was substantially altered, and it has become possible for a generation whose lives and outlook were changed by Cabinet decisions to read and reflect on what were previously State secrets. The Act of 1967 has made available to people knowledge of the inner Cabinet decisions that were formative of their own lifetime and the future of their children.

Both Acts uphold in Article 5.1 of the 1957 legislation the discretion of the Lord Chancellor to maintain the Fifty Year Rule on exceptional matters and even to decide on longer periods of exclusion. More than one such instance has come to my notice in writing this book. Without this ultimate discretionary power, the Wilson Cabinet would probably not have supported the latter Bill. It is thus possible for the Lord Chancellor and his Cabinet Office advisers to exclude certain papers on security grounds from becoming available to the historian for a hundred years or indeed in perpetuity. Nevertheless, the 1967 Public Records Act has made a mass of papers, memoranda and minutes immediately available. It has shaken out a cornucopia of Secret and Most Secret documents that most of us would otherwise have never seen, together with the letters of Ambassadors and Ministers, the papers of the Committee of Imperial Defence, and the records of the Cabinet. Political learning and the writing of history will undoubtedly benefit greatly, in that those whose work or experience associated them intimately with a period can now study it in full depth with the advantage that later historians cannot share, that of human memory.

The year 1969, in which the most significant collection of papers began to become available in the London Public Record Office, gives us a perspective of the equivalent thirties when a firmly established national government, that of Mr Neville Chamberlain, had to use every endeavour between 1937 and 1939 to keep the peace in Europe and elsewhere in the world, and to prepare the United Kingdom and Commonwealth against the contingency of war on three fronts. No similar Cabinet records exist for the First World War, or for the period of tension that preceded it, for the strange reason that until 1916 there was no Cabinet Office and no Secretariat. The records of 1937 to 1939 are therefore unique, in that they enable us to observe a British Cabinet in action and inaction during crises and immediately before a world war. This book thus becomes rather more than a work of research on Mr Chamberlain and his Ministers. It is also an examination of the Cabinet in the context of world history.

One of the last survivors of the Chamberlain Cabinet of 1937–9 to write his memoirs was the Earl of Avon, who as Anthony Eden resigned from it in 1938. Even he was not able to relate fully what went on in Cabinet, since he was writing before the 1967 Public Records Act was passed. When he wrote *Facing the Dictators*, the Fifty Year Rule still existed, and it prevailed strongly and perhaps conveniently in the years when elder Ministers were producing their autobiographies about the Munich period. Cabinet officials were able to rule what might and might not be published. Sir Samuel Hoare (Lord Templewood), Viscount Simon, the Earl of Halifax, the Earl of Swinton and others avoided breaking the established convention that matters in the Cabinet, particularly disagreements, should not be discussed in newspaper articles or memoirs. Their memoirs tend, therefore, to be thin in content in so far as they refer to affairs of State. Some subsequent biographers were also unable to exploit fully the mass of papers suddenly released to researchers after 1968.

An exception to this tendency to be abstract or trivial in writing of their political careers was Alfred Duff Cooper, Viscount Norwich, who left in his unpublished diary a full account of one critical Cabinet meeting in 1938, which I was able to quote in part in a previous work, *Vansittart in Office*. But the Duff Cooper Diary was also subject to the then existing Fifty Year Rule, and in his autobiography *Old Men Forget* he was restrained by the same powerful convention of reticence that has been observed by others before and since. Sir Winston Churchill, who like Duff Cooper had a literary flair and a sense of history, was under similar constraint. Summaries or paraphrases only were permitted by the Cabinet Office to appear in his six volumes of *The Second World War*. In the period of which I write, he was outside the Cabinet, a mistrusted backbencher. On the other side of the House of Commons, the same reticence was observed. In a later period of modern history, when I was asked by Lord Beaverbrook to sound out Mr Herbert Morrison about a post-war Cabinet disagreement, I remember how sharply came the retort—"I am not going to talk about what went on in the Cabinet."

The history of the pre-war period has thus remained incomplete until now (despite the partial probing of the Nuremberg International Tribunal), with 1938, the year of Munich, in public memory as the year of decision. As the papers now available are studied, 1937 emerges more and more as the important year, and the true character of the British policy of appeasement becomes apparent.

The pattern upon which the Documents on British Foreign Policy[1] were edited and issued may have strengthened the impression of sudden and unexpected crisis in 1938, as the Third Series begins with the invasion of Austria on March 11th 1938. The year 1937, together with the first two critical months of 1938, remained severed from the period of which they formed a part and were relegated to another Series. The 1938 Foreign Office Documents were published in 1949. The 1937 Documents were in 1970 not yet on the publishers' horizon. The volumes and files from which they will be drawn were actually moved to the Public Record Office as a result of the 1967 Act before they could be perused and edited by the Foreign Office. They thus provide original material for research. When I have discussed the disadvantages of this historical grouping with the Foreign Office historians, they have represented that no year and no month is an ideal starting point for any Series. I, however, have no choice under the title of this book but to commence it in May 1937, though, with the latitude that a complete view of the documents gives, I have probed back towards the early months

[1] Documents on British Foreign Policy, Third Series 1938–9, edited by E. L. Woodward and Rohan Butler.

of 1937 for their special interest in containing both the Cabinet review of international affairs for the year and the prelude discussions to the defence estimates, those estimates that were to come too late to save Europe from war.

An explanation is due about the Cabinet Minutes that form the vertebrae of this study. These were the responsibility of Colonel Sir Maurice Hankey, a seconded Royal Marine Officer whose long service to the Cabinet and the Committee of Imperial Defence went back to 1914. The minutes were presented in draft form to the Prime Minister's office and customarily approved by him before being committed to the Cabinet Office files. They are not great prose, being the painstaking record of the conversation of men not given to parliamentary language, much less to oratory. Sometimes a date is amiss. Often a passage of heated debate is tactfully summed up: "After some discussion". A name—usually a foreign name—is spelled wrongly. The homeric Secretary to the Cabinet nods occasionally, as when passing the minutes of March 1938, when he recorded that a memorandum was sent to "the French Ambassador, M. Cambon". Monsieur Paul Cambon was French Ambassador to the Court of St James in 1914; in 1938 the French Ambassador was M. Charles Corbin. The minutes are thus not infallible, though they are "best evidence" of what went on.

It is impossible not to admire the scope of subjects with which the Cabinet dealt, while regretting sometimes that a Rembrandt was not present to depict the Anatomy Lesson. Even in the latter months of the Baldwin Administration, which are supposed to have been marked by inertia, the range of these Wednesday meetings was astonishing. In the early months of 1937 the Cabinet dealt with Commonwealth responsibilities regularly as they came up for review through the machinery of Downing Street. Although the most serious and disagreeable topic of defence was often postponed or adjourned, a good deal of smaller home business and some fairly remote foreign questions filled the agenda. We note Cabinet concern with the lot of 30,000 Assyrian Christians in Iraq, with ideas for an amalgamation of Southern Rhodesia, Nyasaland and Northern Rhodesia, though it is recorded that in any such amalgamation "Britain must reserve its solicitude for the natives of those territories".

The Cabinet was solicitous also to prevent the users of methylated spirits in Scotland from obtaining it without signature. It had before it the recommendations of the Air Raid Precautions Department. It was concerned with the Spanish Civil War, with Japan's refusal to limit the calibre of heavy naval guns, with the refusal of the Congress Party in India to accept the responsibilities of office for six States in which it had a working legislative majority. The Cabinet received a secret report from the High Commissioner for Palestine on the situation there, and it had to hear some acrimonious words from the Secretary of State for War, Mr Duff Cooper, about the inability of the Treasury to finance the equipment for five Territorial divisions in support of the Regular Army. As Chancellor of the Exchequer, Mr Chamberlain was concerned with most of these problems.

It is clear that this study of the Chamberlain Cabinet, supported as it is by the general release of Cabinet, Foreign Office and Committee of Imperial Defence documents, could not include them all. Nor need there be quotations from those documents relevant to foreign policy that may have already appeared elsewhere, as in the Foreign Office Series of Documents on British Foreign Policy or in private papers. The purpose is rather to show with what information on the Cabinet table, and with what arguments, minds were made up in 10 Downing Street; what were the long-term considerations; and what was improvised or added under the pressure of events. The reader should be aware that an immense amount of Cabinet work is not covered by this study. Home affairs and overseas matters unrelated to the central problem of diplomacy are not dealt with, nor are trade, commerce, supply or the continuous review of current legislation to be supported or opposed in the House of Commons. I am studying the least workable aspect of Cabinet governments, i.e. foreign affairs, which in the nature of things are, if at all, under never more than the partial control of any government, either in Britain or anywhere else.

In my previous book, *Vansittart in Office*, I illustrated this intractability from Vansittart's Foreign Office reports, written with prescience and pessimism for the Ministers who kept "Van" waiting outside the Cabinet door. Now that door is open and their table-talk may be compared with the advice they were given by him.

This book may be thought by some to be a criticism of the system of Cabinet government or to be an exposure of defects in its many workings. That was not my intention, though, in the course of scrutiny, human failings or faults in the machinery did come to light.

There is, of course, the Churchillian description from the debate in the House of Commons on March 24th 1938, of a system of government ill adapted "to the present fierce, swift movements of events. Twenty-two gentlemen of blameless party character sitting round an overcrowded table, each having a voice. Is that a system which can reach decisions from week to week and cope with the problems descending upon us?"

No doubt enough is already known to convict Mr Chamberlain in a general way of having afforded opportunities to both the Dictators at a time when it was still possible to deter or divide them. Why and how his government made these mistakes, and how this serious, upright Englishman came to deserve such an unenviable niche in history, is something that we come closer to understanding when we have read through the Cabinet papers of the time.

Britain and her Empire were never the same again after the Chamberlain Administration. The decisions taken then were those of the leading world power, possessed of some freedom of choice and leadership. In subsequent Cabinet papers that the Thirty Year Rule will bring to the Public Record Office, we will not easily find other such momentous decisions affecting so deeply the rest of the world. It was the end of the grand epoch, and to understand it fully we must first study the large powers of the British Cabinet and the way in which its business was managed.

THE CHAMBERLAIN CABINET

CHAPTER I

The Cabinet Room

Beyond the fanlight and lion-headed door-knocker of Number 10 Downing Street, a long corridor leads through glass swing doors and then a red baize door into the Cabinet Room. This corridor runs through the breadth of what were once two separate houses; the Cabinet Room is in that part first inhabited by an illegitimate daughter of Charles II, and later by Count Bothmar, the Hanoverian representative at the Court of Queen Anne. When Bothmar died in 1732, the house was offered by George II to his principal minister, Sir Robert Walpole, who declined it as a gift, but accepted it as the future official residence of the First Lord of the Treasury. Since that office was almost invariably joined to that of the Prime Ministers of Great Britain, Number 10 became theirs, though in the first two centuries of its official existence some Prime Ministers preferred to live in their London houses, vacating Number 10 to the Chancellor of the Exchequer. None has done so since the Marquess of Salisbury was Prime Minister.

When Stanley Baldwin moved out in May 1937, Neville Chamberlain was living next door at 11 Downing Street, the official residence of the Chancellor of the Exchequer, having let his London House in Eaton Square to the German Ambassador, Herr von Ribbentrop. The Chamberlains did not at once move in, as Mrs Chamberlain had decided ideas about the lay-out of Number 10. She found it unsettling to have the main bedrooms on the first floor, too close to the State rooms and offices, so a new staircase was built enabling them to be moved to the second floor, while the first floor became offices, reception rooms and a private study for the Prime Minister. She planned with Sir Philip Sassoon, Minister of Works, to redecorate and re-furnish the three main drawing rooms, recarpeting and hanging new curtains, obtaining the loan of pictures from the National Gallery cellars, and discovering others about the house. In these reception rooms she entertained three times weekly during the Parliamentary sessions. The 1937 transformation

took four months and cost £25,000, including a modernisation of the basement kitchen. These were the preparations of
people who meant to stay. Chamberlain was vigorous and confident. As Chancellor of the Exchequer and previously Minister
of Health, he had become thoroughly familiar with the Cabinet
and its proceedings. None of his colleagues imagined that any
man among them had a superior claim to be the next Prime
Minister.

The Cabinet Room, long, narrow and lofty with a table at
least twenty-five feet in length, surrounded with sabre-legged
and leather-upholstered chairs, had been extended in 1781 with
the aid of two Corinthian supporting pillars. In 1937 it contained, in every recess, tall mahogany bookcases, some of which
have since been removed. Blotters of worn black leather, with
the gilt imprint of the First Lord of the Treasury lay in front of
every Ministerial chair. Each place had a water carafe and
tumblers. The table was traditionally decorated with Georgian
and Queen Anne candlesticks, one of which had been the
personal property of four Prime Ministers before being be-
queathed to the Cabinet Room. A portrait of Sir Robert
Walpole by Van Loo hung over the marble fireplace, in front of
which the Prime Minister's armchair and inkstand marked the
centre of the table. The addition of telephones must at some
time have been the subject of perturbed discussion between
Ministers, but they were already there in the day of Neville
Chamberlain and have been added to since with various
security devices. The tall shuttered windows of the Cabinet
Room look out over the low garden wall of Number 10,
through plane trees on to Horse Guards Parade and St James's
Park.

The Cabinet, which evolved out of the Privy Council of
Queen Elizabeth I, is the executive body directing British
policy. Government Departments can thereafter carry it out.
The Cabinet is responsible to Parliament, but because Parliament is essentially the place for discussing public affairs, some
realms of statecraft remain outside its scope. Sir Ivor Jennings
has described the Cabinet as a "Board of directors for Great
Britain and all those parts of the Commonwealth that do not
possess self-government". Its decisions may be revealed to
Parliament and to the press, but need not be, if there are reasons

for withholding them. We know that its papers and proceedings during the period of their virility are strictly private. Consequently, as it receives State and diplomatic papers and may be presumed to have the fullest knowledge, it is a considerable instrument of power. "Whether legislation is required to carry out an administrative policy is a technical question," says Jennings. "The Cabinet has to decide on the policy." Very often that policy needs to be justified to Parliament in only general terms and is carried forward in detail by Government Departments and foreign missions. The Government may be overtaken by electoral vengeance now and then and may be harassed by Parliamentary questions. Betwixt these interruptions it may pursue its courses in secret.

The Cabinet has probably never been a forum of experts, though in the first Chamberlain Administration beside the Foreign Secretary sat two previous Foreign Secretaries.[1] It resembles more a jury panel of men with experience and sagacity, prejudices and aversions as well as an ability to measure the public interest and public opinion. It is noticeable that rarely were the senior civil servants, the real experts, invited into the Cabinet. Sir Robert Vansittart, the powerful Permanent Under-Secretary of State for Foreign Affairs, who had between 1931 and 1935 used his influence with Ramsay MacDonald and Baldwin to make and unmake more than one Foreign Secretary, was seldom invited to be present. Each Minister was briefed by his Departmental Chief before a meeting on what concerned him in it. Only Sir Maurice Hankey, as Secretary to the Cabinet, and after him Mr E. E. Bridges, were permanent figures. On the other hand, in the pyramidal structure of committees that served and informed the Cabinet, the civil servants and senior officers of the Services took their regular places. This pyramid may be thus described in the time of the Chamberlain Administration (page 20 overleaf).

Committees or sub-committees might be added or subtracted, as the need arose. Mr Chamberlain dropped the Political Committee and let lapse the General Purposes Committee as well as the Committee on Political and Economic Relations with Japan. The Foreign Policy Committee was of recent creation, starting its life after the cold shock of Hitler's march into the

[1] Sir John Simon, Sir Samuel Hoare

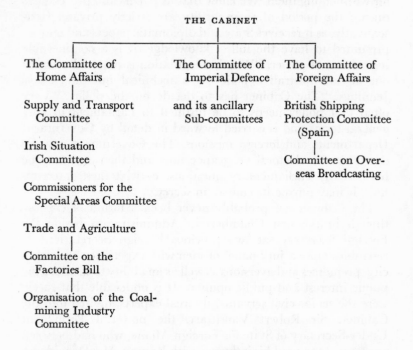

THE CABINET

The Committee of Home Affairs	The Committee of Imperial Defence	The Committee of Foreign Affairs
Supply and Transport Committee	and its ancillary Sub-committees	British Shipping Protection Committee (Spain)
Irish Situation Committee		Committee on Overseas Broadcasting
Commissioners for the Special Areas Committee		
Trade and Agriculture		
Committee on the Factories Bill		
Organisation of the Coalmining Industry Committee		

Rhineland in 1936. It was usually composed of the Prime Minister, the Foreign Secretary, the Lord President of the Council, the three Services Ministers, the Minister for Co-ordination of Defence, the Ministers for the Colonies and Dominions, the Lord Chancellor, the President of the Board of Trade and occasionally the Home Secretary. Ministers were invited or not, depending on the weight of advice or opinion that the Prime Minister required at the moment.

With this committee our narrative is closely concerned. It began its life with regular meetings which lapsed after July 1937, and received fresh impetus in January 1938 as the European nations began to move towards a crisis.

The Committee of Imperial Defence, of which the Prime Minister has since 1936 always been Chairman, was in some fields more powerful and more closely organised than the Cabinet itself. Prior to the 1916 reorganisation into a Cabinet Secretariat, the secretarial services of the Cabinet were actually

provided by the Committee of Imperial Defence. The need for
exact minuting and recording in defence matters had been
obvious for many years. The C.I.D. in its reorganisation of 1936
departed from the constituting Treasury minute of 1904 and
established itself as the Prime Minister, the Lord President of
the Council, the Chancellor of the Exchequer, the Secretaries of
State for Foreign Affairs, Home Affairs, the Dominions, the
Colonies, India, War and Air, the First Lord of the Admiralty,
the Parliamentary Under-Secretary of State for Foreign
Affairs, the three Chiefs of Staff and the Permanent Secretary to
the Treasury. To this body was added the new post of Minister
for Co-ordination of Defence.

The array of sub-committees which acted as watchdogs,
reporters, ears and eyes and statisticians to the C.I.D. were some
twenty-five in number. The Defence Plans Committee and the
Defence Policy and Requirements Committee may be mentioned as among the most important of these. The Chiefs of
Staff Committee and the Joint Intelligence Committee may be
regarded as something apart and primarily responsible to the
Minister for Co-ordination of Defence. The Defence Plans
Committee consisted of leading members of the Cabinet, giving
political guidance to the Defence Policy and Requirements
Committee, which, late in 1937, Sir Maurice Hankey proposed
should be merged into one committee under the supervision of
the Committee of Imperial Defence. This met on Thursdays,
the day after the regular weekly Cabinet meeting.

"There is time, but not too much time," Sir Robert Vansittart had warned in 1934 as he watched the quickening pace of
German rearmament. Members of the Cabinet were reminded
of the time by two mantelpiece clocks in the Cabinet Room and
a grandfather clock by William Whichcote outside the red
baize door. There in the ante-room, brass-framed labels
indicated where each Minister might hang his hat. There, like
the school groups in a Common-room, hang the photographs of
bygone Cabinets. Curiously, the Chamberlain Administration
of 1937–9 is nowhere to be found among them, though Baldwin's is there, as well as the first (Chamberlain) War Cabinet of
1939, and other Cabinets before and after, which have played a
less significant role in the history of England. Somehow the
twenty-one men who took office with Chamberlain on May 28th

1937 were never photographed together for posterity in Whitehall, just as the year 1937 was relegated by the Foreign Office
historians to the end of another era, though it was formative of
all those that followed, and, as we look deeper into the documents of the Cabinet, surely the year of decision.

CHAPTER II

The Year 1937

THE YEAR 1937 was marked by no calamitous event. Hitler had marched his army into the Rhineland in 1936, and the outbreak of the Spanish Civil War lay also in 1936. The abdication crisis over King Edward VIII and Mrs Simpson, a subject still excluded from the Public Record Office, lay also in the near past. In 1937 the Spanish Civil War was the field chosen for increasing attacks in Parliament on the Baldwin Government. Mr Attlee and the Labour Opposition paid less attention to the menacing visage of Japan in the Far East and the stealthy growth of German armaments. It seemed that they thought the immediate issue to be whether Germany and Italy should succeed in supplanting Great Britain as the paramount influence in the Iberian peninsula. Some respite might appear to have been won in the arms race by the Anglo-German naval agreement of 1936, and Mr Baldwin, though disturbed by evidence that German air strength had already overtaken that of the Royal Air Force, may have felt that he was handing over to Mr Neville Chamberlain a situation by no means impossible to manage. Shortly before the Coronation of King George VI on April 11th, he announced his decision to retire from the Premiership. He was on record in a January debate in the House of Commons as pledging air parity with Germany, and the public believed that the military strength of Britain would not be allowed to fall short of the strategic requirement. There had indeed been an energetic attempt at the start of the year to assign a bigger future role to the British Army. The proposal had been embodied in a (Most Secret) Chiefs of Staff report to the Cabinet on January 28th. This envisaged Britain being able to land four divisions of the Regular Army on the Continent within two weeks of Zero day, and a follow-up force of eight Territorial divisions within four months. This was an effort in the right direction, but, like many such, including the announcement by the Chancellor of the Exchequer that Britain would have to be prepared to spend £1,500,000,000 on armaments in the next five years, the endeavour was on paper only. It contained a serious warning against delay.

THIS DOCUMENT IS THE PROPERTY OF HIS BRITANNIC MAJESTY'S
GOVERNMENT

MOST SECRET

APPENDIX I

TO BE KEPT UNDER LOCK AND KEY

It is requested that special care may be taken to ensure the secrecy of this document.

ROLE OF THE BRITISH ARMY.

Summary of Conclusions by the Chiefs of Staff Sub-Committee.
38. Our conclusions may be summed up as follows:—

(i) We re-endorse the definition of the role of the British Army which was included in the Statement of Defence issued in March 1936, and we emphasise that the essential functions stated therein cannot be performed without an Army.

(ii) The strength of the Army at home is in the main dictated by our normal overseas requirements in peace. These forces at home constitute the only immediately available Imperial Reserve and are so organised that a maximum striking force of four Divisions and one Mobile Division may be available for despatch overseas if required.

(iii) The Units of the Regular Army are interchangeable and interdependent. All should, therefore, be equipped to the same scale. The mandate for the modernisation of the Regular Army must therefore extend to every Unit and not only to those who happen at any given moment to constitute the striking force referred to in (ii) above.

(iv) We are agreed that it is doubtful whether the German Army could be stopped by the sole agency of any air forces which the French and ourselves could ever oppose to it and that the Allies must therefore be capable of putting considerable land forces into the field for this purpose.

(v) We assume that any idea of leaving to our Continental Allies the exclusive burden of providing these land forces, and thereby of limiting our contribution to air forces however greatly expanded, is out of the question for political reasons.

(vi) It is therefore impossible to discount altogether the contingency of having to send military forces to the Continent at some stage of the war and perhaps at its very outset.

After some technical observations the report continued:

(xii) Modern developments enable our potential enemies to develop a maximum scale of attack immediately on the outbreak of war. Consequently, the earlier all our forces can be brought into action, the better.

(xiii) Since it might be necessary (vide (vi)) to despatch land forces overseas at the earliest possible date after the outbreak of war, the preparedness of our land forces should be as far advanced as is possible without prejudicing the naval and air programmes of re-equipment.

(xiv) So far as the Territorial Army is concerned, it should be our ultimate aim to equip it to a scale which would enable it to be ready four months after the outbreak of war.

(xv) It is impossible to equip the Territorial Army on any considerable scale in a short time, but if the principle of its modernisation is accepted, the present basis of production of supply can be broadened. Meanwhile, such modern equipment as can be made available for it should be spread evenly throughout the Territorial Army.

(xvi) Plans are being prepared which would, if the situation at home permitted, enable us to land on the Continent the whole of our Regular Field Force by Z + 15 days. We consider that the movement of this force would not be prevented by enemy action.

(xvii) It is impossible to equate land and air forces. Their roles are not exclusive but complementary.

(xviii) In view of the importance of the time factor we wish to emphasise the serious effect that the delay in reaching a decision on the role of the British Army is causing. This delay gives us the gravest concern.

> (Signed) ERNLE CHATFIELD
> C. L. ELLINGTON
> C. J. DEVERELL.

1 Whitehall Gardens, S.W.1.
January 28, 1937.

This memorandum came before the Cabinet for consideration on February 3rd 1937. Behind the concern of the Chiefs of Staff lay the facts stated in a memorandum from Engineer Vice-Admiral Sir Harold Brown, Director General of Munitions Production at the War Office, which Mr Duff Cooper had circulated to the Cabinet in the first week of January 1937.[1]

[1] C.P. 2 (37)

Sir Harold Brown had written: "I understand that the general question of the role of the Army and its equipment has been referred back to the Chiefs of Staff for further consideration, and that it cannot come forward again to the Cabinet until the middle of January. I gather also that the Committee of Imperial Defence have not approved our proposals relating to further equipment for Air Defence of Great Britain, the A.A. defence of Ports Abroad and the new A.A. guns for the Field Force.

"I can, of course, appreciate the magnitude of the issues involved and the difficulties of arriving at definite conclusions, but I must point out the danger in delay from the point of view of material.

"If we are to get within the next two years any substantial quantity of major equipment other than that already approved, e.g. guns and mountings, it is essential to take the necessary steps to provide at once for their production. Even now it is difficult to see how this can be done with any reasonable economy, and in a few months' time under normal conditions and with the usual limitations, it will probably be impossible.

"I am given to understand that the present international situation is one that causes grave anxiety, and I should be failing in my duty if I did not draw attention to the position before it is too late. I have, as you know, put forward repeated requests to have the ultimate requirements settled, pointing out the necessity for a definite long-term production programme. I have made provisional arrangements for meeting such forward requirements as I have been able to ascertain, but, so far, none of these forward requirements has received the necessary approval, and I cannot proceed with schemes which are now becoming very urgent without such approval as will satisfy the Treasury."

Sir Robert Vansittart, Permanent Under-Secretary for Foreign Affairs, seized upon this printed circular and minuted on January 8th, to Mr Eden, this vehement appeal:

"I beg you to take this into immediate and most serious consideration. It cannot, I feel sure, be even yet fully realized what sort of world we are living in. I share to the full Sir Harold Brown's very grave apprehensions, which have already been echoed by the Principal Supply Officers and to me personally by

the Chief of the Imperial General Staff. We are all most pro-
foundly depressed at the leisurely way in which these problems
are being faced. The loss of time does not seem to be fully
appreciated, whereas every week counts and counts most
urgently.

"The C.I.G.S. informs me that all fruitful action is superseded during this controversy. In the Defence Requirements
Committee Report of March 1934, I wrote: 'There is time, but
not too much time.' I would not write that three years later. All
the expert advisers to H.M.G. are really depressed that we
should be in this position after so many warnings as to the
urgency of time; for we have all repeated those warnings, and
this last one from Sir Harold Brown is 'a cry from the heart'—
and head."

Sir Robert suspected that the Treasury was delaying for the
sake of delay, in hope of a change of attitude in Germany or an
alteration in the constellation of powers. "I do not feel that this
particular controversy need have been endured," he pursued.
"For it is obviously impossible to limit our military effort in
advance without receding into impotent isolation. Were we
really going to do anything so foolish, *we should be wasting our
time here at the Foreign Office in endeavouring to arrest a landslide in
favour of the dictators. The controversy is in fact the negation of your
policy.*

"I beg of you most earnestly to end this fruitlessness by a
decisive intervention at the next Cabinet. . . ."

Anthony Eden was sometimes perplexed at the length and
vehemence of his Departmental Chief's minutes. In *Facing the
Dictators* he described "Van" as "more like a Secretary of State
than a permanent official". (On the distaff side of the Vansit-
tarts there was Palmerston blood, and Sir Robert had a powerful political mind.)

"I am as anxious as Sir R. Vansittart to see this controversy
ended," Eden minuted on January 11th. "I have already said
something behind the scenes to help matters. The Cabinet on
Wednesday may be made by me into another occasion for an
effort by me."

"The Cabinet on Wednesday" to which Eden referred was
that of January 13th 1937. The record tells us that "as this was
the first meeting of the Cabinet in the New Year, the Secretary

of State for Foreign Affairs made a brief statement on the international situation. This, he said, was likely to be a critical year in foreign affairs. Many reports reaching the Foreign Office indicated that Germany was unable to face the prospect of another winter in conditions similar to those existing there today. It looked therefore as if this year would determine Germany in following a policy alternatively of co-operation or foreign adventure. There were two schools of thought in Germany. The first and more cautious school including the Army, the Foreign Office and, among others, Dr Schacht. The second and more aggressive school of thought was the Nazi Party. Our object must be to try and restrain the latter."

This restraint, Mr Eden thought, could best be achieved "by our present policy of being firm but always ready to talk". He said that it would assist the Foreign Office in its difficult task if British determination to press forward the armaments policy was made evident, as this would have a steadying effect. It might tell in their favour if the Minister for Co-ordination of Defence were able to make an encouraging statement on the progress of defence programmes before Herr Hitler made his own policy statement to the Reichstag on January 30th.

Lord Halifax, then Lord Privy Seal, suggested other reasons for the difficulties of the European situation. He saw them as the result of the different nature of contacts between British and French and between Britain and Germany. With France they were good, but with Germany tenuous. "Probably the Foreign Secretary could write privately to Monsieur Delbos if he wished; but he certainly could not do so to the German Foreign Secretary without arousing all kinds of difficulties. . . ."

Eden replied that in fact he did not correspond with M. Delbos and that the official contacts with Germany were the same as those with France. However, "he agreed with the Lord Privy Seal's desire to improve contacts with Germany".

Mr Chamberlain pointed out that the differing systems of government in France and Germany made the closest contacts with the latter more difficult. "There were really only two people in Germany who counted for much, namely Herr Hitler and General Goering."

Lord Swinton, Secretary of State for Air, then gave the Cabinet some information on the relative performance of

German, Russian and Italian military aircraft in the Spanish Civil War, after which "some discussion . . . took place as to the desires of the Lord Privy Seal for improving contacts with Germany". . . . Mr Eden "told the Cabinet that he was making as much use as possible of the German Ambassador, Herr von Ribbentrop", who would shortly return from Berlin and inform him of the position there. Mr Baldwin summed up by saying that he shared the desire expressed by several of his colleagues for improving relations with Germany. He knew that this was ever present in the mind of Mr Eden, but the difficulties were very real. The Cabinet accepted a proposal that it "might be given information at rather shorter intervals as to progress with the armaments programme". "When international affairs were discussed on January 13th 1937," wrote Lord Avon, "some of my colleagues appeared to imagine that our difficulties with the Nazi Government sprang from minor causes."[1] He thought that the elder men of the Cabinet were, even in 1937, not convinced of the need to rearm.

In Cabinet, Eden could not voice the Vansittart warnings quite as if they were his own. He felt awkward at the amused looks of senior Cabinet Ministers, who suspected Van's ascendancy over the youthful Foreign Secretary and disliked his pessimistic outlook. Grounds for pessimism were plentiful. On a Chiefs of Staff Sub-Committee Memorandum of February 9th 1937, comparing the probable military strength of Great Britain with that of "certain other nations in May 1937",[2] Vansittart commented to Eden: "I have little to say except that this is a dreadful record of all-round improvidence. Most staggering of all is that the Air Ministry can only show 48 long range bombers against 800 German."

Thus as the year 1937 commenced we see a laudable attempt to form a British Army which could play a part on the Continent, but Treasury strictures and delays in approval wasting the passing weeks. On February 19th Mr Chamberlain said in a public speech that £1,500,000,000 might not be enough to complete the rearmament of Britain. The Chancellor appeared brisk and businesslike compared with the lethargic Baldwin. How would he be in the office of Prime Minister?

To understand the Chamberlain policy, we must first read an

[1] The Earl of Avon, *Facing the Dictators*   [2] C.P. 2 (37)

extract from his diary on the subject of the British Army and rearmament. As far back as October 1936 the Chancellor of the Exchequer had recorded:

> I must really have some decision as to the future function of the Regular and Territorial Armies. . . . In my view apart from any other consideration we had not the man-power to produce the necessary munitions for ourselves and perhaps, if the USA stood out, for our Allies, to man the enlarged Navy, the new Air Force and a million-men Army. We should aim at an Army of four divisions plus one mobile division, and the necessary drafts to maintain its strength, and no more for overseas work. Territorials should be left for A.A. defence.

A little later in 1936 he had written in a letter that "if we were now to follow Winston's advice and sacrifice our commerce to the manufacture of arms, we should inflict a certain injury on our trade from which it would take generations to recover, and we should cripple the revenue".[1] Mr Chamberlain affirmed these views again when still Chancellor of the Exchequer soon after Mr Baldwin had announced on April 11th his intention to resign the premiership. In a Cabinet meeting on April 28th 1937, Mr Duff Cooper, as Secretary of State for War, presented a memorandum in which he asked the Cabinet to confirm three decisions taken on February 3rd 1937. These were that:

(i) The Regular Army and the two A.A. Divisions of the Territorial Army must be provided with the most complete and efficient equipment.
(ii) The remainder of the Territorial Army must be trained in the use of the same weapons as the Regular Army.
(iii) For this purpose they must be given sufficient equipment for training purposes which would be spread evenly over the whole of the twelve (T.A.) Divisions.

Mr Duff Cooper contended that it would hardly be practicable to take away this training equipment at a time when recruits were pouring into the Territorials simply to equip a couple of Divisions in support of the Regular Army. As it appeared, the Army Council were still not permitted to do more than provide

[1] Keith Feiling, *The Life of Neville Chamberlain*

training equipment for the Territorials, he said, and that was not a policy on which the Cabinet could stand permanently. Consequently the Army Council had proposed that war equipment and reserves should be provided to enable a Territorial Army contingent of four Divisions to be sent out four months after the outbreak of war.

The Director General of Munitions Production had informed him that little more could be done in the next three years than to equip the Regular Army and to meet the Training Requirements of the Territorial Army. He asked for this programme to be accelerated, as it was difficult to give the Territorial Army confidence on a basis of equipment for training only.

Sir Thomas Inskip, Minister for the Co-ordination of Defence, spoke briefly, and Mr Chamberlain then proceeded to give the Cabinet a foretaste of the views that he would shortly maintain as Prime Minister.

"The present proposal, Mr Chamberlain said, really went back to much earlier proposals. It began by doubling the original decision in favour of two divisions, substituting four divisions and then went on to suggest a further eight divisions. . . . He recalled that for some time he had urged that the manpower problem was getting continually more important and he was very doubtful as to whether the War Office were right in assuming that the manpower for their proposals would be available. . . . He questioned whether history would support Mr Duff Cooper's assumption that 'it is axiomatic that a formation cannot take the field until it is provided with its full scale of war equipment.'

"The War Office proposal began with the proposition that we should have a very small but perfectly equipped Regular Army which would be of real value even among the large armies of the Continent. Then it argued that it is axiomatic that equipment and armament must be the same for the Territorial Army, and that four Territorial Divisions must be kept fully equipped on the same scale as the Regulars. Eventually this was doubled again. He recalled that a report of the Defence Requirements Committee in 1934 had contemplated an expenditure of £146,000,000 for the Army. The Cabinet, however, had decided to postpone the Territorial Army part of the expenditure and had cut the total to £100,000,000. In July 1936, this

figure had been raised and in December 1936 it had reached
£177,000,000. Now the figure for the Army (excluding the
proposed twelve Territorial Army Divisions) was more than
£204,000,000. The figure contemplated in 1935 had been
doubled. That was for the Army alone, but he thought it only
right to warn the Cabinet that an approach by the Admiralty
for a much larger Naval programme was foreshadowed. The
Royal Air Force had already had many increases and now Air
Raid Precautions were very persistent. Expenditure was also
likely to be asked for food storage or food production. Not only
were all these demands additional to the expenditure of
£1,500,000,000 foreseen in his five-year defence programme,
but they involved immediate additions to current expenditure.
He warned the Cabinet that we were approaching the time
when he would have to propose a fixed limit to which the
Services would have to conform. In these circumstances, he felt
that further time was necessary to examine these questions and
that they should be reviewed in the light of both the financial
position and the manpower position."

The Cabinet conclusion was that "the Chancellor of the
Exchequer should discuss with the Minister for Co-ordination
of Defence and the Secretary of State for War, what was the
extent of the Programme to which, in present circumstances, he
could agree".

The Baldwin Cabinet met for the last time in the late afternoon of Wednesday, May 26th 1937. The Ministers were
twenty in number, and included two who were to leave the
Cabinet with their chief. These were the former Prime Minister,
Ramsay MacDonald, Lord President of the Council, by then no
more than a vague and ornamental figure, and the shipping
magnate Walter Runciman, President of the Board of Trade.
The meeting was taken up with a variety of subjects, a coal
dispute in Nottingham, a London omnibus strike, arrangements
for the Coronation, of which the Home Secretary, Sir John
Simon complained that the Earl Marshal had in his seating
arrangements "scattered the Cabinet about in galleries and
corners", giving precedence of place to the Peerage. They fell to
discussing the salaries of Members of Parliament, which at
£400 per annum were considered inadequate and proposed an
increase to £600. At this stage in their discussion the Lord

President wandered out of the meeting, apparently unaware that this was the last Cabinet that he would ever attend.

As soon as the business of salaries was concluded, Mr Baldwin turned his attention to the change of leadership that was about to take place.

It was no secret, he said, that changes would be taking place in the Cabinet within a few days. He proposed after a short discussion of the method of securing resignations on these occasions that the prospective Prime Minister, the present Chancellor of the Exchequer, "should be authorised to assume that all members of the Cabinet present placed their resignations at his disposal" when he was sent for by King George VI on Friday. Then his successor spoke.

Mr Neville Chamberlain, as the Cabinet minutes record, "thought it would be the wish of his colleagues that someone should say a few words on the present sad occasion when Mr Baldwin was presiding at the Cabinet for the last time. . . . Perhaps the time had not come to weigh up his position in history, but all knew how much the country owed to him in raising the whole standard of political life since he first came into office as Prime Minister." He referred to "the events of November 1936", the crisis over the marriage of King Edward VIII, and the characteristics shown by Mr Baldwin which earned him the respect and admiration of the country and the world. Mr Chamberlain spoke some eulogistic words of Mr Ramsay MacDonald, who was still and finally absent, and then thanked Mr Runciman for his political services in the Board of Trade.

Mr Baldwin replied that "he had long looked forward to being rid of his heavy responsibilities, but now that the moment had come he found it hard to part from his colleagues. . . . He knew it was right that a new leader of the Government should occupy his post for at least two years before a General Election. . . . They had had their ups and downs, and that was true of himself also."

His final words might be interpreted as reflecting some reluctance to accept that a Prime Minister who had himself just unthroned a monarch ought not himself to remain in office.

"He felt it was rather hard that he himself was going out of office in fairly good health, though admittedly tired" . . . but

B

"he was not in future going to interfere in any way with the Government", and would make no political speeches in the remainder of 1937. "He felt, however, that he still had some good work in him and he hoped that his services to the State would not entirely cease."

So in a very English way ended the Cabinet career of Stanley Baldwin. Neville Chamberlain was left with the resignations of all his colleagues in his hands, the undisputed master of the field.

CHAPTER III

Seeking Appeasement

THE RESHUFFLE WAS SO promptly done that, a week after the last Baldwin Cabinet, Mr Chamberlain had kissed the hand of the Sovereign and seated himself in the Cabinet Room in the armchair in front of the mantelpiece. Viscount Halifax had moved from the Privy Seal to be Lord President of the Council in place of Ramsay MacDonald, who sent them a regretful note. This was read out, with his apologies that he had not remained present for the "doxology" of the previous week. Sir Thomas Inskip remained Minister for the Co-ordination of Defence. Sir John Simon moved from the Home Office to the Treasury. Sir Samuel Hoare moved from the Admiralty to the Home Office, and this enabled Mr Chamberlain to shift the reluctant Mr Duff Cooper, who was becoming troublesome with his demands for the Army and the Territorial Army and place him as First Lord of the Admiralty in calmer waters. Into his place at the War Office he moved Leslie Hore-Belisha. As Minister of Transport Mr Hore-Belisha had recently created a sensation by saying that motorists might at some time no longer be able to leave their cars just where they pleased on the street kerbs; and his orange-bulbed crossing beacons had earned for him the reputation of a man of drive. His sort of brilliance and social background did not commend this young Liberal-National to the military caste at the War Office, but soon he commended himself to Mr Chamberlain by putting Army expansion second to Army reforms and so avoiding conflict with the Treasury. Viscount Swinton remained Secretary of State for Air, and Mr William Ormsby-Gore and Mr Malcolm Mac-Donald, Secretaries of State for the Colonies and the Dominions respectively. Earl Stanhope moved to the Board of Education and Mr Oliver Stanley went to succeed Viscount Runciman in the Board of Trade. Earl De La Warr became Lord Privy Seal and the Marquess of Zetland remained Secretary of State for India and Burma. There were in all twenty-one Ministers of Cabinet rank with twenty junior Ministers and Under-

Secretaries not in the Cabinet. Five Ministers, Simon, De La Warr, Hore-Belisha, Burgin and Ernest Brown (Minister of Labour) were Liberal National[1] and Malcolm MacDonald the residual National Labour Minister. They met at 4 p.m. on June 2nd 1937, in the Prime Minister's room in the House of Commons for a first Cabinet meeting unmarked by any special event. Mr Eden had to report that a bombing incident off Spain, in which the German pocket battleship *Deutschland* had been damaged, had upset British plans to get foreign contingents withdrawn from the Spanish Civil War. There was a routine request from the British High Commissioner in Palestine and a report on penetration of the Near and Far East by German civil aviation. The salaries of Ministers of the Crown and a Rating and Valuation Bill were discussed, as well as the forthcoming conference of Commonwealth Prime Ministers to be held in London. This meeting brought no surprises or innovations. As for foreign policy, this had since April 30th 1936, soon after Hitler's march into the Rhineland, been handled in detail by the already described Foreign Policy Committee of the Cabinet, a compact group of six or nine Ministers. This had already met eleven times before Mr Chamberlain became Prime Minister and he had been present at its inception, feeling his way in foreign affairs.

The course of these meetings may be instructive, as it was in this committee that the policy of appeasement was pushed forward. Meeting with less formality or notice than the Cabinet it was a convenient place for the secret discussion of British diplomacy. At its first meeting on April 30th 1936, Mr Eden took note of Hitler's Rhineland move, but proposed no momentous changes of policy. He said that the League of Nations and its Covenant must go on. The second was concerned with getting together a meeting of the Locarno Treaty powers, i.e. the West European allies of the 1914–18 War, to search for a general settlement. By the third meeting in July 1936, the Ministers were down to a discussion of a transfer of colonial mandates as a means of tempting Germany back into the League. At the fourth meeting Mr Chamberlain spoke against any sort of blunt declaration that there could be no such transfer, and Mr Eden

[1] The proportion of Conservatives to National Liberals in the 1936 General Election had been 385 to 32.

adopted instead a formula for a statement in the House of Commons on July 27th 1936, that there were "grave, moral, political and legal difficulties in any transfer of a colonial mandate."

This subject was not exclusively discussed in the Foreign Policy Committee. We find the Committee of Imperial Defence on July 10th 1936, with Sir Thomas Inskip in the Chair, studying a C.I.D., 'paper' on the Transfer of Colonial Mandate to Germany.[1] On this occasion the Earl of Plymouth, Parliamentary Under-Secretary for the Colonies, pointed to the last general conclusion that there was no chance of satisfying Germany in the colonial sphere alone and that "efforts in this direction must be combined with an attack on wider and more fundamental problems", while Sir Robert Vansittart thought that "nothing short of the return of all her colonies had any chance of satisfying Germany".

At the fifth meeting of the Cabinet Foreign Policy Committee, on August 25th 1936, Mr Chamberlain expressed the opinion that "it seemed not unlikely that Germany would return to the League of Nations". The Committee had to face up to powerful and insistent German propaganda both for a return of former German colonies and a free hand in Europe. The Committee adopted a conclusion put forward by a Foreign Office policy paper:[2]

> We should decline to disinterest ourselves from the East and Centre of Europe and continue to insist on the need for a general settlement, while urging France not to wreck a Western settlement by maintaining impossible demands in the East and Centre.

Herr von Ribbentrop, as Special Envoy and later Ambassador to the Court of St James spread the idea in London of letting Germany go East—whether this meant the Russian Ukraine, Poland or Czechoslovakia, it was difficult to tell. In London society, where dislike of regicides and revolutionaries was still strong, there were some ears in clubs and soirées attentive to such suggestions. The Foreign Office had to be on the alert against attempts to upset its main lines of policy, which had never favoured the abandonment of Russia. But in the sixth

[1] C.I.D. Paper 1236 B   [2] F.P. (36) 9

meeting of the Cabinet Foreign Policy Committee, on March
10th 1937, Lord Halifax, then Lord Privy Seal, asked whether
it might not be possible to outflank the real obstacle to a general
settlement—the Franco-Soviet pact—"on the lines originally
suggested by the Chancellor of the Exchequer. Germany
declined to deal with Russia. Was it possible to persuade her to
make a multilateral guarantee pact with all her eastern neighbours, whose territories lay between Russia and herself? If so,
would such an arrangement be a material contribution to a
general settlement? Could we say to Germany that no western
settlement seemed possible while Eastern Europe remained un-
settled, and that if she could make the suggested pacts with her
eastern neighbours, the position on the West might thereby be
substantially eased?"

Mr Eden replied that "Germany might offer to agree provided that in return we undertake to secure the termination of
the Franco-Czechoslovak and the Franco-Soviet pacts. This we
surely could not do."

The original outline of Mr Chamberlain's policy, to which
Lord Halifax referred, is not included in the Foreign Policy
Committee record, but in this meeting Mr Chamberlain spoke
too and repeated his views.

"Germany and Russia were potential enemies", he said. "If
it was possible to neutralise the intervening states, the dangers
of war might be greatly reduced. His suggestion had been
that Germany might make a pact, non-aggression and non-
interference, with all her Eastern neighbours and that Russia
should make a similar pact with the same countries. This
scheme would take the place of the Franco-Soviet pact."

Others listening at the meeting to this curious proposition
were Stanley Baldwin, then still in the Chair, Ramsay Mac-
Donald, Sir John Simon, Ormsby-Gore, Malcolm MacDonald
and Sir Thomas Inskip. Sir John Simon thought the Chamberlain plan "admirable as an answer to Hitler's fears of Russia,
but it did not seem to meet the German objections to the
Franco-Soviet pact". Eden, who realised the simplicity of the
proposal, contented himself with pointing out "one serious
obstacle, that relations between themselves of some countries
between Russia and Germany were far from good".

The seventh meeting of the Foreign Policy Committee, which

had invited the presence of Sir Frederick Leith-Ross, British
Treasury Adviser at the League of Nations, dealt seriously with
the problem of colonial restitution. Dr Schacht and Sir
Frederick had in a series of confidential talks on raw materials
and colonial mandates discussed a "comprehensive settlement".
Sir Thomas Inskip, however, reminded the meeting that Mr
Eden had warned the House of Commons of "grave legal,
political and moral difficulties" in the way of colonial
restitution.

Mr Chamberlain persisted. He said that he gathered that
Mr Eden shared his view that "if a full, final and general
settlement could be got by return of the Cameroons and Togoland, a deal should not be ruled out". Lord Halifax supported
him, saying that "there should be some repartition of Africa".
Tanganyika had been ruled out as in too commanding a
position[1] and South West Africa would never be relinquished by
South Africa. Mr Ormsby-Gore observed that this "repartition"
would in fact mean taking part of Portugal's African colonies
and that Germany might raise "black armies" against her
neighbours. South Africa and Australia, added the Secretary of
State for the Colonies, were against colonial restitution.

Neville Chamberlain was not thus to be thwarted. He
formulated to the Committee on Foreign Policy a memorandum, dated April 2nd 1937, and entitled "Anglo-German
Relations".[2] In the first four paragraphs he laid bare his
political thinking on appeasement by negotiation:

It will, I think, be admitted that the general situation in Europe is
such that we cannot afford to miss any opportunity of reducing
the international tension. The present rulers of Germany and
Italy have been organising their nations systematically for war:
but they justify these measures to their people on the ground that
they are surrounded by enemies and that they have no alternative
means of self-preservation. For there are sections in both countries
which are anxious to restore good international relations and
thereby alleviate the economic difficulties with which these
countries are faced and our rearmament programme has rein-
forced their arguments. It is difficult for a dictator to climb down
publicly, but Herr Hitler's last speech contains certain definite

[1] The exploits of General von Lettow Vorbeck were still remembered.
[2] F.P. (36) 23

assurances in regard to the peaceful intentions of Germany, and Dr Schacht's approaches, which have been made with the approval of Herr Hitler, cannot be regarded as anything but an invitation to a general discussion.

Any Government which turned down this invitation without at least exploring the possibilities sufficiently to make sure that there was no possible basis of agreement would incur a very heavy responsibility. Even a slight improvement in the international atmosphere may lead gradually to a general *détente*, whereas a policy of drift may lead to general war. M. Blum, who should be alive to the difficulties of any negotiation with Germany, appears anxious to pursue the conversations as rapidly as possible, and if this is not done we may be sure that the responsibility for failure will be laid at our door.

It seems to me that the notes submitted by the Foreign Secretary and by the Colonial Secretary both need reconsideration in the light of this possible turn of events. The general political questions outstanding between Germany and the Western democracies are scarcely touched upon. The notes concentrate entirely on the colonial question, which is the last one which should be tackled. If as the result of such notes it were decided not to pursue the discussions, the reason for the breakdown would clearly be our refusal to discuss Colonies. Surely this is exactly what we want to avoid.

Our objective should be to set out the political guarantees which we want from Germany as part of any general settlement; and if the discussions have to break down, we want the breakdown to be due to Germany's refusal to accept our reasonable requirements in the political field.

To this was attached an outline programme to be communicated to the French Government, which was becoming sensitive at the idea of Britain making a separate deal with Germany over colonies, or indeed over the balance of power in Europe.[1] The French could rightly object to any proposals that would ingratiate Britain with Germany at the expense of French territory overseas.

Dr Schacht in his biography *Account Settled* made fleeting references to his endeavours for colonial restitution without, even in the dock at the Nuremberg International Tribunal on War Crimes, revealing the full scope of his conversations with

[1] F.P. (36) 23

Sir Frederick Leith-Ross. These aimed at a settlement in which
Soviet Russia would in the first instance have been left aside,
and this is plainly shown by the preamble to the British,
"Outline Programme to be communicated to the French
Government", which the future Prime Minister attached to his
memorandum:

> His Majesty's Government in the United Kingdom have con-
> sidered with care the suggestions which have been put forward by
> Dr Schacht that tripartite conversations should take place
> between representatives of the British, French and German
> Governments, with a view to exploring the possibility of a general
> settlement of outstanding questions between Germany and the
> Western Powers. While His Majesty's Government feel some
> uncertainty as to the precise authority which Dr Schacht may
> have in this matter, they consider that the interests of all countries
> in an appeasement of the European situation are so preponderant
> that no opportunity should be missed of trying out the possibilities
> of an agreement by whatever means may be best calculated to
> secure this object.
>
> Dr Schacht formulated in some detail the requirements of
> Germany, but, naturally enough, left it to the French and
> United Kingdom Governments to formulate their requirements
> in the political field. The next step, therefore, is for the French and
> United Kingdom Governments to outline the political questions
> on which satisfactory assurances would have to be obtained from
> Germany before progress can be made on economic issues.
>
> In this spirit His Majesty's Government would suggest that the
> following should be the lines on which, on behalf of the French
> and British Governments, there should be further communication
> with Dr Schacht.
>
> (1) The conclusion of a treaty or treaties of non-aggression and
> guarantee for Western Europe to replace the treaty of mutual
> guarantee signed at Locarno. (This might be expanded by
> some reference to the recent German Note on this subject.)
>
> (2) Measures by Germany in treaty form or otherwise which will
> reassure the Governments of Central and Eastern Europe of
> Germany's intention to respect the territorial integrity and
> sovereign independence of the various States in those parts of
> Europe. (In this connexion we should request confirmation of
> the readiness of Germany to negotiate a non-aggression and
> non-interference Treaty with Czecho-Slovakia, and to enter
> into an indirect arrangement with regard to the Soviet Union.)

(3) The return of Germany to the League of Nations; (on this it might be added that we have already proposed that the Covenant of the League should be separated from the Treaties of Peace and embodied in a self-contained Convention, and that we should want to know whether the German Government would stipulate for any further changes); and

(4) An international arrangement for the limitation of armaments. (Some indication should be given of what we consider to be practicable in this sphere.) . . .

The Chamberlain memorandum then pointed out that as no other Governments were willing there would be insuperable objections to the transfer of Tanganyika to Germany:

There remains, therefore, only the West African mandates, viz., French and British Togoland and Cameroons, and if the suggestions made by Dr Schacht are to be pursued, a satisfaction of the German demands must be found in this area. . . .
Such concessions could only be contemplated if they were accepted by Germany as a full and final settlement of all her territorial claims, and if thereby a permanent basis could be found for European appeasement.

Dr Schacht has explained in *Account Settled*, that Hitler's forward policy in Spain brought these discussions to naught, but Chamberlain and Halifax continued to pursue their aim of a general settlement. Mr Ormsby-Gore was told by them that "it would be very unwise to make an enemy of Dr Schacht at this juncture".[1] Confronted with the Chamberlain Memorandum on Anglo-German Relations, Ormsby-Gore said that "if essential to the peace of Europe we should have to acquiesce [on colonies] though with very great regret".

Colonies would come last in his proposed deal, Neville Chamberlain explained. He favoured continuing talks with Dr Schacht rather than recommencing them with Baron von Neurath, the German Foreign Minister (which would keep the subject in his own grip). Twice more the subject of colonial restitution was raised in the Foreign Policy Committee. On May 10th 1937 it was suggested that Gambia be given by Britain to France in the repartition to compensate her for the

[1] Eighth meeting of Foreign Policy Committee, April 6th 1937

loss of the French Cameroons to Germany. At Baldwin's last appearance in the Chair of the Committee, on May 19th, the opinion of M. Yvon Delbos, the French Foreign Minister, was quoted. Delbos thought that colonies should come last in any general discussion. Leakages to the press and in the House of Commons on the possibility of a deal on colonies combined meanwhile with the hardening attitude of Hitler to make colonial restitution an even more difficult subject. The subsequent two meetings of the Foreign Policy Committee at which Neville Chamberlain took the Chair and invited his Chief Industrial Adviser, Sir Horace Wilson, to be present, were more concerned with a policy of access to raw materials for all nations. On June 21st 1937, the Committee met at 10 Downing Street to take note that after an incident in which a torpedo had been fired in the direction of the German cruiser *Leipzig*, off Spain, Baron von Neurath had postponed his London visit. The fifteenth meeting of the Committee on June 28th in the Prime Minister's room at the House of Commons could see no immediate hope of appeasement, but was able to comfort itself with a report from a Portuguese diplomatic source that in answer to specific questions General Franco "gave assurances of collaboration with Great Britain, within whose political orbit he considers the two peninsula nations should maintain themselves. He had entered into no engagements with third countries." This windfall to British policy had to remain a Cabinet secret.

After July 1st 1937, there were no more meetings of the Foreign Policy Committee until January 1938, a seasonal break due partly to the absence of Eden at conferences in Brussels and Nyon, and to the summer vacation. However, the main Cabinet continued to meet regularly. Mr Malcolm MacDonald reported to it on June 16th that Commonwealth Prime Ministers at the London Imperial Conference had been inclined "to look rather more critically at British involvement in Europe than His Majesty's Government itself cared to." Even the Australian Government had rather criticised our opposition to the *Anschluss* [the proposed union of Germany and Austria]. General Hertzog of South Africa felt that the attitude of Britain towards France was too warm and towards Germany too cold. . . . Mr Mackenzie King intended to play the Canadian role of intermediary in situations of international tension. . . . He would visit Hitler and express sympathy with his constructive work, but he intended to add that if Germany ever turned to destructive efforts against the United Kingdom, all the Dominions would come to the United Kingdom's aid." None of the Prime Ministers, except Mr Savage of New Zealand, was prepared to back Britain to the hilt in every circumstance, even that of war in Europe in a cause that did not appear to raise a direct threat to the existence of the British and their Commonwealth.

After the first meeting of the Chamberlain Cabinet on June 2nd 1937, there were three others of minor importance. Then on June 30th a more notable meeting was held at 10 Downing Street, at which the granting of belligerent rights in the Spanish Civil War was discussed. This would help General Franco, Mr Eden objected, but Lord Halifax put forward the view that "we should not lose sight of our main desideratum of not allowing relations with Germany and Italy to deteriorate . . . play for time . . . keep in view the granting of belligerent rights as a possibility".

The Treasury grip that Mr Chamberlain had exerted on the Services Ministers in the Baldwin Cabinet of April 28th, was now reasserted by Sir John Simon. On June 30th the new Chancellor presented a memorandum calling for the Defence Departments "to estimate anew the time required for completion of their programmes. These general estimates should then be examined by the Treasury and submitted to the Defence Policy and Requirements Committee of the Cabinet. Meanwhile decisions on new projects of major importance should be postponed."

Mr Chamberlain supported Sir John Simon with the dry observation that "it will be necessary to arrive at a global total".

Even Sir Thomas Inskip, described by Eden as "the placid Sir Thomas", expressed anxiety at this procedure "lest questions already decided should be reopened, and all decisions held up till the global term was arrived at".

The three Services Ministers spoke with the same concern, and it was finally decided that since both the Admiralty and the Air Ministry had entered new standards of strength for approval, they would each enter two total figures, that already approved and that for which they sought approval.

On the following Wednesday, July 7th 1937, the Cabinet noted that the British Ambassador in Rome had written a letter to Sir Robert Vansittart on "the truculent and aggressive attitude of Italy in the Mediterranean". The Cabinet had already noted with alarm increases in Italian military strength in Libya, and Sir Robert had circulated the Ambassador's letter to the Chiefs of Staff. How far, asked Sir Thomas Inskip, ought this letter to be treated as a warning from the point of view of our defensive arrangements?

Mr Chamberlain spoke: "The Prime Minister thought there was very little that could be done to improve matters. The real counter to Italy's disquieting attitude was to get on better terms with Germany."

Lord Halifax urged that "in carrying out the Prime Minister's idea of bettering relations with Germany, we should avoid putting forward proposals as Anglo-French proposals, and that close contact should be preserved with Berlin in the development of such proposals". Mr Eden is recorded in the Cabinet Minutes as "expressing agreement with this method of approach".

The minutes then record this conclusion:

"The Cabinet agreed with the Prime Minister's proposal that the best way of countering the disquieting attitude of the Italian Government was to cultivate better relations with the German Government."

CHAPTER IV

The Road to Berlin

IN THE CABINET meetings of the summer and autumn of 1937, the Chamberlain conception of diplomacy unfolded. Baldwin had avoided short cuts in foreign policy and regarded with scepticism all offers of personal encounter with the dictators. He did not trust himself in the foreign context. He listened to his Ministers and weighed impatience against caution, confessing his ignorance of foreign affairs and allowing other opinions. Not so the new Prime Minister.

"Chamberlain made it quickly clear that he intended to be master in his own Cabinet," wrote Lord Birkenhead.[1] "A man of intense shyness and inner reserve who could not even unburden his thoughts and fears to his own colleagues, but only to his sister and wife and to the secrecy of his diary . . . there appeared in him when crossed, a streak of ruthlessness . . . and an autocratic tendency which led him to exercise an iron control over his Cabinet."

"Chamberlain had the most definite ideas as to what was needed," wrote Sir Samuel Hoare,[2] to whom Chamberlain confessed that he had "no capacity for looking on and seeing other people mismanaging things". Probably since Sir Robert Peel no Prime Minister exercised such supervision over the Departments of his Ministers. Keith Feiling, writing the first biography of Chamberlain,[3] examined his diary and those family letters in which Neville revealed himself to intimates. Feiling quotes a significant sentence from a letter of this period: "I believe the double policy of rearmament and better relations with Germany and Italy will carry us safely through the danger period, if only the Foreign Office will play up."

Lord Avon devotes a chapter of *Facing the Dictators* to delays in rearmament, which in reality could be traced back to March 1934 after Hitler had told him and Sir John Simon in Berlin

---

[1] The Earl of Birkenhead, *The Life of Lord Halifax*
[2] Samuel Hoare, Viscount Templewood, *Nine Troubled Years*
[3] Feiling, *The Life of Neville Chamberlain*

that Germany had achieved air parity with Britain. In November 1934, Baldwin had claimed that the R.A.F. expansion programme would give Britain a margin of superiority over Germany of "nearly 50 per cent". He was later content with the pledge of air parity with Germany, but the margin of superiority was clearly lost in January 1937 when General Erhard Milch revealed to a member of an R.A.F. Mission in Berlin that the *Luftwaffe* by the autumn of 1938 would have a total of 1,755 first line aircraft while Britain would have 1,736. Moreover, in the course of 1937, information reached Britain that German aircraft production was being speeded up. It soon became plain from Mr Chamberlain's remarks to his Cabinet that he would not consider himself bound to maintain an exact numerical parity of strength with Germany or even to maintain in public the pledge of air parity that Baldwin had given.

He told Eden that he meant as Prime Minister to take "a good deal more interest in foreign affairs" than his predecessor had done. One of the manifestations of this interest was an attempt by Sir Horace Wilson to undermine the powerful influence of Sir Robert Vansittart, "who hampered all attempts of the Government to make friendly contact with the dictator states".[1]

Sir Horace, Chief Industrial Adviser to the Government, must be counted among those few intimate friends to whom Chamberlain revealed his thoughts. His ideas of foreign policy exactly reflected those of his master and he was assiduous in procuring the means of furthering them, relying on the assistance of Sir Warren Fisher, Permanent Secretary of the Treasury and Head of the Civil Service. In this instance they were successful in removing Vansittart by the end of 1937 from his commanding position in the Foreign Office to a post of no responsibility as Chief Diplomatic Adviser to the Government.

At a meeting of the Cabinet on July 28th Mr Chamberlain expressed his hope that Mr Eden would be able to take a holiday and Eden did go to Fawley in Hampshire with his family. On July 29th the Prime Minister told the Cabinet that during the parliamentary recess in case of urgency "he would summon those Ministers within easy reach of London". This tendency was in 1938 to become injurious to the idea of Cabinet

[1] Avon, *Facing the Dictators*

responsibility. The Cabinet in fact met five times in the twelve
weeks of the 1937 summer vacation, debating among other
subjects a proposal from Lord Halifax for a settlement with
Germany and Italy over intervention in the Spanish Civil
War. The Cabinet also discussed a proposal of the Prime
Minister for a naval "demonstration of force" to induce a less
aggressive attitude in Japan, then in the middle of its war with
China. On October 27th the Cabinet met to consider the new
estimates on defence expenditure prepared by the Services
Departments.

These Services estimates were shortly to become the subject
of a memorandum[1] from Sir Thomas Inskip, in which the
anxieties and priorities of the Treasury were once more
emphasised. It is noteworthy in giving priority to economic
resilience above military preparedness. The Minister for
Co-ordination of Defence recalled that:

... this review was set on foot as a result of a study undertaken by
the Prime Minister, in the concluding weeks of his Chancellorship,
of the Defence Programmes as a whole, present and prospective,
in terms of our resources. It is desirable to state at the outset what
is involved in the statement that our Defence Programmes must be
in relation to our total available resources.

In considering whether we can afford this or that programme,
the first question asked is how much the programme will cost; and
the cost of the programme is then related to the sums which can be
made available from Exchequer resources, from taxation, or
exceptionally from the proceeds of loans. But the fact that the
problem is considered in terms of money, must not be allowed to
obscure the fact that our real resources consist not of money, i.e.
paper pounds which are nothing more than a symbol, but of our
man power, and productive capacity, our power to maintain our
credit, and the general balance of our trade.

Owing to its shortage of native raw materials and foodstuffs,
this country is particularly dependent upon imports which have
to be paid for and can only be paid for if the volume of our export
trade is not impaired. This factor of the general balance of our
trade is closely connected with our credit. The amount of money
which we can borrow without inflation is mainly dependent
upon two factors: the savings of the country as a whole which are
available for investment, and the maintenance of confidence in

[1] C.P. 316 (37), December 1937

our financial stability. But these savings would be reduced and confidence would at once be weakened by any substantial disturbance of the general balance of trade. While if we were to raise sums in excess of the sums available in the market, the result would be inflation; i.e. a general rise in prices which would have an immediate effect upon our export trade.

The maintenance of credit facilities and our general balance of trade are of vital importance, not merely from the point of view of our strength in peace time, but equally for purposes of war. This country cannot hope to win a war against a major Power by a sudden knockout blow: on the contrary, for success we must contemplate a long war, in the course of which we should have to mobilise all our resources and those of the Dominions and other countries overseas. This is no new conception. The report of the Chiefs of Staff Sub-Committee on Planning for a War with Germany (D.P. (P) 2) was based on the general conception that Germany is likely to be the aggressor and will endeavour "to exploit her superior preparedness by trying to knock out Great Britain rapidly, or to knock out France rapidly, since she is not well placed for a long war in which the Sea Powers, as in the past, are likely to have the advantage." We must therefore confront our potential enemies with the risks of a long war, which they cannot face. If we are to emerge victoriously from such a war, it is essential that we should enter it with sufficient economic strength to enable us to make the fullest uses of the resources overseas, and to withstand the strain. . . .

The Inskip Memorandum concluded:

The problem before the Cabinet is, therefore, to strike a proper balance between these factors, and to determine the size and character of the forces which will suffice to ward off defeat in the early days of war, and will enable us to exercise our rightful influence for peace, without making demands on our resources which would impair our stability, and our staying power in peace and war.

Sir John Simon already spoke in this sense to the Cabinet on October 27th of "the magnitude of the defence requirements asked for by the fighting Services. At that moment he did not propose to mention a figure which the nation could afford. He only wished to draw attention to a consideration of gravity . . . that it was not going to be so easy to borrow the necessary money as had been contemplated." The Minister for Co-ordination of Defence was then directed to preside over a panel consisting of such officials as Sir Maurice Hankey, Sir Horace Wilson and two representatives of the Treasury. "On the military side Sir Thomas would consult with the Services Ministers who could bring with them their professional advisers."

The next Cabinet meeting on November 3rd 1937 dealt principally with Spain. It noted that General Franco had proposed to appoint the first nobleman of Spain, the Duke of Berwick and Alba, as his representative in London and that the Foreign Office was using "discreet efforts to secure the appointment of a more suitable person".

On November 24th there was a matter of some importance when Lord Halifax, Lord President of the Council, gave his "account of what had passed during his recent visit to Germany, as well as his general impressions of the attitude of the German Government". He had been offered the opportunity of making those contacts in Germany that he had advocated in Cabinet. The Prime Minister, as we have seen, had obtained Cabinet agreement on July 7th 1937, "to cultivate better relations with the German Government". Somehow a gilt invitation card reached Lord Halifax early in October via the editor of *The Field*, inviting him as Master of the Middleton Hounds to attend a Hunting Exhibition in Berlin. The patron was Reich Master Huntsman, Hermann Goering.

There was a foxy scent about this invitation, but Eden did not find it easy to say outright that it should not be accepted. Winston Churchill, who occasionally saw Eden at this time, had the impression at dinner with both men that the overture did disconcert the Foreign Secretary.[1] Lord Halifax declared afterwards that it did not. He related that he popped the card into an envelope with a note to Eden, saying that he proposed to accept the invitation unless Eden thought that he should not.[2] Halifax relates further that when he introduced the subject at the dinner table on October 14th, Eden "said quite seriously that he was not sure that it might not be of some advantage for me to go to Germany under this cover". Looking back on it, Halifax did not

[1] W. S. Churchill, *The Gathering Storm*
[2] The Earl of Halifax, *Fulness of Days*

think the visit "did any harm". "My own recollection," wrote Lord Avon, "is that when I first heard of this proposal I was not eager, but saw no sufficient reason to oppose it."[1] Mr Chamberlain, as might be expected, approved thoroughly of the plan.

The Cabinet record of Lord Halifax's visit to Germany is vague. "His impressions were", as the Most Secret Memorandum[2] rightly noted, "subject to the considerations that his visit was very brief, that he might have been deceived, or his judgment might have been at fault, or the German attitude might change. . . ."

He had seen Herr Hitler, Baron von Neurath, General Goering, Dr Goebbels, Dr Schacht, and General Blomberg.

He had encountered friendliness and a desire for good relations.

They had agreed that there was no more desire to separate France and ourselves than to upset the Berlin–Rome Axis.

Our rearmament had been of assistance.

General Goering, with Herr Hitler's approval, had said that "even with the colonial question in the field he could see no circumstances in which the two countries would fight", and General Blomberg had said that good relations between Germany and the United Kingdom were the only thing that mattered. Italy and France were secondary. . . .

With all those mentioned he had discussed the problems of Central Europe, Austria, Czecho-Slovakia and Danzig. Herr Hitler had expressed satisfaction with the Austro-German Agreement of July last.[3] Of Czecho-Slovakia he had said, "She only needed to treat the Germans living within her borders well and they would be entirely happy".

Herr Hitler had strongly criticised widespread talk of an imminent catastrophe and did not consider that the world was in a dangerous state. Herr Goering had said that not one drop of German blood would be spilt in Europe unless it was forced on them.

Lord Halifax's general conclusion, therefore, was that the Germans had no policy of immediate adventure. They were too busy building up their country, which was still in a state of revolution. Nevertheless he would expect a beaver-like persistence,

[1] Avon, *Facing the Dictators*
[2] Cab. 43(37), Summary of Discussion
[3] An error in the minutes. The Austro-German Agreement of July 1936 is meant.

pressing their aims in Central Europe, but not in a form to give others cause—or probably occasion—to interfere.[1]

As to the League of Nations, Herr Hitler regarded the present system and conception as unworkable and unreal. To a direct question he had replied that the matter was not one to which any answer could at present be given. But Germany would not join the League as at present constituted and functioning. Baron von Neurath had thought the League useful for social questions, labour matters and as a meeting-place where Foreign Secretaries could get to know one another.

On the question of disarmament Herr Hitler said that "we had missed every bus with his label on". He had indicated the possibility of an abolition of bombing aeroplanes, which, he said, had previously been rejected by the Colonial Powers, who wanted the right to bomb natives.

Lord Halifax thought, therefore, that the basis of an understanding might not be too difficult as regards Central and Eastern Europe, and that the question of the League could be discussed.

The Cabinet Summary did not record in detail what Halifax had said to Hitler when they met at Berchtesgaden. It does record that Mr Eden, who had read the Halifax report and also the notes of the German interpreter "expressed great satisfaction with the way that the Lord President had dealt with each point in his conversations with the Chancellor". Lord Avon comments differently in *Facing the Dictators*: "I noticed too that Lord Halifax in the words of Schmidt's record had spoken of 'possible alterations in the European Order which might be destined to come about with the passage of time. Among these questions were Danzig, Austria and Czechoslovakia' . . . I wished that Halifax had warned Hitler more strongly against intervention in Central Europe." Another Cabinet Minute of November 1937[2] notes, however, that Eden described Lord Halifax as making "a favourable impression" on the visiting French Ministers, M. Chautemps and M. Delbos with an account of his visit to Germany.

We may note the trend of the Cabinet discussion on November 24th recorded in the minutes after Lord Halifax had told his story:

[1] This wording recurs in a later explanation by Lord Halifax.
[2] Cab.23.90

"The Lord President agreed that the Germans had not suggested a *quid pro quo*, but neither had they given any impression of bargaining Central Europe against a colonial settlement, as some British newspapers had suggested. Herr Hitler himself, however, had suggested an advance towards disarmament by the possible abolition of bombing aeroplanes. . . . The idea of abolishing bombing aeroplanes interested the Cabinet. It was suggested that it might have the result of enabling the German Army to dominate Europe, particularly if the risk of war with the United Kingdom was eliminated. It would, however, have the advantage of removing the risk of a knock-out blow at the outset of a war."

The Prime Minister "recalled that the object of the visit had been not to reach an agreement, but to make contact and to bring back to the Cabinet an impression of the German outlook, and the possibilities of a settlement. . . . For his part he would not make any offer in the colonial field except as part of a general settlement. . . . The difficulty was to find what contribution the Germans could make.

"Some satisfactory assurance would have to be sought that the Germans did not mean to use force in Central Europe. . . . An agreement on limitation of bombing aircraft and the size and power of some weapons might save a great deal of expenditure."

The Cabinet were puzzled that Hitler had not taken the bait of colonies in Africa, the only field in which they could legitimately satisfy his aspirations.

To hear about the Halifax venture into secret diplomacy, M. M. Camille Chautemps and Yvon Delbos[1] arrived in London on November 28th. If Mr Eden had privately uneasy feelings about the wisdom of the Halifax visit to Germany, as Foreign Secretary it was his business to satisfy the French, who may have arrived with some apprehensions, that British diplomacy was in order. The Cabinet Minutes record that after the French visit:

"The Secretary of State for Foreign Affairs reported that the Anglo-French conversations of the two previous days had begun with a statement by the Lord President of the Council on his visit to Germany, which had been as full and as frank as that

[1] The British Cabinet record persists in spelling the name of the French Minister wrongly with the addition of a German diaeresis, Delbös.

given to the Cabinet. The statement had obviously made a favourable impression. The French had noted that Herr Hitler had made the point that there was no connection between the colonial question and that of Central Europe and the other questions raised. The Lord President had explained that he made clear that this was not his attitude.

"On the subject of Central Europe the French Ministers had said that there were two possible policies: (1) to disinterest ourselves, and (2) to interest ourselves in a spirit of conciliation. On the question of the Sudeten–Deutsch in Czecho-Slovakia, the British Ministers had urged the importance of meeting legitimate grievances, and had asked M. Delbos, on the occasion of his coming visit, to try and find out what concessions Dr Beneš was willing to make, as this would be most useful in our approaches to Berlin. The French Ministers had agreed, but had pointed out that the Germans preferred bilateral negotiations with Czecho-Slovakia and had doubted what sort of reception they would give to our friendly and pacific efforts.

"On the subject of Austria it had been agreed that the situation was rather different. The last declaration had been that of Stresa, when Great Britain, France and Italy had agreed on the maintenance of the integrity and independence of Austria as a necessary element in European peace. The French Ministers had pointed out that the Italian interest in Austria had somewhat weakened, but did not think that they had entirely disinterested themselves in that country. They agreed that the Austrian Government had shown great courage, and their information corresponded to ours, that Dr Schuschnigg's position had improved. They had agreed also that Austria must take a place in the negotiations with Germany and that it might be useful to obtain a repetition of the German declaration of last July.[1]

"Disarmament was considered by the French Ministers to be of capital importance in a settlement. The British Ministers had expressed the view that qualitative disarmament held out better prospects than quantitative, and the French Ministers had undertaken to look into this. The French Ministers had insisted that some measure of disarmament was essential to any arrangement.

"On the subject of the League of Nations and its constitution and powers, the Lord President had pointed out that the Ger-

[1] July 1936 is meant, date of the Austro-German Settlement.

mans could not face rejoining so long as the nominal powers of coercion were maintained. On this point the French Ministers had not been so rigid as had been anticipated. They wanted, however, to keep Article 16 [of the Covenant] for regional agreements even if it was not retained for general use. They had not rejected a suggestion to consider a solution proposed by the Scandinavian Governments in favour of leaving to the League the faculty to apply sanctions. At the outset, however, the French Ministers thought it would be better not to raise these particular issues. They recalled that Herr Hitler himself had asked why other nations were so anxious to have Germany in the League when the United States of America was not a member, and had suggested that a League without Germany was a possibility."

Mr Eden's memoirs give a more vivid account of the Chautemps and Delbos visit, relating that M. Delbos "begged the British not to encourage any German venture in Czechoslovakia", explaining that it was with the new techniques of subversion in view that he had recently restated the French guarantee to Czechoslovakia.[1]

The minutes of the Cabinet do not convey truly the importance of the three meetings with the French Ministers, and omit one emphatic opinion by M. Delbos. It is to the Cabinet Office record itself that we must turn for a more illuminating and less reassuring account of the conversations of the Heads of Government on November 29th and 30th.[2] This shows that Lord Halifax, describing at the first meeting to Chautemps and Delbos his visit to Germany, said that "the Germans gave him the impression of being convinced that time was on their side and of intending to achieve their aims in an orderly fashion . . . in comparatively orderly fashion, but not take any action in any matter that would give other Governments cause to oppose or interfere".

M. Delbos, mentioning that he had special information, "saw the methods of German expansion as a plebiscite in Austria; in Czechoslovakia the introduction of Ministers with Nazi tendencies . . . a kind of federation . . . a quasi-autonomy . . . and then attachment to Germany."

Mr Chamberlain then asked the crucial question whether

[1] Avon, *Facing the Dictators*   [2] F.P. (36) 40

this course of events would bring into operation the treaty between France and Czechoslovakia.

Delbos: "If there were no acts of aggression the treaty would not come into operation. If there were risings provoked by Germany and if there were armed intervention, it was evident that the treaty would apply."

Chamberlain: "Did M. Delbos see any way of preventing German expansion in Central Europe short of using force?"

Delbos: "If Great Britain and France manifested their will to impose respect for law, this would make Germany more and more reasonable.[1] There were two courses—to let things slide, and the result of that would be obvious, or to take an interest in the problem in the spirit of conciliation. If we did the latter the situation would not be altogether desperate."

Since the murder of Chancellor Dollfuss in July 1934 Herr von Schuschnigg had sought to maintain the precarious independence of Austria. The subject of Austria, the record noted, was discussed at the request of M. Delbos. Mr Eden began by pointing out that neither France nor Great Britain had treaty obligations to Austria. M. Delbos, however, reminded the British that Great Britain, France and Italy had asserted at Stresa that the independence and integrity of Austria was a necessary element of European peace. Mr Eden then agreed that "Austria would have to figure in the final arrangement". Mr Chamberlain concluded that as the object was a general settlement, it was impossible to take no account of Austria. "He would have thought it possible to explore the situation with Germany; and he did not think it out of the question to ask her to give an assurance not to use force."

In what circumstances force was not to be used the British record does not explain. It adds that "M. Delbos agreed".

France at this time relied on a British military contribution to the defence of Western Europe under the Locarno Pact which French Ministers put no higher than two mobile divisions in support of the French Army. The Inskip Memorandum on Defence, already quoted for its homilies on strength through economic health, contained other paragraphs setting forth the priority of strategy as the Committee of Imperial Defence now saw it:

[1] Omitted in the Cabinet Minutes account of the meeting.

The corner stone of our Imperial Defence Policy is to maintain ①
the security of the United Kingdom. Our main strength lies in the
resources of man power, productive capacity and the powers of
endurance possessed by this country. Unless these can be maintained substantially unimpaired, not only in peace but particularly in the early stages of a war, when they will be subject to
continuous attacks, our ultimate defeat in a major war would be
certain, irrespective of what might happen in other and secondary
spheres.

It follows that our first and main effort must be directed to two
principal objectives, namely, ② to protecting this country against
attack, and to preserving the trade routes on which we depend for
essential imports of food and raw material.

Our third objective is the maintenance of forces for the defence of
British territories overseas, against attack by sea, land or air. One
of the main features which distinguishes our defence problems
from those of certain Continental countries is that we require not
only to maintain in peace garrisons and defences at naval bases
and other strategic points throughout the world, but also to have
available at all times forces for despatch overseas for the performance of what may be described as Imperial Police duties. It is
obvious that in time of war the demands for reinforcements of our
peace-time Imperial garrisons might well be very considerable.
At the same time, the strength of the forces available for such
reinforcement is not a matter of such vital importance as the
defence of this country, since so long as this country remains
undefeated we may hope in time to repair any losses or defeats
suffered elsewhere.

Our fourth objective, which can only be provided after the other
objectives have been met, is co-operation in the defence of the
territories of any allies we may have in war.[2]

I deal in the ensuing section with the detailed application of this
policy to the programmes of the three Services. It is clear, however, that, if this policy is adopted, and the survival of Great
Britain herself is accepted as the primary condition of success, the
greatest danger against which we have to provide protection is
attack from the air on the United Kingdom, designed to inflict
a knock-out blow at the initial stage of the war, and that our first
endeavour must be to provide adequate defence against this
threat.

To complete the task assigned to me by the Cabinet, it is obviously

[1] C.P. 316 (37)
[2] These priorities were not communicated to any prospective ally.

necessary that the Defence Departments should be invited to submit revised forecasts of the cost of their programmes, if the basis of the policy outlined in the preceding paragraphs is approved. These revised forecasts, together with the forecasts of defence expenditure borne on civil votes, must then be considered in relation to the conclusion set out in paragraph 31, that, if we are to avoid heavy increases in taxation and permanent annual defence maintenance expenditure after 1942 substantially in excess of any sum which we can make available for defence purposes, every effort must be made to bring the total defence expenditure within the 5 years 1937–41 within a total of £1,500 millions. . . .

I must, however, warn my colleagues of the possible consequences of this proposal in order that they may share my responsibility for the decision to be taken with their eyes open. Notwithstanding recent developments in mechanised warfare on land and in the air, there is no sign of the displacement of infantry. If France were again to be in danger of being overrun by land armies, a situation might arise when, as in the last war, we had to improvise an army to assist her. Should this happen, the Government of the day would most certainly be criticised for having neglected to provide against so obvious a contingency.

Nevertheless, for the reasons indicated, I am of opinion that there is no alternative but to adopt the more limited role of the Army envisaged in this report.

The Defence Requirements Committee in their Third Report proposed that the Regular Army should be supported by three contingents of the Territorial Army, each of 4 divisions, fully equipped on a modern scale, and able to proceed overseas 4, 6 and 8 months respectively after the outbreak of war.

This recommendation was not endorsed by the Cabinet who decided that the decision as to whether and when the proposals for reconditioning the Territorial Force can be implemented should be reserved for 3 years, or until such time as the industrial situation of the country and its capacity for output brought this proposal within the range of actual possibilities.

This report was not in the hands of British Ministers till early in December 1937 and the ideas that it expressed on strategy were evidently in turmoil. It remains true that no inkling was given to Chautemps and Delbos of current rethinking on the British Continental role. As companion reading for the Cabinet in December there was another document that bore the

Chamberlain imprint, a Most Secret Memorandum[1] printed on December 3rd, "A Comparison of the Strength of Great Britain With Certain Other Nations As At January 1938". This was to be discussed by the Cabinet on December 8th and at subsequent meetings in which Mr Chamberlain sought active expression for his conception of what British policy ought to be.

[1] C.P. 296 (37), December 3rd 1937

CHAPTER V

Cunctation

"Marking Time" delay

M<small>R</small> E<small>DEN</small>, <small>WHO</small> first saw this paper in draft at the 300th meeting of the Committee of Imperial Defence on October 28th, sensed at once that the Foreign Office must have time to examine its strong political implications.[1] He obtained a postponement of further discussion and by December 2nd, Sir Robert Vansittart, Sir Orme Sargent, Assistant Under-Secretary, Mr William Strang and Mr Laurence Collier of the Central and Northern Departments, had worked out the related comments of the Foreign Office.

The main document was signed by the three Chiefs of Staff, Admiral Sir Ernle Chatfield, Field-Marshal Sir Cyril Deverell and Air Chief Marshal Sir Cyril Newall. It was in fact the product of the Joint Intelligence Committee working under their direction. It showed that Britain and France would have a marked superiority of naval strength in 1938, that Germany and Italy together would possess a numerical superiority on land, and in the air would have an even larger advantage over France and Great Britain. The conclusion was, however, that no country mentioned would be able to conduct a land offensive in Europe by January 1938 with any great prospect of success.

Russia would dispose of 17 divisions, rising to 53 within a week of a mobilisation, a fleet of 184 submarines and 3,050 first-line aircraft, but "could not employ any of these forces against Germany or Italy without violating neutral territory. . . . Only if Poland is friendly and willing to co-operate could Russian intervention on behalf of France and England quickly develop into a real menace for Germany." The paper seemed to attach much less importance to co-operation from Czechoslovakia.

Germany would in January 1938 be able to mobilise the same number of divisions as France, it was stated. In 1939 she was

[1] The Most Secret Memorandum, "A Comparison of the Strength of Great Britain With That of Certain Other Nations As At January 1938", classified as C.P. 296 (37), began as C.O.S. Paper 639, printing date November 12th 1937.

likely to achieve a marked superiority. In January 1938 Germany would be far ahead of Britain and France in her power to stage an air offensive and in her preparations for resisting air attack, especially in the readiness of her anti-aircraft artillery.

The very great superiority of Britain and France over Germany at sea "must render the latter apprehensive of the ultimate effect of economic pressure which she must expect us to develop against her". Germany would hesitate to embark on hostilities against Britain early in 1938.

The memorandum set forth these views on Britain's principal allies in war, France and Belgium:

There is ample evidence that the position in France, and even more so in Belgium, in regard to war reserves is bad. The partial nationalisation of the French peace-time armament and aircraft industries has been completed on paper, but so far these measures, combined with labour troubles, have had the opposite effect to that desired. Financial, economic and social difficulties have jointly conspired to damp down the pace of French production of armaments and to reduce capacity for rapid expansion, and the present condition of the French aircraft industry is deplorable. Moreover, present reports indicate that lack of equipment, inefficiently executed reorganisation and political interference in the Service, has very seriously affected the fighting value of the French Air Force. The effective power of the Belgian armament industry is less than that of the French; war reserves are very seriously deficient, and the fact that the bulk of the armament factories are close to the German frontier makes it impossible to rely upon their output in war. In 1938 neither France nor Belgium is likely to obtain much outside assistance as regards supplies of munitions.

Against these considerations may be set the fact that French mobilisation in 1938 would enable her to put approximately the same number of divisions as Germany in the field, whereas, by 1939, this will no longer be the case. France must also consider that her fixed land defences are now relatively as strong as they are ever likely to be, and looking ahead she may forsee the danger of military encirclement by three dictator Powers. None of these considerations, however, is likely to outweigh French determination not to seek war.

Belgium's attitude is always purely defensive. The recent statement of her policy indicates a desire to keep clear of commitments and guarantees, and to preserve her neutrality in a war in the West of Europe. At the same time, Belgium is engaged in putting her defences in order; the completion of these will increase her chances of remaining neutral, an attitude which, from the military point of view, is to the advantage of France and ourselves.

The value of Russia was of no less concern and was the subject of cautious assessment:

Armed Forces.
Although the U.S.S.R. has very great man-power and large stocks of equipment, including aircraft, it is doubtful whether her military staff would consider her organisation sufficiently developed to enable her to embark on an offensive war with confidence. The Soviet forces have as yet made little progress in tactical training with the modern arms which they have acquired. The armament industry is still young and has fundamental weaknesses which influence output. In war it could not yet maintain for any length of time the maximum forces that the U.S.S.R. can mobilise, while the transportation system of the country, though improved, has not yet been developed to a pitch where it could stand the strain of anything but a short war. The rebuilding of the Soviet Navy is still in its infancy except so far as submarines are concerned. It is considered that the Russian Air Force would rapidly deteriorate when it began to suffer heavy casualties, since, although there is an enormous so-called reserve of pilots, practically the whole personnel reserve is poorly trained in all respects. This weakness is giving the Russian Staff much concern. . . .

The main conclusions of the Chiefs of Staff were that:

Great Britain, France and Belgium would be much stronger at sea than Germany and Italy, and would be able to exercise considerable economic pressure. Neither Germany nor Italy is likely to be in a strong financial or economic position, and the allied pressure would probably reduce them both to a very weak condition in the course of a long war. It is therefore unlikely that Germany or Italy, either singly or in conjunction, would embark on war unless they believed that they could achieve victory quickly.
To make economic pressure effective within a reasonable time, it would be important for it to be applied immediately on

the outbreak of hostilities, and for it to include an adequate system for the rationing of neutrals.

The German Army will not have either the numbers, equipment or training to justify a belief that she could overrun France quickly. Even with the co-operation of Italy on the Franco-Italian frontier she would not be justified in anticipating a rapid decisive success on land. *y. strength*

Although there have been indications that in some quarters the belief is held that success in war can be achieved by the exercise of air power alone, there is no proof that this represents German military opinion as a whole. Nevertheless, if internal difficulties should force her leaders to consider war as the only alternative to loss of prestige, they might decide to gamble upon the effect of air attack. The scale of her attack in 1938 would be lower than that of which she may be capable in 1939, but, on the other hand, she may become aware of our deficiencies in modern bomber aircraft and the backward state of our air defence measures and the industrial weakness of France.

The internal situation in the U.S.S.R. has deteriorated to such an extent during the past year, as a result of political and industrial troubles, that she is unlikely in any circumstances to embark on an offensive war unless she is directly threatened. . . .

In any event, the intervention of the U.S.S.R., while Poland and Czechoslovakia remained neutral, would confer little immediate benefit on the Allies' cause. If Germany and Italy believed themselves justified in counting upon a quick decisive success against France or Great Britain, the fear of Soviet intervention would not, therefore, necessarily deter them from war. . . .

In considering their chances of success in war, Germany and Italy would probably take account not only of their own state of preparedness, but of the internal conditions in France and Russia, and the consequent effect on the military strengths of those countries, as factors which increase the danger of war.

Then came the significant paragraph in which the military men ventured a view which appealed strongly to the thinking of Neville Chamberlain.

From the above Report it will be seen that our Naval, Military and Air Forces, in their present stage of development, are still far from sufficient to meet our defensive commitments, which now extend from Western Europe through the Mediterranean to the

Far East. Even today we could face without apprehension an emergency either in the Far East or in the Mediterranean, provided that we were free to make preparations in time of peace and to concentrate sufficient strength in one or other of these areas. The lack of a defended Fleet base and dock in the Mediterranean, other than at Malta, is a serious deficiency; the defences and dockyard at Singapore are also uncompleted. So far as Germany is concerned, as our preparations develop, our defence forces will provide a considerable deterrent to aggression. But the outstanding feature of the present situation is the increasing probability that a war started in any one of these three areas may extend to one or both of the other two. Without overlooking the assistance which we should hope to obtain from France, and possibly other allies, we cannot foresee the time when our defence forces will be strong enough to safeguard our territory, trade and vital interests against Germany, Italy and Japan simultaneously. We cannot therefore, exaggerate the importance, from the point of view of Imperial defence, of any political or international action that can be taken to reduce the numbers of our potential enemies and to gain the support of potential allies.

When Sir Ernle Chatfield explained the memorandum to the Committee of Imperial Defence on December 2nd 1937, he dwelled at some length on the concluding paragraphs and especially on the assertion that Britain was in "the very serious situation that we were not yet in a position to fight two of our potential enemies simultaneously and it was impossible to foresee the time when it would be possible to fight all three". Admiral Chatfield repeated that it was "impossible to exaggerate the importance of any political or international action that could be taken to reduce the number of our potential enemies or gain the support of potential allies".

Mr Duff Cooper had only been waiting for this naval distress signal to exclaim that the time had come "to reconsider the basis of our defensive preparations".

The Prime Minister observed tartly that "to contemplate basing our defensive preparations on the possibility of a war with Italy, Germany and Japan simultaneously was to set ourselves an impossible problem".

The Committee then examined the views of the Foreign Office upon this memorandum.

"I am in general agreement with the arguments and con-

clusions of the memorandum," Mr Eden's written comments
began. He added, however, that he had some observations to
make. Britain appeared to be in no position to fulfil her Locarno
defence obligations to France and Belgium. He noted that the
Chiefs of Staff had not stated in what effective force Britain
could attack Germany by air direct or what weight of bombs
she could drop on Germany.

If there was to be an effective economic blockade of Germany
"we might have to stretch our belligerent rights well beyond the
limits allowed by international law".

The Foreign Secretary then dealt with the last sentences in
the memorandum that seemed most to impinge on his domain:
"I agree it is of supreme importance to maintain a close and
confident relationship with the French Government and to co-
ordinate our efforts. It is of almost equal importance so to
conduct our relations with the U.S. Government that the latter
shall raise as few obstacles as possible, in case of grave emergency, either to the use of our naval power in exercise of
economic pressure or, in spite of present neutrality legislation,
to the grant of financial accommodation and the supply of
munitions to this country and her allies from the United States.
To go further, it must always be our constant aim in peacetime
to increase as far as possible the likelihood of the U.S. giving us
armed support in case of war."

Finally, of the hints of appeasement or dividing potential
enemies contained in the last lines of the memorandum, the
Foreign Office paper remarked:

"The Chiefs of Staff also rightly emphasise the importance of
doing what we can to reduce the number of our potential
enemies.

"Germany, Italy and Japan have recently associated themselves in a pact, the ostensible purpose of which is common
resistance to the spread of Communism. . . . There is no reason
why contacts should not be maintained between His Majesty's
Government and the three Governments in question, to seek a
settlement of outstanding issues and establishment of har-
monious relations, if that is possible. But it would, I think, be
a mistake to try to detach any one member of the German–
Italian–Japanese bloc by offers of support or acquiescence in
the fulfilment of their aims. The aims of all three are in varying

c

degrees inimical to British interests and a surrender to one might well be the signal for further concerted action on the part of all three Powers."

The Foreign Office paper then reflected on the alternative—"it might be more in keeping with our honour and dignity to pursue a policy of armed strength. This might continue for years without either peace or war in Europe. This policy has in the past been described as 'cunctation',[1] and might be the penalty to be paid now for having failed to resist aggression since 1931."

Sir Thomas Inskip criticised a suggestion in the Foreign Office paper that, provided Britain played for time and was given time, all would be well, whereas the Chiefs of Staff had emphasised that she would never be able to fight Germany, Italy and Japan simultaneously. Sir John Simon was irritated by the word cunctation, which Mr Eden explained as meaning "marking time". "We are not marking time," snapped Sir John, "we are in process of spending £1,500 millions on our defence." He thought that the Foreign Office paper "insufficiently recognises the importance of reducing the number of our potential enemies. . . . It is clear that we cannot go on spending at this rate forever, and a political adjustment with one or more of our political enemies is absolutely vital."

Mr Eden argued that the Chiefs of Staff memorandum had failed to take full account of the economic weaknesses of the three potential enemies. It was not correct to assume that Italy would be as strong in a military sense a year hence as she was in 1937. The main contention that he had tried to bring out, however, was that the basis of British foreign policy could not be changed. Nothing could be done to alter the situation with Japan. So far as Italy was concerned no reliance whatsoever could be placed on her promises. As regards Germany, he said, the Committee were well aware what was being done to reach an understanding with her, and it was unnecessary to go into details.

Lord Halifax offered the opinion that Foreign Office pessimism on the chances of reaching conciliation with Germany might not be justified. Mr Chamberlain summed up that the Chiefs of Staff had addressed some warnings to the Committee

---

[1] The action of delaying, delay, tardy action, *The Oxford English Dictionary*.

of Imperial Defence and had been "perfectly right to do so. . . . On the other hand their conclusions were in some respects reassuring. It would be a mistake to count too much on assistance from France or the United States in the event of war. The French Army was good but their Air Force was deplorable. The United States on the other hand had almost incalculable power. The difficulty was to get it into the open and it was impossible to rely on the Americans delivering the goods. They would probably come in on our side eventually, but they would probably come too late. It was also a mistake to count too much on the co-operation of minor powers."

The Chiefs of Staff, pursued Mr Chamberlain, had appealed to the Foreign Office to detach one or other of our potential enemies. He could himself see no prospect of success by methods that would shame us in the eyes of the world . . . and ultimately land us in worse difficulties. He preferred the present policy of the Foreign Office to that of doing nothing. He preferred active diplomacy to cunctation. Our Ambassador in Tokyo was trying to keep the door open. So far as Germany was concerned, the Committee was well aware what was being done. As for Italy, everything was being attempted to initiate conversations. He felt that the policy which he had summarised should put Britain in a better position.

The Prime Minister plainly did not like the Foreign Office memorandum, in which the use of the obscure word cunctation and some cutting phrases about failing to resist aggression, suggested the hand of Vansittart, who had indeed revised it on November 23rd with Mr Strang. Chamberlain proposed that the Committee of Imperial Defence note the warnings of the Chiefs of Staff and the *oral* statement of the Foreign Secretary himself "which took proper account of the situation". The inference was that the written comments of the Foreign Office did not do so.

The "Comparison of Strength" was then referred on to the Cabinet itself which met on December 8th to consider this appeal for greater use of diplomacy. The Prime Minister explained both the Chiefs of Staff paper and the reactions to it of the Foreign Secretary. He thus precluded any prolonged discussion, and gave the matter the emphasis that he desired.

"The Foreign Secretary", declared Mr Chamberlain, "had

circulated a short paper to the Committee of Imperial Defence dealing with certain aspects of the Chiefs of Staff paper, but not pretending to give any general account of our foreign policy. At the meeting of the Committee, however, the Foreign Secretary had made a verbal statement, the general effect of which had been summarised in conclusion." He then repeated the main considerations that had been brought to the notice of the committee. It was true, as the Chiefs of Staff had pointed out, that we could not hope to confront satisfactorily Germany, Italy and Japan simultaneously and, when we looked round as to what help we could get from other nations, the results were not very encouraging. France was our most important friend. Though she was strong defensively and possessed a powerful army, the French Air Force was far from satisfactory. During the Anglo-French visit, M. Chautemps had admitted to an output of aircraft that was only about one-fifth (60–300) of our own.

"A long time must elapse before France would be able to give us much help in the air. The Power that had the greatest strength was the United States of America, but he would be a rash man who based his calculations on help from that quarter. Our position in relation to the smaller Powers was much better than formerly, but he did not think that they would add much to our offensive or defensive strength. In time of peace their support was useful, but in war less so. The Chiefs of Staff, as he had mentioned, said they could not foresee the time when our defence forces would be strong enough to safeguard our territory, trade and vital interests against Germany, Italy and Japan simultaneously. They had urged that our foreign policy must be governed by this consideration, and they had made rather a strong appeal to this effect. Of course, it would be possible to make an effort to detach one of the three Powers from the other two and it might even succeed. This, however, could only be done at the cost of concessions which would involve humiliations and disadvantages to this country by destroying the confidence of other nations. No one would suppose, therefore, that we should try and bribe one of the three nations to leave the other two. What the Foreign Secretary was doing was to try and prevent a situation arising in which the three Powers mentioned would ever be at war with us.

"As he himself had pointed out before, however, Germany was the real key to the question. In view of the recent consideration given by the Cabinet to the question of improving relations with Germany, it was unnecessary to develop that theme any further. He thought, however, that he had said enough to show that the strategic considerations urged by the Chiefs of Staff were fully taken into account in our foreign policy.

There was then what is described as a "short discussion" in the Cabinet. According to the record,[1] one of the Ministers drew attention to the undertaking given in 1936 by Mr Baldwin to maintain air parity with Germany. Sir Thomas Inskip argued that Lord Baldwin's statement required to be interpreted. "He had never taken it to mean that Britain must have exactly the same number of fighters and bombers as Germany in order to carry out the contemplated equality." Mr Chamberlain then said that he did not intend to repeat the pledge of Mr Baldwin. "If the question were raised, he would make it clear that the Government did not consider it necessary to have precise equality in every class of aircraft."

In this way he stepped his policy towards the understanding that he sought with Germany. The discussion on air parity may have arisen from a Most Secret Defence Plans Policy Sub-Committee Report submitted by Lord Swinton on October 27th 1937. In this the Secretary of State for Air reported that General Erhard Milch on a visit to London admitted that Germany had already completed the construction programme of aircraft that, according to his earlier statements, was only to have been completed by the autumn of 1938.

Lord Swinton dryly observed that "General Milch promised that if an expansion (of the Luftwaffe) took place we should be informed. Judging by the past, I cannot place much reliance on this undertaking and I think the information would be given after and not before the event."

To this disturbing report was attached a memorandum from the Air Staff, "The Requisite Standard of Air Strength". This recommended that the existing programme of 124 R.A.F. squadrons be increased by 30 squadrons to provide a first-line metropolitian air strength of 2,331 aircraft, including 1,442 bombers.[2] The memorandum repeated a saying of Sir Edward

---

[1] Cab. 46 (37), p. 268   [2] Referred to as Scheme J

Grey, British Foreign Secretary in 1912, to which an Admiralty paper had already drawn the attention of the Cabinet. On the subject of appeasement as a substitute for military preparedness Sir Edward had said:

"In the first place you must not rely upon your foreign policy to protect the United Kingdom. That is to say, if you let your margin of naval strength fall below that which may be brought to bear against you rapidly, you are setting foreign policy a task which you ought not to set it. The risk of an attack on the United Kingdom stronger in force than we could meet with the ships we keep in Home waters is not one to be settled by diplomacy."

This dictum could in 1937 be extended to air as well as naval strength. The ensuing Cabinet of December 22nd 1937 would show how much this advice was being ignored, and that the Chamberlain Cabinet would follow an opposite course to that preferred by Sir Edward Grey.

CHAPTER VI

A Fateful Session

WHETHER MR CHAMBERLAIN actually slowed down the momentum of rearmament at the end of 1937 is open to some doubt; for rearmament had not yet gathered momentum, despite the agonised appeals of Admiral Sir Harold Brown and Sir Robert Vansittart in January. It would be more accurate to suggest that his deliberate and methodical handling of both financial approval and policy prevented an immediate expansion and acceleration of the rearmament programme. The slow pace is well illustrated in the introductory paragraph to the "Report on Defence Expenditure in Future Years"[1] already quoted in Chapter IV, which was printed and circulated to the Cabinet on December 15th 1937. This recalled that the Cabinet meeting of June 30th asked the Minister for Co-ordination of Defence to estimate anew the period of time required for the completion of defence programmes on the basis already sanctioned and extending over the years 1937–41. The total demands of the Services Ministers, taking into account rising prices, were to be submitted year by year for consideration by the Treasury. It was observed that "additions have been made to the programme without any attempt to find countervailing economies".

The Treasury view was that "on the average £220m. a year can be found for defence over the 5 years 1937 to 1941. But the present position in regard to borrowing is now more difficult than in the Spring. If it were decided that it was necessary to spend substantially more than £1,500m. on defence over this period of years, it would probably be found necessary that the excess should be found by an increase in the level of taxation, rather than by increasing the total sum made available for defence from borrowed money above £400m. . . . The broad conclusion to be drawn from this summary is that it is necessary to take under review the whole range of the Defence Programmes in order to determine which items are essential, and

[1] C.P. 316 (37)

which items are of lower priority and can be postponed, curtailed or dispensed with."

Another increase in income tax, raised in April by 3*d*. to 5*s*. in the £1, would be unpopular. So Mr Chamberlain sought again to bring the Service Departments into line when the Cabinet met three days before Christmas to consider this lengthy report. It had also an unusually heavy agenda of eight parliamentary Bills and one Order-in-Council. Many of these had to be discussed later in the Christmas recess.

There was first an incident in the Far East to consider. H.M.S. *Ladybird* had just been hit by Japanese gunfire and the U.S. gunboat *Panay* sunk in China waters. Mr Eden reported that President Roosevelt had told the British Ambassador in Washington that there might be a blockade of Japan "*after* the next incident", and that he was meanwhile willing to have naval staff conversations with Britain. Mr Chamberlain, Mr Eden and Mr Duff Cooper agreed that they would have liked more immediate Anglo-American action as a preventive to another incident of the same kind. Mr Eden, however, warned his colleagues against too optimistic a view of any immediate action and the Prime Minister added that the President and Mr Morgenthau were "still contemplating the possibility of sanctions without war. . . . It was necessary to convince them that it was impossible to apply a blockade without being ready to support it by force". There was a distinct British reluctance to make a show of force alone, but the Cabinet appeared to agree that Britain would be prepared to make a joint demonstration with the United States if she was willing. After deciding, despite fresh difficulties with Ireland, to continue to treat the Irish Free State as remaining within the Commonwealth, the Cabinet turned its attention to the Inskip "Report on Defence Expenditure in Future Years" and Sir Thomas summed up the issues upon which he asked for Cabinet approval.

He laid emphasis upon the shortage of financial resources; upon the desired priorities in defence; upon the need for the Royal Navy not to expand its programme beyond the already approved standard of strength; and upon the proposal in his report that the primary role of the Regular Army should be that of Imperial Commitments coupled with anti-aircraft defence duties at home. He proposed that the Air Defence of

Great Britain and Fighter Squadron dispositions should be extended beyond their existing northern limits and that R.A.F. expansion should concentrate on the Metropolitan Air Force rather than overseas—another way of suggesting that fighters rather than bombers were the necessary arm of the future. Sir Thomas acknowledged the assistance that he had received on the proposed pattern of defence from the Treasury, the Foreign Office, the Committee of Imperial Defence and Sir Horace Wilson. He then drew attention to paragraph 31—"every effort must be made to bring the total Defence Expenditure over the five years 1937-41 within the total of £1,500m."—and again to paragraph 37—"that in the long run the provision of adequate defence will only be achieved when our long-term foreign policy has succeeded in changing the present assumptions as to the number of our potential enemies".

Sir Thomas quoted Mr Hore-Belisha, the Secretary of State for War, as having said at an earlier Cabinet meeting that France no longer looked to Britain in the event of war to supply an Expeditionary Force on the scale hitherto proposed. This had led him to suggest that the Army outside the United Kingdom should be related to the defence of Imperial commitments. Sir Robert Vansittart, added Sir Thomas, had written a letter to him on the possible consequences of this policy, and with the Air Staff he had experienced considerable difficulties over the question of bomber aircraft. His own view was that parity (with Germany) was more important in fighter aircraft, resisting aggression, than in the offensive role of bombers. The Air Staff had described this policy as inadequate and defeatist.

The Prime Minister adjourned the morning Cabinet and invited them at 5 p.m. to his room at the House of Commons. In the interval Mr Duff Cooper remained unshaken in his pursuit of expanded rearmament and contended in the afternoon session that the Navy's building programme, as then approved for 1938-9, represented an actual reduction on the previously agreed standard of strength. Mr Hore-Belisha on the other hand paid an obedient tribute to the Chamberlain–Inskip line. He thanked Sir Thomas for sympathising with the difficulties of the Army Council in the matter of priorities and declared that he was himself coming to the same conclusion about the Army's role. He acknowledged that the Cabinet had never accepted the whole of the proposed War Office programme for developing a large field force for service in Europe. A Continental expedition was for him last in the list of priorities. The international situation was not, he said, analogous with 1914. He had been impressed with the French Maginot Line which required only 100,000 men to hold it. If Britain was to scrap the idea of an Expeditionary Force, he said, that would encourage France to extend the Maginot Line to the sea.

It then fell to Viscount Swinton to speak for the R.A.F. The Secretary of State for Air said that he agreed with the views of the Prime Minister that the key to the problem of British safety was Germany, but he pointed to the inevitable risk involved in relinquishing the bomber programme. The calculations of the Air Staff were more scientifically based than Sir Thomas Inskip had allowed. What was not possible, said Lord Swinton, especially with the Air Force, was to improvise at short notice. The object of a bomber force was to reduce the enemy's power of attack by bombing his aerodromes, factories, etc. He did not think it possible to have an Air Force that did not provide an effective deterrent by its offensive power.

As for the question of striking a balance between the effort to be expended in accumulating reserves of war material and that devoted to expanding the war potential, he must point out that even a fully equipped shadow factory like Austins would take six months to get into production of aircraft. *The only alternative to building up war reserves and developing war production potential simultaneously was for the Air Force to go slow during the first six months of a war.*[1]

Lord Swinton then conceded that as it seemed to be impossible to make every preparation simultaneously, it was better to reduce the piling of reserves in future programmes and increase the war potential. He reflected that the existence of shadow factories was itself a strong deterrent to war.

In the light of what must be anticipated as to the strength of the German Air Force, concluded the Secretary of State for Air, and taking into consideration the announced British commitment (to parity in the air) he would suggest that the Government could not accept less than the expanded Scheme J for the R.A.F. without a complete reversal of policy. They ought to

[1] Author's italics

build, and above all, recruit the personnel up to that basis of strength and prepare plans for a real war potential.

Sir John Simon then put the Treasury case. The Chancellor of the Exchequer said that the scheme of the Minister for Co-ordination of Defence would have the effect of containing the Admiralty for next year on its present basis of naval construction and that in twelve months a decision would be taken as to whether the naval programme was to be increased. The Air Force was to be increased by the adoption of part of Scheme J, but the largest changes were to be made to the role of the Army which, he hoped, would save many millions. He pointed out that the authorised programme for the Air Force was at present Scheme F and not Scheme J.

The paper before them, Sir Thomas Inskip's "Report on Defence Expenditure in Future Years", proposed to establish a reserve of 225 per cent of war material in store against the risk of war. Sir John described this as "an intelligible proposition", but he objected that "in five to seven years it might mean that we should possess a mass of obsolete machines, whereas if the money was put into war potential, the factories would be able to produce up-to-date machines". He thought therefore that there was great force in the argument that an increase in war potential was better than an exaggerated production of reserves.

Many factors made up parity of military strength, he argued, not merely a counting of machines. On a numerical basis it would quite easy to reach a point where we could not compete any longer. Sir John thought that the proposals of Sir Thomas Inskip did in fact carry out the pledges previously given by Mr Baldwin of air parity.

No pledge could last forever, observed Mr Chamberlain. He was prepared to defend a departure from previous pledges in the House of Commons, if the Cabinet thought it necessary.

Sir John Simon asked the Services Ministers for early defence estimates, as he had this year for the first time to consider what part would be met out of taxation and what out of loan. The estimates must be published by the end of February 1938. The Cabinet would consider them on February 16th, so that time might remain for the Treasury to make its calculations. Moreover he wished the Service Ministers also to send forecast estimates for the next five years to the Minister for Co-ordination of Defence, so that he might consider the loans necessary.

Mr Hore-Belisha murmured a complaint that all this extra work meant the officials of the War Office giving up any idea of a Christmas holiday. Sir John had a final admonition for the Services Departments. "Until the total was known, he did not know whether the programmes would be within the financial capacity of the country to carry them out."

The tide of argument was then turned a little in favour of urgency by Sir Samuel Hoare. As a former First Lord of the Admiralty, the Home Secretary stated his view that without an improvement in Anglo-German relations, it would be necessary to complete at least twenty capital ships. He suggested a surplus allowance for the training of more naval personnel. He also declared himself reluctant to go directly against the advice of the Air Staff and was against approving the proposals of Sir Thomas Inskip that war reserves should come second to war potential. "In a future war the enemy's efforts were likely to be devoted towards a knock-out blow. That brought out the importance of first-line strength." He hoped that the question would be considered further from that point of view.

Mr Eden acknowledged the general argument of the memorandum that defence should be related to economic capacity. It appeared to him "irresistible", though he had "some apprehensions as to the stated inability to assist allies on land". These were aroused by those paragraphs of the report which defined the Continental role of the Army as fourth in order of priority.[1]

This definition is put forward by reason of the increasing demands made on our manpower and industrial resources by the risk of air attack [the report stated], which necessitates increases in the Air Force and in the Air Defence of Great Britain. It may be noted, however, that a number of recent events have occurred which go far to justify this change in policy. Thus it has been suggested that France no longer looks to us in the event of war to supply an expeditionary force on the scale hitherto proposed in addition to our all-important co-operation on the sea and in the air. Secondly Germany has guaranteed the inviolability and integrity of Belgian territory and there seems good reason for thinking that it would be in Germany's interests to honour this agreement.[2]

[1] C.O.S. 316 (37) paras 68, 69, 70

[2] This December assessment by Sir Thomas Inskip is more optimistic about Belgium than the assumptions in the November C.O.S. memorandum

Mr Eden objected that the report was concentrating too much on the defensive. "The Army was to have an entirely defensive role and it was proposed to deprive the Air Force of part of the offensive power advocated by the Secretary of State for Air. He agreed with the Home Secretary that the Cabinet should not interfere with the Air Ministry as to the distribution of our resources between offensive and defensive. He had also been disturbed by the suggestion of the Secretary of State for War that the country was opposed to sending forces abroad until it was safe at home. If the Channel ports fell into the hands of Germany, the country would not be safe. If war was to take place in Western Europe, an attack on France by Germany was the most probable operation to be envisaged. He did not under-rate the value of the Maginot Line, but might we not be called on to help? It was true that M. Delbos had said that France only expected us to provide two mechanised Divisions and M. Daladier had said something of the same kind to the Secretary of State for War, but both statements had overlooked Belgium and had been made on the assumption that Belgium could look after herself. If, however, there was an invasion of Belgium or Holland, the position would be different and the Chiefs of Staff had shown again and again that this would be the chosen method to break through into France. He would not ask to change the order of priority, but he thought it essential that when a decision had been taken, the French Government should be told, so that the two countries might consider together how their countries were to be defended.

"From an international point of view, the strength of the Air Force was of the first importance, as illustrated by the impression made on the Milch Mission. From this point of view, he would very much like to see Scheme J adopted for the R.A.F. He would like to know also whether the Secretary of State for War contemplated being in a position to provide the two mechanised Divisions desired by the French. If, however, there should be any margin of expenditure, he hoped that priority would be given to the Air Ministry's Scheme J and that there

on the comparative strength of certain nations in January 1938. These regarded Belgium merely as increasing her chances of remaining neutral as she rearmed and in making their calculations of military strength the Chiefs of Staff ranged Belgium with Britain and France.

would be no revision or watering-down of our pledges."

Mr Hore-Belisha embraced the Inskip doctrine. He replied that "if British resources were larger, he could provide a bigger Army but, having regard to the effort being made at sea, in the air and in finance, he did not think that the French ought to expect we could furnish an Army as well, though he agreed that the French ought to be told of our decision. So far British conversations with the French had been confined to the subject of Belgium. He thought they ought to extend over the whole world. France would then be brought to realise that if the United Kingdom were subjected to air attack, it would be wrong for them to count on Expeditionary Force from this country. The only way he could supply two mechanised Divisions was by dividing the existing Division into two, which was conceived on lines rather larger than in some countries."

Lord Swinton sought to clarify the position. He understood that it was the intention of the Minister for Co-ordination of Defence to leave Scheme F intact and to increase the fighters of the Metropolitan Air Force up to the scale of Scheme J. In addition there was to be some increase in the first-line strength of bombers to meet an increase by Germany of 50 per cent in her bomber strength. Further, the case for larger war reserves rather than higher war potential was again to be considered. Sir Thomas agreed that this was broadly the case. Sir Samuel Hoare thereupon expressed the opinion that the question of maintaining air parity or abandoning it was thus avoided for the time being.

The Prime Minister then spoke his preference for war potential rather than the accumulation of 225 per cent in war material reserves. Lord Swinton reiterated that without strong aircraft reserves, it was impossible to make good the losses incurred during the early months of a war. Even if the machines in reserve were not of the very latest type, he said, they would be better than none. The estimate of a 225 per cent reserve of aircraft had been worked out on a most careful computation of the rate of casualties.

Lord Halifax supported Lord Swinton, Mr Eden and Sir Samuel Hoare on the question of air strength. As to the role of the Army, he hoped that the Cabinet would not overlook the warning contained by the Inskip Report that:

If France were again to be in danger of being over-run by land armies, a situation might arise when, as in the last war, we had to improvise an army to assist her. Should this happen, the Government of the day would most certainly be criticised for having neglected to provide against so obvious a contingency.

Lord Halifax continued that Sir Thomas had been right to emphasise the importance of relating diplomacy to rearmament (a point of policy on which Mr Eden had said that he refrained from comment). The fact that Britain must work to an expenditure of about £1,500m. over the next five years—a sum that Lord Halifax deduced was inadequate—brought out clearly that the limitations imposed on defence by finance threw a heavy burden on diplomacy.

"In spite of all the efforts of the Foreign Secretary, the Prime Minister and others," said Lord Halifax, "we have arrived at a position which above all we wished to avoid, in which we are faced with the possibility of three enemies at once. The conclusion which I draw—and no doubt it will be shared by the Foreign Secretary—is that this throws an immensely heavy burden on diplomacy and that we ought to make every possible effort to get on good terms with Germany. I realise the great pressure on the Foreign Secretary but, after this discussion, I feel it is of great importance to make further progress in improving relations with Germany."

Mr Eden did not allow himself to be drawn by this appeal and commented briefly that the first task would be to review with the French Government what offer could be made to Germany in the colonial field. Evidently he felt that there was no room for appeasement in Europe alone. The Prime Minister concurred that no move could be made with Germany until after further explorations. He emphasised that whatever Britain could do in the colonial field must be counter-balanced by some move by Germany. Public opinion would not tolerate an arrangement on any other lines. He recalled that it had been thought that the German contribution to a settlement might take the form of some measure of disarmament. Herr Hitler had made a statement in November to Lord Halifax which opened the possibility of some advance on these lines. Mr Chamberlain

[1] C.O.S. 316 (37) para 75

said that "he had accordingly taken on himself to ask the Minister for Co-ordination of Defence to go into the technical aspects of the question of limitation of bomber aeroplanes, as well as of other forms of qualitative disarmament. So far as the general question was concerned, he hoped to address himself to the matter during the Recess with a view to a meeting of the Committee on Foreign Policy in the New Year."

This hint of a form of deal by Mr Chamberlain gave rise to a discussion of "the difficulties of air limitation". Finally the Prime Minister summed up. He attached great importance to those paragraphs of the Inskip Report that stressed the necessity of maintaining economic stability as an essential element in defensive strength. This had often been spoken of, but he did not recall seeing it put forward as a vital consideration on defence. Mr Chamberlain said: "In my view, this is a matter of first importance. It may be that in the next war our enemy would aim at a 'knock-out' blow, but the evidence before me does not show that it would be likely to succeed. . . . If that view is correct, the factor of our staying power must be present in the minds of other Governments as well as of ourselves. They must be asking themselves what are our chances in a long war."

Mr Chamberlain then ran over the priorities of defence as listed by Sir Thomas Inskip and restated various points as he saw them and as he assumed the Cabinet to be agreed with him in seeing them. The fairly fundamental objections of Swinton, Eden and even Halifax to defence limitation he seemed to brush aside by merely conceding that their views were reasonable enough. It was recorded in the minutes by the assiduous Hankey that the Cabinet agreed to approve the "Report on Defence Expenditure In Future Years," with the following observations:

> The Cabinet took note with approval of those parts of the Report stating the factors of economic resources and stability as being essential to the strength and fulfilment of the Defence programmes.
> The Cabinet adopted the proposed defence priorities,[1] but deferred a final decision on an increased standard of naval strength until next year.

[1] C.O.S. 316 (37) Part IV

The primary Army role was to be as stated in the Minister's Report—that of Imperial commitments including Anti-Aircraft defence at home.

Some parts of the Regular Army and Territorial Army might in the scale of attack now envisaged, be used for internal security duties.

No final decision was reached on policy for expansion of the Air Force, but the Minister for Co-ordination of Defence was to consult further with the Secretary of State for Air.

The Cabinet took note that the Chancellor of the Exchequer required a forecast of anticipated expenditure on the Defence Programmes up to March 1942.

Finally the Cabinet were recorded as having agreed that (i) "the limitations which finance imposes on National Defence place a heavy burden on diplomacy, which renders it desirable, as soon as may be, to follow up the conversations between the Lord President of the Council and Herr Hitler, and (ii) that with this in view the Prime Minister has instructed the Minister for Co-ordination of Defence to take up with the Services Departments the possibility of some limitation of bomber aircraft as well as other forms of qualitative disarmament."

It may be noted that these conclusions omitted any resolution to inform the French Government of the forsaken Continental role of the British Army. In none of their autobiographies do the principal Ministers of the Chamberlain Cabinet mention the Cabinet meeting of December 22nd, but Mr Eden records in his memoirs in a general way the fundamental differences between his views and the Inskip Report. "Sir Thomas was inclined to lend too much weight to the Treasury argument," he wrote. "My replies could not be accommodating. I pointed out that Germany, Italy and Japan each had ambitions and we stood in the way of their fulfilment."[1] There might have been a case for resigning over defence limitation and the Chamberlain proposal that Britain should reduce her air striking power in the hope of detaching Germany from the array of hostile powers. Mr Eden's thoughts of resignation would not be long deferred. Thus 1937 ended with a slow emphasis on rearmament and hopes placed on a stretched diplomacy.

[1] Avon, *Facing the Dictators*

CHAPTER VII

The Rift with Eden

Mʀ Cʜᴀᴍʙᴇʀʟᴀɪɴ ᴡᴀs evidently in a hurry in January
1938 and meant to allow no obstacles to his policy. Eden did not
wish to let the initiative in foreign policy pass from the Foreign
Office to less informed Ministers or City groups with access
through Sir Horace Wilson to 10 Downing Street. The Foreign
Office therefore quickly produced a paper, which Eden circulated to Ministers and other members of the Foreign Affairs
Committee of the Cabinet on January 1st 1938, under the title
"Further Steps Towards a General Settlement".[1] He wrote:

> I circulate to my colleagues of the Foreign Policy Committee the
> attached paper prepared in the Foreign Office to indicate some of
> the main points which seem to require an early decision in order
> to enable His Majesty's Government to follow up the recent con-
> versation between the Lord President of the Council and Herr
> Hitler.
> January 1st 1938.   A. E.

The preamble stated that:

> The conversation between Lord Halifax and Herr Hitler showed
> that, if we wish for a general settlement with Germany, it will be
> for us and not for the German Government to take the next step
> by putting forward some concrete proposals. The conversations
> with the French Ministers showed that no progress could be made
> until His Majesty's Government had made up their mind on how
> the problem of Germany's colonial claims is to be tackled. The
> next step therefore lies with us. It is important, if we are really
> anxious to prevent the hopes created by the recent conversations
> from evaporating, that there should be no long delay. We must
> keep moving. . . .

The Foreign Office paper discussed the "present claim of
Germany to all her former colonies, or for equivalent colonial

[1] F.P. (36) 41

territory elsewhere". It declared the Foreign Office to be incompetent to decide on its own either what British territories overseas should be ceded, or what territory now under Allied or friendly mandate (French, Belgian or Portuguese) might have to be added to make an equivalent offer in size and value to the former German colonial possessions.

It had to be borne in mind that neither Tanganyika nor South West Africa could form part of the act of restitution.

The paper then queried in equally general terms the nature of a "general settlement with Germany". Would this embrace a new Peace Conference of Powers; would it consist of a series of bilateral settlements in Europe; or, "as the Germans presumably wish, would it be a purely Anglo-German Settlement, general only in the sense of covering all the points outstanding between the two countries?" These were the alternatives upon which the members of the Foreign Policy Committee would have to decide.

Mr Chamberlain may have considered that this paper savoured rather of cunctation in its approach to an urgent subject. It really did no more than illustrate that thinking in the Cabinet was in extreme disarray and that nobody quite knew how a bargain could be struck. Having put this problem to his Cabinet Committee colleagues, Mr Eden went off to the South of France for a short holiday.

The Foreign Affairs Committee of the Cabinet had not met since July 1937, partly for seasonal reasons and partly also because in his *impasse* between British public opinion, which was unwilling to make concessions to Germany in Africa, and a Foreign Office which was unwilling to make concessions to her in Europe, Mr Chamberlain could see no immediate reason for calling it sooner. He nevertheless entertained high hopes that he could very soon himself take the initiative with Germany and Italy and detach one or other of his formidable enemies from their triple entente with Japan.

These hopes are well illustrated by the reserve and scepticism with which he treated a Most Secret message from President Roosevelt in which Roosevelt told of an initiative of his own of a similar kind, but more censorious and public in character.

Mr Sumner Welles, the Under Secretary of State in Washington, approached the British Ambassador, Sir Ronald Lindsay, on January 11th with an outline of the Roosevelt idea. If Britain by January 17th had decided to give it cordial and open support, the President proposed to make a declaration on the fundamental principles governing international relations when he addressed the Diplomatic Corps at a New Year Reception on January 22nd. He would make some observations on giving all nations access to raw materials and would further speak about the rights and obligations of nations in wartime. He would pursue his aim of improving the rapidly deteriorating situation by inviting the Heads of Government of some European countries, but not Austria or Czechoslovakia, to visit him for talks. The President described this as an initiative parallel to that which Britain was taking in Central Europe.

Since Mr Eden was absent on the Riviera, Sir Alexander Cadogan, who on January 1st 1938 had succeeded Vansittart as the Head of the Foreign Office, alerted his Secretary of State, but meanwhile sent the President's message over to 10 Downing Street. His own Minute on the plan was that "the President certainly has courage. If he wants to advance along this line, the risks may be worth taking." Lindsay in a telegram from Washington on January 13th recommended "a very quick and cordial acceptance of the President's ideas", But Mr Chamberlain, on this delicate diplomatic matter, referred Cadogan to his Chief Industrial Adviser, Sir Horace Wilson, who later described the President's move as "woolly rubbish."[1]

Without waiting for the return of Eden on January 15th, Chamberlain sent a reply to the President on the 13th asking him "to consider holding his hand for a short while"[2] and informing him of his own plans for appeasement. Evidently he doubted whether America would under any circumstances support Britain in a European war and thought that Roosevelt would only irritate the dictators by his long-distance open diplomacy. To soften the rebuff, Chamberlain sent this telegram to Lindsay in Washington:

I do hope the President will not find my message disappointing. He was, of course, not aware of our latest plans here for resuming our efforts at conciliation. The information that I have now given

---

[1] Avon, *Facing the Dictators*
[2] From Mr Eden's Cabinet précis of events.

him may show him that this factor ought to be taken into consideration. His plan, drawn up without full knowledge of all that is going on, risks upsetting all we were trying to do here.

Sir Alexander Cadogan met the returning Eden at Folkestone with the telegrams. The Foreign Secretary read them on the boat train. Before going to see Mr Chamberlain at Chequers, the Foreign Secretary was treated to a lecture on foreign affairs by Sir Horace Wilson, who kept watch in 10 Downing Street while his master was away. There was an awkward interview on the 16th at Chequers between Chamberlain and Eden and another on the 18th at 10 Downing Street, when Eden got wind of family letters between Neville Chamberlain and Lady Ivy Chamberlain, widow of Sir Austen, who was spending the winter in Rome. In these Chamberlain had revealed his mind on the possibilities of a general settlement between Britain and Italy and one such letter had been shown by Lady Ivy to Count Ciano. Three meetings of the Foreign Affairs Committee of the Cabinet were held in rapid succession on January 19th, 20th, and 21st to discuss the President's initiative, to improve on the first messages sent in reply to it, and to discuss Mr Chamberlain's plan to accord *de jure* recognition to the annexation of Abyssinia by Italy, a move on which Roosevelt requested Chamberlain to "hold your horses". The Committee was divided in its views on the wisdom of Mr Chamberlain's first response. We know from the Eden memoirs that at the first of these meetings Mr Chamberlain read long extracts from a letter written from Rome by Ivy Chamberlain. She had conceived a personal mission of mending Anglo-Italian relations.

No full official record of these three meetings appears to exist. The meticulous Hankey was present as Secretary at each and noted that "a full record" or "a full summary of the above discussion is on record in the Secretary's official file of the Minutes". These were not circulated at the time, because the subject was confidential between two Heads of Government, though Mr Eden made a précis of the proceedings for restricted circulation. When I first drew attention to this gap in the Secretary's file at the Public Record Office on December 31st 1968, a thorough investigation was made by Cabinet Office officials which lasted until April 1969, when it was agreed that "no trace has been found among the records of the Cabinet Office of the Summaries of the discussions in the Foreign Policy Committee on 19th/21st January 1938; nor has any trace been found of the Secretary's standard or official file for this Committee."

The reply of President Roosevelt to Mr Chamberlain was that he "greatly appreciated the very frank and friendly spirit" of the Prime Minister's message, but Mr Cordell Hull, the U.S. Secretary of State, let it be known to Sir Ronald Lindsay at dinner that the President was disappointed, and in the swift train of subsequent events his plan was first postponed and finally abandoned. Mr Chamberlain, though he relented to the extent of raising his objection to the American plan being proceeded with, would not have Britain wholly associated with it. He described it as "open to many criticisms" and on the evening of January 24th referred to it in Cabinet as a "rather preposterous" plan. His own preference, it will be seen, remained for secret diplomacy.

Mr Eden was much upset as all prospects of a Roosevelt initiative faded, and upset too at the lack of consultation between the Prime Minister and himself. "I hope we have not discouraged the poor President too much", he minuted in red ink on the Foreign Office file which in the space of two weeks had grown thick with correspondence. The final entry was made by Cadogan after the German invasion of Austria: "I think the time has come when all this story should be entered 'green'." This meant that the correspondence should be filed away with a high degree of secrecy, as befitted an initiative that had never been taken.

It remains an open question whether the Roosevelt initiative could, without full British backing, have done more than irritate the dictatorships. Its main importance in this story is that it deepened the rift between Chamberlain and Eden, the former believing, together with Sir Horace Wilson, that it would have gravely disturbed the chances of a settlement with Germany upon which they were building their hopes. Lord Avon relates that he bitterly reproached the Prime Minister when they met at Chequers on January 16th for having himself sent a reply to Roosevelt although he knew that his Foreign Secretary would be home and available to advise him within twenty-four hours. "For the first time our relations were seriously at odds."[1] — FIRST TIME EDEN REALIZED THE FACT.

After this first flurry of Cabinet Committee meetings in 1938 there was a fourth, also at 10 Downing Street, on the morning of January 24th to consider appeasement and the prospects of a general settlement. Mr Chamberlain told the Committee that "he had been impressed by the desirability of showing the Germans at the earliest possible moment that we were giving serious consideration to the position arising out of Lord Halifax's visit (to Germany). As time went on the Germans might well become suspicious that we had abandoned our intention of following up Lord Halifax's conversations."

He thought that if Britain entered into conversations with Italy, as he now wished to do, such suspicions might be confirmed and intensified. If an announcement had to be made about the opening of Anglo-Italian conversations, it would assist the Government if it were known that it was making efforts towards "general appeasement" with Germany as well as Italy. Chamberlain then unfolded his plan for associating Germany with an entirely new form of colonial administration in Africa on a demilitarised and international basis. Eden stated with some emphasis that it must be made clear to the Germans "beyond any possibility of doubt that there could be no colonial settlement except as part of a general arrangement".

There was some discussion between Ministers, the minutes tell us, on the method of approach to Germany and the sacrifices that other colonial powers would be called upon to make. Sir John Simon said that "a glance at the map of West Africa will show how very extensive are the possessions of Belgium and Portugal in that part of the world".

Mr Eden warned the meeting that on this aspect "we should have to be very careful indeed . . . Portugal is extremely sensitive . . . and . . . very apprehensive . . . that some deal in West Africa at her expense is in contemplation".

Sir Samuel Hoare objected that the Prime Minister appeared to envisage a separate approach to Germany on the colonial issue which, if rejected, would leave the position rather worse than before.

"The Prime Minister did not agree", the minutes record.

[1] Avon, *Facing the Dictators*

"He could not see why the position would be worsened by the submission in outline of his proposals to Germany." Sir Samuel pointed out that Germany would not be content with sharing an international administration and would expect some offer of territory "with full sovereignty" in tropical Africa.

"It is imperative", interjected Mr Ormsby-Gore, Secretary of State for the Colonies, over whose domain this argument was being fought, "that Germany should give some indication of what she would be prepared to contribute towards a settlement in regard to air disarmament and Central Europe."

Chamberlain and Eden then appeared to agree that a colonial settlement should be "in the forefront" of a general settlement. Eden informed the Committee that the newly appointed Ambassador in Berlin, Sir Nevile Henderson, favoured a colonial settlement first, "in the hope that Germany would subsequently meet Britain's requirements for the security of Europe". (This was the method that Chamberlain had just been offering for discussion.) The Foreign Secretary said that he himself assumed that there would have to be "substantial progress' towards a general settlement before Germany was told of British willingness to make a colonial settlement. Ministers noted that Germany had never precisely stated what form of restitution, other than a complete restoration of her pre-war colonial territories, would be acceptable to her.

Mr Malcolm MacDonald pointed out that the southern line of the Congo basin international area, envisaged in the Prime Minister's plan, would pass north of the self-governing territory of Southern Rhodesia, but as at that time there was a British Commission engaged in looking into the case for amalgamation of Northern and Southern Rhodesia, the possibility of such amalgamation should be kept open. Mr Ormsby-Gore expressed the hope that Northern Rhodesia would be excluded from any colonial deal with Germany.

The Committee on January 24th had before it a second Foreign Office paper amplifying the previous memorandum on "Further Steps Towards a General Settlement" and spelling out "the elements of the problem". This attempted to outline what the contribution of Germany might be towards general appeasement.[1]

[1] F.P. (36) 43

It declared that at the meetings of British and French Ministers in November 1937, the solution had been seen as including:

A western pact of non-aggression and guarantee
A disarmament agreement of qualitative character
A return perhaps by Germany to the League of Nations
Renewal by Germany of her previous undertaking of 1936 to respect the integrity of Austria
Concessions by the Czechoslovak Government to the "German minority", enabling Britain and France to seek satisfactory guarantees from Germany of the integrity of Czechoslovakia.

Among other "elements of the problem" that this paper enumerated was a remark which Lord Halifax thought that Hitler had made during their interview in Berchtesgaden in November 1937 that "he still thought it desirable to abolish bombing aeroplanes". The Foreign Office paper recalled that at an audience given in October 1937 to the Aga Khan, Hitler had volunteered the idea that he would "guarantee her independence if Czechoslovakia granted autonomy to the Sudeten regions". A dispatch from Sir Nevile Henderson in Berlin was also attached to the memorandum circulated to Cabinet Ministers. The Ambassador advised that talk in public of a "general settlement" should be dropped, "as it gave the impression that Britain was out to drive a bargain and so made it less likely that she would get it". The Ambassador "doubted the practical utility of asking for fresh guarantees as regards Austria". As to Czechoslovakia, he thought that "a bilateral agreement should be suggested to Germany as part of her contribution to peace". The Ambassador freshened these December impressions[1] with a second dispatch in January 1938 reporting the extreme difficulties that he had experienced during a private talk with Herr von Ribbentrop, then on a holiday in Germany. He had tried in vain to get the German Ambassador to say what contribution Germany could offer to make to a "general settlement". Sir Nevile had impressed on him that when he returned to his London post, this question would certainly be asked again.

[1] The dispatch was dated December 15 1937.

The Foreign Affairs Committee of the Cabinet set about drafting instructions to Sir Nevile on the nice business of seeming to offer restitution of former German colonies, though restitution would in reality only be in the form of an amalgam of African territory, in which Germany would share the administration and possess no real sovereignty. He was to extract from Baron von Neurath in return some idea of the contribution to the appeasement of Europe that Hitler would be prepared to make.

The Ministers became nervous that their instructions might not be understood fully, or that they might not have fully understood the mind of the Ambassador, and so summoned Sir Nevile to attend their next Committee meeting on February 3rd 1938. Sir Nevile, a tall greying and elegant career diplomat, withal a feeble personality, was then heard personally in the Prime Minister's room in Parliament.

A previous draft of his instructions had envisaged that a general settlement should embrace "assurances in regard to the independence and integrity of Austria and Czechoslovakia". This plain language went beyond what Sir Nevile now thought advisable. He repeated the account already given in his dispatches of the extreme difficulty of extracting any promises from Herr von Ribbentrop. Then he related the upshot of his subsequent soundings with Baron von Neurath, at which he had outlined to the German Foreign Minister what British requirements would be in any general settlement. When an assurance regarding Austria had been mentioned, said Sir Nevile, "Baron von Neurath's attitude was that Austria was behaving badly and that he could make no promise of any kind with regard to her". These ominous words provoked no recorded comment in the Cabinet Committee.

Revised instructions to Sir Nevile were drafted that "in order not to create misunderstanding which might give rise to greater difficulties at a later stage, Sir Nevile should remind Herr von Neurath of the observations that he made recently as to the importance that would be attached, not only by His Majesty's Government but by other Governments to German collaboration in appeasement. Mention, but only mention,[1]

[1] This phrase, "but only mention", was dropped from the final instructions.

should be made of Czechoslovakia and Austria as illustrations of the general principle of collaboration." Sir Nevile was also to refer to the question of limitation of armaments and "though full of difficulties" to the colonial question. The condition of Germany returning to the League of Nations as part of the settlement was, in view of Neurath's flat rejection of previous soundings, dropped out as revision proceeded, though figuring as a possibility in the previous draft.[1]

Sir Nevile Henderson warned the Committee that in any case it would not be possible for him to open conversations in Berlin until the present internal crisis in Germany was over.[2] Hitler was engaged in a trial of strength with certain personalities in the German Army. Sir Nevile was in this instance correct, in that the changes made at that time in the Armed Forces Command were accompanied by a significant change in the Foreign Ministry. Baron von Neurath was pushed into a post of no importance and Herr von Ribbentrop appointed Foreign Minister in his place. The changes in the Armed Forces, including new Army Group Command appointments, prompted an inquiry from King George VI as to the probable consequences that Sir Nevile expected. Sir Nevile wrote from Berlin a letter to his Sovereign containing the suggestion that the reforms "left the German Army with a big say in foreign affairs" and "had strengthened the hand of the peace party in Germany," a construction extremely hard to believe even in the confused atmosphere of Berlin during February 1938.

[1] F.P. 36 appendix
[2] Henderson was referring to a fierce struggle between Hitler and Himmler and the German General Staff. The latter body had demanded the retirement of Field-Marshal von Blomberg as an unsuitable person to be Minister of War after his recent second marriage to a woman of inferior reputation. Himmler in turn, sensing the danger to his master in the removal of this Nazi sympathiser at a time when many other Generals were critical of Hitler's forward strategy, had struck a counter-blow. He produced perjured evidence against the Commander-in-Chief of the Army, General Baron von Fritsch, alleging homosexual relations with an obscure person and demanding his dismissal. Hitler accepted these allegations at their face value, suspended the General, and proceeded to a structural reform of the Command of the Armed Forces, timed to avoid further risks to his regime.
These reforms left him as Supreme Commander of the Armed Forces, with General Wilhelm Keitel as Chief of a newly-formed High Command. General von Fritsch was removed without remedy as to his injured reputation.

Their London meeting of January 24th marked the beginning of a flow of personal letters from Sir Nevile Henderson to Mr Chamberlain and Lord Halifax. Henderson thus managed to convey ideas that were read by Cabinet Ministers without being exposed first to the penetrating comments of Sir Orme Sargent, Assistant Under-Secretary of State in the Foreign Office. The Ambassador in Berlin expressed himself freely on matters that required a perspective opinion from the Foreign Office, provided by both Central and Northern Departments. As weak men are apt to do, Sir Nevile delivered himself forcibly of his views. "It would be utterly disastrous to strengthen the French alliance with Russia", he wrote to Chamberlain in February 1938. His visit to London and the meagre prospects of appeasement that he described must have increased the premonition of Eden that there was serious trouble ahead.

CHAPTER VIII

The Invasion of Austria

"IT WOULD BE rash to accept the assurances given that there will be no change in German foreign policy." Thus Mr Eden in the Cabinet of February 9th commented on the internal crisis that had made Herr von Ribbentrop Foreign Minister and Hitler Supreme Commander of the Armed Forces. The February 1938 crisis in Germany was indeed short lived[1] and hardly lost a day to Hitler's plans.

Eden managed to obtain at this meeting that there should be closer co-operation between the British, French and Belgian Armed Forces. He had noted with disquiet that the trend towards Germany in the Cabinet of December 22nd 1937 had infected the Chiefs of Staff with uncertainty. This was evident from their reply to his letter of December 16th asking the Committee of Imperial Defence to advise on ways of maintaining contact with the French and Belgian Staffs.

The response had been a memorandum[2] dated February 4th 1938, in which the Chiefs of Staff drew attention to a previous ruling in 1936[3] that "no provision should be made for staff conversations with any Power". Admiral Sir Ernle Chatfield, Air Chief Marshal Sir Cyril Newall and General Lord Gort then declared that "the recent Cabinet decision on the role of the British Army has ... altered the situation of the Army" ... War commitments and the dispatch of a Field Force to the Continent now take a relatively low priority" ... "It would be more appropriate frankly to inform the French of the new situation. ..." While acknowledging that a commitment to air co-operation with France still existed, the Services Chiefs continued that "we do not advocate that discussion on air questions should be authorised. We feel certain that the opportunity of

---

[1] On February 7th Herr von Papen in Vienna had urged the Chancellor, Dr von Schuschnigg, to make an immediate visit to Hitler in Berchtesgaden, an event to be discussed in the next Cabinet meeting.

[2] C.O.S. 680 of 4.2.38, C.I.D. Paper 1394–B

[3] C.O.S. Paper 511, 1936

turning such conversations to their own advantage would be seized upon by the French with avidity. . . . The temptation to arrange a leakage that such collaboration was taking place would, in our opinion, prove irresistible to them in order to flaunt an Anglo-French accord in the face of Germany. Apart from the deplorable effect of such a leakage upon our present efforts to reach a détente with Germany, it is most important from the military standpoint that we should not at the present time appear to have both feet in the French Camp."

Lord Avon records that he demanded and obtained the withdrawal of this C.O.S. paper, having asked the Prime Minister and Sir Thomas Inskip that the matter be taken to the Cabinet.[1] This was accepted, and at the meeting of February 9th some improvements in military liaison with France and Belgium were agreed.

There was serious news to impart at the subsequent Cabinet meeting of February 16th about the gathering impetus of Hitler's designs upon Austria. Mr Eden summarised it thus: "On February 7th the German Minister in Vienna (Herr von Papen) first proposed a meeting between Herr Hitler and the Austrian Chancellor, but the Chancellor refused to go at short notice and the meeting eventually took place on February 12th. At that meeting Herr Hitler brought great pressure to bear on Dr Schuschnigg with the object of accelerating the absorption of Austria by Germany, and also informed him that Lord Halifax completely approved of Germany's action towards Austria and Czechoslovakia. The Chancellor appears to have put up a good fight, but had to make two concessions of great importance."

Eden named these as the appointment of Dr Seyss-Inquart, a known Nazi sympathiser, to be Minister of the Interior, and the appointment of the Under-Secretary in the Foreign Ministry, Dr Guido Schmidt, to be Minister for Foreign Affairs.

"It was significant that Italy, although she was informed of this meeting, at any rate on the Austrian side, one day before it took place, i.e. February 11th—the same day that we ourselves were informed—did not appear to take any action either in restraint of Herr Hitler or in support of the Austrian Chancellor." In Berlin the British Ambassador "had been assured by

[1] Avon, *Facing the Dictators*

the Minister for Foreign Affairs that he had every hope that the upshot of the negotiations would be one of appeasement".

Lord Halifax, whose name had thus been utilised by Hitler, confined himself to telling his colleagues "that his general impression as the result of his interview with Hitler had been that the *Führer* would continue his activities in Austria, but in a manner that did not enable any other country to inter-fere. . . ." "This," said Lord Halifax, "is what appears to be happening."[1]

Mr Eden concluded by saying that he did not want any decision from the Cabinet at that moment. "He did not want to put himself in the position of suggesting a resistance which we could not in fact furnish."

The Cabinet passed on to studying the Services estimates requested for this date by Sir Thomas Inskip in presenting his "Report on Defence Expenditure" at the Cabinet meeting before Christmas. The Minister for Co-ordination of Defence repeated on February 16th his previous conclusions that "it was beyond the resources of this country to make proper provision in peace for the defence of the Empire against three major Powers. He therefore desired to repeat with fresh emphasis his opinion as to the importance of reducing the scale of our commitments and the number of our potential enemies." He told the Cabinet of his disappointment that the Services departments were not bringing the scale of their expenditure in the years 1937–41 within the total of £1,500m. Sir John Simon referred again to "this enormous figure" and said that this expenditure "was as serious a matter as any Cabinet had ever had to face in times of peace". But he would abandon the figure of £1,500m. and accept the new estimates amounting to £1,650,000m. for

[1] Mr Michael Palairet, British Chargé d'Affaires in Vienna, in a further dispatch to Mr Eden on February 20th refers again to the emphasis that Hitler put on the views of Lord Halifax in his attempts to browbeat Dr Schuschnigg. In paragraph 10 of this dispatch Mr Palairet reported that he saw Dr Guido Schmidt by appointment at 6 p.m. on February 14th. "He described the violent nature of the meeting and results of it: but he told me nothing of the time limit. Nor did he tell me that Herr Hitler had quoted Lord Halifax to Dr von Schuschnig as saying that His Majesty's Government approved of his policy towards Austria and Czechoslovakia. I learned this from Herr Hornbostel, the Political Director at a party given that evening by Dr and Frau Schmidt in the Hofburg, the old Imperial Palace."

these five years, "though he did so with a heavy heart".

Lord Swinton explained that after Scheme J for the Air Force had been turned down on grounds of excessive expense, he had drawn up Scheme K which included the full number of fighter aircraft in Scheme J with the minimum number of bombers considered by the Air Staff to be consistent with safety and the full provision of trade protection and reconnaissance. Even that Scheme had resulted in a figure in excess of £560m. He had then attempted a scheme falling short of the provision deemed necessary for the Metropolitan air force, but coming within the financial limits available—"not what the Air Staff think ought to be done, but what they think would be the best value for the sum. I hope the Cabinet will be under no illusion in this matter.'[1]

It was essential to the Air Ministry, said Lord Swinton, if they were to obtain the production they required, to have a programme looking forward four or five years ahead. Up to 1939 the Air Ministry were already committed to contracts entered into and some contracts went beyond that year. Unless they could give orders extending beyond 1939 there would be a gap in production, as some eighteen months had to be allowed for the production of jigs and tools for new types. Moreover, unless they could give orders on a large scale they would not be able to obtain the necessary speed of production. He urged that orders should be given for a longer period and argued that the break clauses in contracts would mean only small waste if contracts were later altered or cancelled.

The Cabinet accepted the revised figure of £1,650,000,000m. for defence in the five-year period 1937–41, but recorded its misgivings at this sort of spending. It also resolved that this total would be reviewed in 1939 with a view to possible reductions.

The policy decisions of December 1937 had left them in a quandary about France. The Cabinet came finally to the conclusion that it was "an obligation of honour to inform the French Government of the effect of the recent Cabinet decision on the role of the British Army". It authorised the Foreign Secretary to inform France that the maximum force that could be sent to Europe "in certain circumstances" to comply with

[1] Cab. 23. 92

British obligations was "two Regular divisions within three weeks and one mobile division".

Even that effort at the time seemed beyond fulfilment, since a Continental expeditionary force was now a fourth priority in British policy planning. The Prime Minister remarked to the Cabinet that the British message "could hardly come as a shock to the French, as they had already informed us that two divisions was all that they expected."[1]

At the next Cabinet meeting, that of February 19th, the personal crisis between Eden and Chamberlain came suddenly to a head. Chamberlain was persisting with his own plan to negotiate a settlement of outstanding differences with Italy, and Eden objected that there must first be some sign of Italian good faith. Eden sent in his letter of resignation on February 20th and Mr Chamberlain accepted it with alacrity. Lord Halifax was appointed Secretary of State for Foreign Affairs in his place. The differences between the Prime Minister and his Foreign Secretary have been fully described in *Facing the Dictators*, and figure at length in the Cabinet records. They arose from the determination of Mr Chamberlain to handle certain foreign policy initiatives himself or through his own confidential agents; but there is no indication in the Cabinet Minutes that a clear disagreement was admitted at this time between Chamberlain and Eden over the main policy towards Germany of playing for time and a settlement.

After other Ministers had appealed for compromise in vain, Mr Malcolm MacDonald summarised the differences between the two men in their last Cabinet meeting on January 20th.

"The differences have been in such matters as the Roosevelt letter," he said, "and the Italian conversations, and it has been said that further differences would arise over Central Europe. Could not the Foreign Secretary and the Prime Minister sit down and consider whether these anticipations as to Central Europe are justified? Cannot the matter be explored?"[2]

After an adjournment for tea and discussion in a small group of Ministers, the Cabinet resumed at 6.10 p.m. and met again

[1] France had asked that the British contribution to European security should take the form of two armoured divisions, of which in 1937 none yet existed in the British Army.

[2] Cab. 23. 92

D

at 10 p.m. At this last meeting Mr Chamberlain read out Eden's letter of resignation and the Cabinet proceeded without Eden, to approve the basis proposed by Chamberlain for tentative talks with Italy.

Whatever his misgivings on Central Europe may have been, the official papers show that Mr Eden pursued the accepted line on Germany to the last. Significant is his reply on February 16th to Sir Eric Phipps in Paris, who had put forward a proposal from the French Government for firm joint diplomatic action in the crisis over Austria. Eden wrote:

> I am extremely doubtful of the wisdom of any separate or joint communication by the British and French Ambassadors in Berlin of the kind suggested by M. Delbos. You should, however, now tell M. Delbos that His Majesty's Ambassador in Berlin, when he left London, was authorised to inform the German Chancellor that His Majesty's Government were considering what steps might be taken to bring about a measure of appeasement which would include *inter alia* Austria.

So Mr Eden was not pressing for a stand on Austria, and he left office too soon to read a letter addressed to him by the Earl of Perth, British Ambassador in Rome, who reported on February 19th, at the height of the resignation crisis, an interesting interview.

The Soviet Ambassador had called on Lord Perth at the British Embassy in Rome on 18th February, and in the course of general conversation, said that "it would be no secret to me that the Soviet Government would much prefer to see an agreement between Italy and Great Britain rather than an agreement between Britain and Germany".

The inner papers of the Central Department of the Foreign Office show how clearly the predicament of the British Government over Austria was understood there in the days immediately before Mr Eden resigned.

On a minute sheet of February 16th[2] commenting on an urgent appeal from Dr von Schuschnigg that "it would be of the greatest help to him if we would speak firmly in Berlin", Sir Orme Sargent dryly remarked: "Neither Herr von Schusch-

---

[1] F.O. 371. 22311   [2] R. 1442. 171. F.O. 371. 22311

nigg, nor M. Delbos, nor Mr Palairet know that we are about to make proposals to Herr Hitler for an Anglo-German settlement, which includes a vague and tentative reference to Austria as an instance where Germany could collaborate."

"It is important", he continued, "that if Britain is prepared to contradict Hitler, Sir Nevile Henderson should have fresh instructions," but Sir Orme concluded that Hitler had "successfully called the British bluff" and that "it would be more dignified to leave the subject alone".

Mr William Strang, Head of the Central Department of the Foreign Office, wrote a broad appreciation of the situation as he saw it, quoting the words of Canning that "a menace not intended to be executed is an engine which Great Britain could never condescend to employ".[1] Strang added that "we do not possess the means to prevent Germany from treating Austria and Czechoslovakia as satellite states", an observation on which an unsigned hand, resembling that of Sir Robert Vansittart, in pencil in the margin commented: *"Don't we?"* Mr Strang described the Stresa declaration as "the high water mark of Allied resistance over Austria . . ." "The Germans are clearly not in a position to fight a great or a long war," he wrote. "But on the other hand neither we nor the French possess the offensive power to prevent Germany from working her will in Central Europe."[2]

Sir Alexander Cadogan agreed that "the time for talking big about Austria has gone by (probably some time ago) and Britain could only say more if she accepted further commitments". A Foreign Office memorandum of February 19th declared that "Hitler's coup in Austria (the Berchtesgaden talks) has created for us a completely new problem in Central Europe which we will have to face forthwith. We must assume that Austria is doomed as an independent State. Hitler can now bring about complete Nazification, followed by annexation, whenever he wants to, without military intervention."

---

[1] Chamberlain in September 1938 goes to the same source of inspiration and quotes in his diary from Professor Harold Temperley's *Foreign Policy of Canning* that "Over and over again Canning lays down that you should never menace unless you are in a position to carry out your threats."—*The Life of Neville Chamberlain.*

[2] R. 1657/137/3. F.O. 371. 22312

The public attitude of Mr Chamberlain over Austria is evident from his reply on March 2nd to Mr Arthur Henderson, who raised the question for the Labour Opposition whether there had been an ultimatum to Austria during the Berchtesgaden meeting between Hitler and von Schuschnigg. He asked the Prime Minister to endorse a recent declaration by M. Delbos that "the independence of Austria is an essential element of European peace". Mr Chamberlain's reply was that his advisers found no grounds for saying that there had been any violation of Article 88 of the Treaty of St Germain, "making the independence of Austria inalienable otherwise than with the consent of the Council of the League of Nations".

"What has happened", said Mr Chamberlain, "has been that two statesmen have agreed to certain measures being taken with a view to improving relations between their two countries ... I may say that His Majesty's Government obviously cannot disinterest themselves in the events in Central Europe ... and will continue to watch what goes on in Austria with the closest possible attention."

This statement in the House of Commons was made in disregard of Mr Palairet's letter of February 20th (Dispatch no. 50 from Vienna) which was circulated to the Cabinet and sent to the King. It reported that Hitler "raved like a madman ... with violence and unscrupulous bullying . . . saying that 'nobody could stop him if he chose to put Austria in order'."

A memorandum handed by Sir Orme Sargent to M. Corbin on February 25th stated Britain's preference for her own unilateral diplomatic action in Berlin rather than increasing Anglo-French pressures.[2]

As to Lord Halifax's role in the Berchtesgaden talks with Hitler in November 1937, Sir Orme wrote on February 23rd[3] that "I have now seen Lord Halifax's minute on this question". The case for a possible rejoinder to Hitler's allegation, that Halifax agreed with Hitler's policy on Austria, was under consideration in the Foreign Office. Sir Robert Vansittart and Sir Alexander Cadogan were both active in this matter, but Sir

---

[1] F.O. 371. 22312   [2] R. 1657/137/3

[3] R. 1982/137/3. British Interest in the Fate of Austria. This minute is not retained in the Foreign Office file and Lord Halifax was not talkative about his discussions on Austria with Hitler.

Orme recorded that the Halifax reply was "to the effect that if the matter is taken up, it should be so handled as not to prejudice the other side of our policy" (appeasement).

A week after succeeding to Eden's post, Lord Halifax, remembering the views attributed to him as approving Hitler's attitude on Austria and Czechoslovakia, sent further instructions to Sir Nevile Henderson on February 27th. These were to be repeated when the Ambassador saw Herr Hitler and Herr von Ribbentrop on March 3rd. "You should maintain the reference to Austria by name and the reference should take the following form," Halifax told his reluctant Ambassador.[1]

"You should say that in our view appeasement would be dependent among other things on measures taken to inspire confidence in Austria and Czechoslovakia and to establish better relations between these countries and Germany." . . . "Recent arrangements between Germany and Austria . . . have aroused apprehension in many quarters."

Henderson was later instructed to present these views to the Fuhrer in writing, and this he duly did, with absolutely no success. In a Very Confidential Report of March 5th 1938, Henderson described the meeting to Lord Halifax. Hitler was brusque and truculent, accusing Vansittart and the British press of sowing discord between Germany and Great Britain. At one stage the Ambassador asked whether Germany was seeking a plebiscite in Austria. Herr Hitler replied ambiguously that he demanded "a process of just evolution for that country". Henderson at once took up this point and reported his own words thus to London:

The British Ambassador pointed out that the present British Government had a strong sense of realities. Mr Chamberlain himself had taken over the leadership of the people and was not led by them. He had displayed great courage in exposing the impracticability of certain international phrases such as collective security and the like. . . . History had showed that seldom had anything been more difficult than to find two men who not only wanted the same thing but above all meant to carry it out at the same moment. For this reason England had declared her readiness

[1] F.O. 408. 68, p. 191

to clear up the difficulties, and she now put the question to Germany whether she too on her side is ready.

This plain suggestion that Chamberlain would help to arrange a plebiscite in Austria and might have met Hitler in March 1938 was recorded by Hitler's interpreter, Schmidt, but Hitler did not take up the offer. He had on November 5th 1937 secretly briefed his Army Chiefs that the annexation of Austria and Czechoslovakia would be his first objectives in a grand project to solve the crucial problem of *Lebensraum* for the German people. Although Hitler can hardly have believed that Halifax would approve of his methods over Austria and Czechoslovakia, the *Führer* most probably realised during their November interview British readiness to accept a *fait accompli* in Austria. In concluding his dispatch of March 5th, Henderson declared himself discouraged by his interview with Hitler, but he soon took refuge in second thoughts.

On March 11th, in a further analytical dispatch about their stormy interview, Henderson reported his views to Halifax on a remark by Hitler that the time for a colonial settlement was not ripe. This was "solely because of the conditions which we now seek to impose about Austria and Czechoslovakia". . . . But Henderson qualified this. "There again, I do not believe that at this stage Hitler is thinking in terms of *Anschluss* or annexation. Both today would merely add to his present difficulties rather than simplify them. I fancy he was telling the truth when he assured me that if the Berchtesgaden agreement (with Schuschnigg) worked, he would be satisfied with things as they are."

On the day after the British Ambassador sent this dispatch, Hitler marched his troops into Austria.

[1] C. 1657/E. F.O. 408. 68

CHAPTER IX

A Rather Dangerous Position

THREE DAYS BEFORE the invasion of Austria the Cabinet met to consider Sir Nevile Henderson's report on his "discouraging" interview with Hitler on March 3rd. Lord Halifax commented at the Cabinet of March 9th that it was his impression that "Herr Hitler had been at his worst and that Herr von Ribbentrop had been thoroughly unhelpful. . . . The German Government appeared to be set head-on to achieve its aims in Central Europe and did not want to tie their hands by talks. That left Britain in a rather dangerous position." Lord Halifax told the Cabinet that on March 8th he had received "rather a sharp rejoinder" from the French Government to the note in which he had explained that Britain should pursue its own course of appeasement in Berlin in preference to any further joint Anglo-French *démarche*. The moral that he drew was that all this emphasised the importance of an agreement with the Italian Government. He told the Cabinet that in his forthcoming interview with Herr von Ribbentrop his attitude would be "a mixture of disappointment, reproach and warning. His warning would not take the form of threats."

Lord Halifax then ran over the German attitude towards a settlement. "He proposed to speak very frankly. He would not conceal his disappointment, though he would intimate that this made no difference to the British desire to improve relations."[1]

The Foreign Secretary went on to formulate in advance his proposed comments in a form which, with slight variants, was the essence and limit of British public warnings that year:

The last thing that he wanted to see was a war in Europe, but the experience of all history went to show that the pressure of facts was more powerful than the wills of men, and if once a war should start in Central Europe it was impossible to say where it might not end, or who might not become involved. His general line would be

[1] Cab. 23. 92, p. 327

not to give the Germans the impression that we were running after them, but to show that we were not shutting the door. He would appeal to Herr Ribbentrop's well known desire for an understanding and would intimate that conditions were now comparatively favourable and might not return. If therefore, they wanted progress, it was up to them (the Germans) to take advantage of so favourable an opportunity.

What, asked an unnamed Minister, did Lord Halifax mean by "a favourable opportunity"?

The Foreign Secretary replied that the Prime Minister had shown himself anxious for an understanding and he himself "had the reputation of being in favour of something of the kind". Mr Chamberlain then explained after some discussion that it was not proposed to say that this was the last opportunity for an understanding. The Cabinet appeared to him to be agreed that it was important to avoid anything so drastic as a warning that it was "now or never". Mr Chamberlain thought that the Foreign Secretary's way of putting the matter was "admirable".

Some Cabinet Ministers were of the opinion that Sir Nevile Henderson might have adopted a firmer line. It appeared to them also embarrassing that Hitler "had promised a written reply to the soundings on the colonial question". (This might put restitution firmly on the map.) Sir Samuel Hoare, discussing the method of conducting diplomacy with Ribbentrop, emphasised that "the right way to deal with this was to say that if Germany invaded Austria or Czechoslovakia, they raised dangers in Europe of which the end could not be foreseen".

The conclusions recorded by the Cabinet did not contain this wording and approved the less brusque line that Lord Halifax proposed to take.

Such were the proceedings of Wednesday, March 9th. At 10.30 a.m. on Saturday, March 12th, the Cabinet was summoned with "No agenda paper issued" . . . "as a matter of urgency to consider the situation that had arisen in Central Europe as a result of recent events in Austria, where Dr Schuschnigg, the Chancellor, had resigned, his Government had been driven out of power, the Nazis were in charge, and German troops had already crossed the frontier". Mr Chamberlain said that "although there was probably not very much that could be done, he had thought it right that the Cabinet should meet".

Lord Halifax related that on Friday, March 11th, Herr von Ribbentrop had lunched with the Prime Minister and shortly after lunch the news had arrived of the ultimatum to Austria. "He and the Prime Minister had then had a very serious talk with Herr von Ribbentrop, who had professed to be ignorant of the whole situation and had eventually left them to telephone Berlin. . . . Later in the afternoon, in response to a request from Dr von Schuschnigg for "immediate advice from His Majesty's Government", Lord Halifax "after consultation with the Prime Minister . . . had replied that His Majesty's Government could not take the responsibility of advising the Chancellor to take any course of action which might expose his country to dangers against which His Majesty's Government were unable to guarantee protection." He hoped the Cabinet would approve that course. Mr Chamberlain reflected that "Dr Schuschnigg had not asked for advice before announcing the Plebiscite which had caused so much trouble". The Cabinet approved the Halifax reply. Lord Halifax informed them of a diplomatic approach to Signor Mussolini, which had resulted in an obvious rebuff. He then put forward the following questions for Cabinet consideration:

(1) What steps should be taken to guide public opinion?
(2) How were we to prevent similar action being taken in Czecho-Slovakia?

Mr Chamberlain recounted his own impressions of Herr von Ribbentrop as appearing "stupid, vain and incapable of passing on what was said to him". The Prime Minister said that before the arrival of the telegrams from Austria he "had agreed with Ribbentrop's general thesis, but had said that Britain wanted "a peaceful attitude of mind in Europe to which Germany must make her contribution". Then had come the news from Vienna. . . . The Foreign Secretary and he had dealt "rather firmly with Herr von Ribbentrop over the question of the ultimatum".

"Here was a typical illustration of power politics," said Chamberlain. "This made international appeasement much more difficult. In spite of all, however, the Prime Minister felt that this thing had to come. Nothing short of an overwhelming display of force would have stopped it. . . . At any rate the question was now out of the way. . . . It might be said with justice that we had been too late in taking up the conversations with Italy. The next question was how we were to prevent an occurrence of similar events in Czechoslovakia."

The Cabinet record states that "in the subsequent discussion a good deal of consideration was given to the possibility of some expansion and acceleration of our defence forces. The general view was that any such expansion and acceleration should be applied to our Air Force and Anti-aircraft defences." ". . . The Cabinet were informed that the Right Hon. Winston Churchill was intending to attack the Government on the grounds of the inadequacy of their Air Force programme."

Chamberlain warned the Cabinet "against giving the impression that the country was faced with the prospect of war within a few weeks. . . . He was inclined to favour an increase in the Air Force and acceleration of A.A. defences, but was against any reference to the matter in the communiqué to be issued after the meeting of the Cabinet". . . . "The best thing," said the Prime Minister, "would be for the Cabinet to meet again on Monday 14th and if the Government has decided on an increase in air strength, Mr Churchill can be approached with a better prospect of succeeding in getting him to temper his criticisms in the House of Commons."

The Cabinet duly met on March 14th and considered the diplomatic aftermath of the annexation of Austria, after which it discussed the merits of strong or milder language in Parliamentary references to these events. Mr Chamberlain suggested that the condemnation should be applied to the methods used by Herr Hitler, and Lord Halifax agreed "that what it was necessary to condemn was the method". The Prime Minister "thought that no statement ought to indicate that events were leading to war".

Lord Halifax referred to a message from Sir Robert Vansittart and Sir Alexander Cadogan that he had received in the Cabinet, urging that there should be some denial of the allegation that the Germans had acted with the approval of the British Government. The Cabinet decided against a specific explanation, though "it was to be borne in mind when shaping the Parliamentary statements that would be made".

The Cabinet then discussed a letter from Mr Duff Cooper of March 13th. The First Lord, who was unwell and absent from the Cabinet meetings, wrote to suggest an immediate increase in the naval programme, but Mr Chamberlain said that he preferred to think of an increase in aircraft construction. Lord Swinton argued that a new R.A.F. plan known as Scheme K would provide by March 1939 a first line bomber strength of 1,320 and a fighter strength of 542 aeroplanes with a total metropolitan first-line air strength of 2,182 machines. Under this plan there would be the required reserves of aircraft by March 1940, that was to say, one year earlier than had been previously contemplated. Again he met with objections from Mr Ernest Brown, Minister of Labour. Sir John Simon also pointed out that this was "a very grave matter". . . . His firm view was that if the Cabinet were to adopt Scheme K for the R.A.F. it meant an end to fixing a total sum for Defence Expenditure. Despite further arguments by Lord Swinton that unless the foundations of Scheme K were laid immediately it would be impossible to implement any other decision on expansion taken later, Sir Thomas Inskip supported the objections of the Chancellor of the Exchequer. "Scheme K would wreck the armaments programme recently adopted by the Cabinet", he said.

Mr Hore-Belisha then came out with an unexpectedly strong demand for more rearmament, but Lord Halifax objected that "the events of the last few days had not changed his own opinion as to the German attitude towards Britain. He did not think it could be claimed that a new situation had arisen."

"The Prime Minister pointed out that it was now 12.30 p.m. He was due to lunch with His Majesty the King at 1 o'clock. This discussion confirmed him in the opinion that he had already expressed that the Cabinet were not in a position to make any specific statement that day, but his own statement in the House of Commons would recall one already made in the Defence Estimates before the invasion of Austria that 'further stages of expansion will take the form of increasing progressively the strength of the Royal Air Force' and he would forecast a fresh review of the defence programme."

It is noteworthy that the Foreign Affairs Committee of the Cabinet, on March 15th, 1938, its first meeting after the invasion of Austria, was discussing Spain and the Anglo-Italian conversations. It addressed itself on March 18th to the situation in Central Europe, with Czechoslovakia on the agenda —but not Austria, as that country was already off the map. With the Prime Minister in the chair were present Lord Hailsham, the new Lord President of the Council, Lord Halifax, Sir John Simon, Sir Samuel Hoare, Mr Malcolm MacDonald, Mr Ormsby-Gore, Sir Thomas Inskip and a new arrival, Mr R. A. Butler, Parliamentary Under-Secretary in the Foreign Office, succeeding Lord Cranborne who had resigned with Mr Eden.

The Committee had before it a Foreign Office Memorandum setting forth the alternatives of policy open to Britain over Czechoslovakia. This memorandum, "Possible Measures to Avert German Action in Czechoslovakia", assumed that the German Government would "by fair means or foul" work for the eventual incorporation of a Sudeten German minority within the Reich, and argued that Britain had three alternatives, the Grand Alliance as proposed by Mr Winston Churchill on March 14th in his House of Commons speech, a new commitment to France, or no new commitment and peaceful negotiation of a settlement.

There was also a sombre telegram from Mr Basil Newton, the British Minister in Prague,[1] in which Mr Newton gave his view that the political position of Czechoslovakia was not permanently tenable and that she was an unstable unit in Central Europe.

The Prime Minister surmised that a solution was possible, saying that it would not be in accordance with Herr Hitler's policy to seize the whole of Czechoslovakia, since he only wished to have Germans in the Reich. Sir Thomas Inskip "could see no reason why we should take any steps to maintain such a unit in being".

Sir Maurice Hankey twice intervened to point out that Czechoslovakia could only exist if treated as one unit, as the industrial and agricultural areas were mutually dependent, and to remind the Committee that the existing frontier of Czecho-

[1] Dispatch No. 17, March 15th 1938

slovakia had endured for two hundred years. The Germans in the Sudetenland, he said, had moved into those areas from across the frontier. Mr Malcolm MacDonald saw the issue of Czechoslovakia as one on which the Commonwealth "might well break in pieces". South Africa and Canada would not join in a war "to prevent certain Germans from joining their Fatherland".

The Committee reviewed at length the dangers of a situation in which France might drag Britain into a war, because, as the Prime Minister pointed out, "we could not afford to see France destroyed". Sir Thomas Inskip saw no readily effective means of pressure on Germany except a naval blockade, "but this would take from two to three years", and the Prime Minister added that if Germany were blockaded, she would over-run Hungary and Roumania. The Ministers regarded France as unable in a war to go to the aid of Czechoslovakia and there was speculation whether she would rely on military assistance from Soviet Russia. "The more closely we associate ourselves with France and Russia," said Lord Halifax, "the more we produce on German minds the impression that we are plotting to encircle Germany." He did not accept "the assumption that when Germany had secured the hegemony of Central Europe, she would then pick a quarrel with ourselves. . . . He did not credit a lust for conquest on a Napoleonic scale."[1] Mr Ormsby-Gore thought that to assume a new commitment to Czechoslovakia would be "bad and dangerous" and "would split public opinion in this country from top to bottom". Sir Samuel Hoare said that he would prefer a new commitment to France rather than one tied up in any way with Central Europe, but even that, objected Lord Halifax, "might also involve us in war in the very near future when in certain respects, such as supply of A.A. guns, we were very unprepared". Halifax then came to the heart of the argument.

Either we must mobilise all our friends and resources and go full out against Germany or we must remind France of what we have often told her in the past, namely that we are not prepared to add in any way to our existing Commitments and that therefore she must not count on military assistance from us if she gets embroiled

[1] Cab. 27. 623, p. 164

with Germany over Czechoslovakia, and that she would be well advised to exert her influence in Prague in favour of an accommodation.

The Prime Minister enlarged on the physical difficulties of aiding Czechoslovakia in war. "If Germany could obtain her *desiderata* by peaceful methods, there was no reason to suppose that she would reject such a procedure in favour of violence." "During the Austrian adventure," he pointed out, "Herr Hitler had studiously refrained from saying or doing anything to provoke us." The Prime Minister saw no reason to suppose that the United States were prepared to intervene actively in Europe. Sir John Simon was "much struck" by the suggestion of Mr Newton[1] that even after a successful war the Allies "could certainly not contemplate the re-creation of Czechoslovakia . . . a very modern and artificial creation with no real roots in the past".

The Prime Minister expressed himself most uneasy at a situation in which French Ministers could decide whether Britain went to war or not. A proposal by Lord Halifax that Britain should both seek a negotiated settlement and assure France of British assistance in case she became involved in a war over Czechoslovakia met with dissent. The Committee adjourned the whole matter till March 21st and in the interval Lord Halifax produced a memorandum[2] containing a draft communication to the French Government to the effect that:

> His Majesty's Government do not see their way to undertaking further obligations either in respect of Czechoslovakia direct or in respect of France in connection with Czechoslovakia.

They considered the idea of a guarantee to France, but it did not commend itself. Sir William Malkin, Legal Adviser to the Foreign Office, pointed out that there would be no obligation upon Britain under the Locarno Treaty if France became involved in a war over Czechoslovakia, because there would have been "no attack upon France by Germany". The Prime Minister, however, thought that the draft communication was "stiff and unsympathetic" in tone and the Committee was told

[1] Prague Dispatch 17, March 15th 1938   [2] F.P. (36) 56

that in the opinion of Sir Robert Vansittart it would have a "catastrophic effect" upon Anglo-French relations. Lord Hailsham suggested that Sir William Malkin should re-examine his legal opinion on Locarno obligations, since in the case of a war between France and Germany arising over Czechoslovakia, it would be for Britain to decide whether France or Germany had been the first to attack and whether France was the victim of "unprovoked aggression". Lord Halifax thought that the French did not like facing up to realities and "delighted in vain words and protestations". He said, however, that "he was quite prepared to warm up the memorandum,[1] provided that its substance was not materially altered."[2]

Lord Halifax had fastened upon a public statement just made by M. Delbos that the Franco-Czechoslovak treaty of 1925 would come into force "if an aggression were real, *whatever form it took*". This was meant to deter Hitler from attempting a solution in Czechoslovakia by infiltration of para-military forces.

The Committee thereupon adjourned after asking Lord Halifax to prepare a revised communication to France "in warmer and more sympathetic language", which would be verbally communicated to the French Ministers by Sir Eric Phipps and sent simultaneously to the Dominions governments. A statement by the Prime Minister would be made in the House of Commons on the 24th. In the course of discussing the draft of this statement in Committee, Mr Oliver Stanley had stated his view that "80 per cent of the House of Commons are opposed to new commitments but 100 per cent favour our giving the impression that we will stand up resolutely to the Dictators". Mr Chamberlain replied that he did not disagree with this estimate. It was at the same time evident that both he and Lord Halifax were guided by the maxim of Canning, quoted by Mr Strang in his minute on Austria, that Britain should never employ a threat "not intended to be executed".

A report written by the Chiefs of Staff lay before the full Cabinet on March 22nd, as well as the draft statement on acceleration of defence production which the Prime Minister must make to the House of Commons and the "warmed-up" message to be conveyed verbally to the French Government.

[1] F.P. (36) 56   [2] Cab. 27. 623, p. 217

The dominant conclusion of the Chiefs of Staff was that no pressure which Britain and her possible allies could exercise would suffice to prevent the military defeat of "Czecho-Slovakia." (By this time a hyphen, hitherto sporadically used in official print had become fairly established in usage and implied the feasability of partition or a federal existence. The Prime Minister described the Chiefs of Staff report as "an extremely melancholy document", envisaging as it did that an armed conflict over Czechoslovakia would become a world war with Italy and Japan also.

The Prime Minister said that, in view of this Report, "he he was not in a position to recommend a policy involving the risk of war". We should endeavour to induce the Government of Czechoslovakia to apply themselves to producing a direct settlement with the Sudeten Deutsch. We should also persuade the French to use their influence to obtain such a settlement. The settlement to be contemplated was between the Czecho-slovak Government and the Sudeten Deutsch, and not Germany. If the Cabinet would agree to such a policy, he would instruct the Ambassador in Paris to talk quite frankly with the French on the basis of an *aide-memoire*. He preferred the idea of a conversation rather than a note. He argued that if Germany used economic pressure on Czechoslovakia instead of force, Britain would find herself in a humiliating position, if she had accepted a fresh commitment. He thought "it was difficult to believe that the French would not be relieved to discover some method to relieve them of their engagement". He spoke of speeding up existing plans for rearmament and "the sooner we can reach agreement with Italy the better".

Sir Maurice Hankey recorded a fairly lengthy discussion in the Cabinet "from various points of view", but without identifying the Ministers who differed from the policy proposed. The main objection to it was that "it would be tantamount to inviting Germany to take the next step in her programme".

The minutes record alternative policies then suggested. These were:

(1) To tell the House of Commons that the whole situation in Europe had been changed by recent events; to announce that the Government were in touch with the French Government

with a view to an early Conference and would propose Staff
conversations.

(2) To inform the Czecho-Slovak Government that Britain
would support reasonable proposals for dealing with the
Sudeten-Deutsch and would act as a go-between with Germany.

(3) Adopt a firm line towards Germany, including perhaps a 12
month guarantee for Czecho-Slovakia to allow a settlement to
be worked out.

(4) If not possible to help the Czecho-Slovak, British policy
should be to keep the Germans guessing.

(5) The statement in Parliament and the *aide-memoire* for the
French Government should be redrafted to show the utmost
goodwill and cordiality to France and sympathy with Czecho-
Slovakia.

"The view that was accepted more generally and increasingly
as the discussion continued was that the policy proposed by the
Foreign Secretary and supported by the Prime Minister was
the best available in the circumstances. Several members of
the Cabinet, including the Prime Minister and the Foreign
Secretary, admitted that they had approached the question
with a bias in favour of some kind of guarantee to Czechoslovakia, but the investigation at the Committee on Foreign
Policy had changed their views. It was suggested that the policy
had changed their views. It was suggested that the policy
proposed by the Foreign Secretary was likely to be generally
approved by Parliament and the country. It was becoming
increasingly clear that the people were not in favour of any new
commitment. A recent expression of views by important
representatives of the City of London was mentioned in this
connection. It was agreed, however, that there was an underlying resentment at the idea of constantly having to knuckle
under to the dictators for lack of sufficient strength."

Among the disadvantages of following a policy of risk, it was
stated that "at least two months would elapse in a war before
the United Kingdom could give any effective help to France. . . .
Meanwhile the people of this country would have been put in a
position of being subjected to constant bombing, a responsibility
that no Government ought to take. . . . In regard to the position
two years hence, the Cabinet were reminded that the Royal Air
Force would at any rate be armed with up-to-date aeroplanes

and the anti-aircraft defences with modern weapons. . . . In all
the above circumstances it was generally felt that any policy of
bluff would be dangerous, and that it would be better to proceed on the idea that our performance was almost better than
our promise."

The Cabinet finally approved the line of policy proposed by
the Foreign Secretary—no new commitment involving the risk
of war, and a settlement to be sought inside Czechoslovakia.
There was to be a statement on improvements in British
defences with "full priority for rearmament work".

Lord Halifax explained the British view to Monsieur Corbin
with some difficulty on March 22nd. The absence of a clear
British policy of support for France over Czechoslovakia was
sufficient to overthrow the Chautemps Government, in which
M. Delbos had stated publicly its absolute support for Czechoslovakia. Mr Chamberlain read to the Cabinet on March 30th
a friendly letter from M. Léon Blum, the new President of the
Council, but added that M. Corbin at dinner the previous
evening had expressed the view that the Blum Government
would not last very long and that the Daladier Government,
which would probably succeed it, would also not be of a durable
character. It may be assumed that this instability in French
Governments would have been less marked if a British assurance
had been forthcoming that enabled M. Delbos to maintain his
declared policy on Czechoslovakia.

The statement of Mr Chamberlain in the House of Commons
on March 24th set an unalterable pattern for the rest of the
year 1938. He repeated the obligations to assist France and
Belgium under the Locarno Pact against "unprovoked aggression" and described the reasons for refusing guarantees that
might automatically involve Britain in a war over Czechoslovakia.

"But while plainly stating this decision I would add this.
Where peace and war are concerned, legal obligations are not
alone involved, and if war broke out, it would be unlikely to be
confined to those who have assumed such obligations. It would
be quite impossible to say where it would end and what
Governments might become involved. The inexorable pressure
of facts might well prove more powerful than formal pronouncements and in that event it would be well within the bounds of

probability that other countries, besides those which were parties to the original dispute, would almost immediately become involved."

Mr Churchill may have known or may have sensed the subterfuge. In his speech on the same afternoon he said, "The Nazification of the whole of the Danube States is a danger of the first capital magnitude to the British Empire. Is it all to go for nothing? Is it all to be whistled down the wind? If so, we shall repent in blood and tears our imprudence and our lack of foresight and energy."

Mr Chamberlain's stance was strongly defended by his supporters in the House of Commons and on his peace and war statement, British diplomacy walked a tightrope in the months to come. It was said in the Cabinet that in Berlin Mr Chamberlain's warning was to be given a strong emphasis, but that British diplomats in Paris and Prague would be instructed to give it a more cautious interpretation. The Chamberlain Government kept a careful watch on the effect that its public warnings might produce. At the Cabinet of April 6th 1938, "The Foreign Secretary noted a tendency in France rather to overrate the likelihood of our rendering assistance to that country in coming to the aid of Czechoslovakia. He proposed to take the opportunity to instruct His Majesty's Ambassador in Paris to correct this view."

CHAPTER X

Haggling over Defence

At the emergency meeting of the Cabinet on March 12th we have seen that there was a sense of urgency about rearmament. Lord Swinton had recalled his recent offer of Scheme K for the Air Force, which was below the minimum R.A.F. strength considered necessary by the Air Staff, but which the Cabinet had decided was more than the nation could afford. After the invasion of Austria he recommended that immediate steps should be approved so that Scheme K could if necessary be put into operation in 1939, enabling the Government to say that they were taking all the steps necessary for a further expansion. Instead Mr Chamberlain preferred to refer to defence measures that were already agreed, in such a way as to allay public concern.

It was probably at this meeting that Lord Swinton made the revelation that he had so equipped the Shadow Factories that they would be able immediately to accept any expansion of the aircraft programme that the Cabinet might approve. The incident is not mentioned in the minutes, but was vividly described by Lord Swinton twenty-eight years after.[1] To the question how soon a further expansion of production capacity could be put in hand, Lord Swinton replied to the Cabinet:

"Tomorrow morning."
"Where would the order be carried out?"
"In the Shadow Factories."
"But," said Sir John Simon, "they are fully occupied."
"No, the factories have been built and equipped large enough to take all the new expansion." He had done this without or with very nebulous authority.
Lord Swinton added: "I await the censure of my colleagues."

Although on March 14th the Air Ministry's Scheme K had again been rejected, the haggling still went on in Cabinet between those in favour of military preparedness and those who

[1] James Margach and the Earl of Swinton, *Sixty Years of Power*

regarded the economic strength of Britain as her first line of defence. The Services Ministers, Lord Swinton, Mr Duff Cooper and Mr Hore-Belisha, were pitted against the Treasury, the Ministry for Co-ordination of Defence, the Ministry of Labour and, though this was no more than a case of personal bias, also the Minister of Health, Sir Kingsley Wood, who was in line with the views of Mr Chamberlain, Sir John Simon, Sir Thomas Inskip and Mr Ernest Brown in resisting any show of strength or rapidly accelerated movement in war production.

During the Cabinet debate on March 22nd about Czecho-slovakia and the risks of war, one anomaly was brought to light in their proposals. "The Cabinet were reminded that at the present time the Defence Services were working under instructions to cut down estimates and it was suggested that this was hardly consistent with an announcement that we were accelerating our armaments."[1] This schism is still evident on April 6th when Lord Swinton argued for yet another programme of aircraft production, R.A.F. Scheme L, to keep pace with Germany, and was told by Sir John Simon that the approved total of defence costs could not be exceeded.

Sir Thomas Inskip first reminded the Cabinet that:

Scheme F had been approved by the Cabinet and was in force at that time.
Scheme J had been put forward by the Air Staff as the minimum scale essential for security at a cost of over £600m. in five years. This had been rejected as too expensive.
Scheme K would cost £567m. over five years. It had not been possible to reconcile this Scheme with the Cabinet decision taken in February that the total expenditure of the Services over five years should not exceed £1,650,000,000.

Sir Thomas Inskip dealt then with Scheme L. "After making inquiries he was now satisfied that it was impossible to obtain any sudden and rapid increase of labour. The increase would be slow and spread over months."

Mr Chamberlain observed that "the Cabinet might have to decide that there was a point beyond which expenditure on the Services could not be taken, without too great a general weakening of the nation. . . ." He reminded Lord Swinton that

[1] Cab. 23. 63, p. 43, March 23rd 1938

the Air Ministry was being "rationed" to an expenditure of
£505m., and put some searching questions to him on the merits
of this new Scheme L.

Lord Swinton pointed out that the Government had just
announced its intention to increase the Air Force and anti-
aircraft programmes and to accelerate their completion, even
though it involved some interference with industry and a concentration of labour and material on Defence.

"It is obviously impossible to accomplish this within the
rationing scheme proposed by the Minister for Co-ordination of
Defence, which the Cabinet only agreed to before the Austrian
crisis." Swinton quoted words spoken by Sir John Simon on
November 1st that the objective of air rearmament was "to
create and maintain an Air Force which will form an effective
deterrent and insurance for peace". Even Scheme L, in the
opinion of the Air Staff, would not provide that. Scheme L was
a minimum dictated not by what the Air Staff considered would
give safety, but by political considerations of what was possible
without control and National Service. It was impossible to
improvise in the production of aircraft, said Lord Swinton.
"*Now* is the time, and quick action later will be impossible unless
orders are given and action taken at once." If Scheme L were
approved Britain would be in a better position than otherwise.
"We would not be at the mercy of Germany—as it may be said
that we are today—and we should possess a strong deterrent."[1]

Sir John Simon countered that this question was one in which
every member of the Cabinet had a responsibility and not one
Department alone. He repeated at length his previous arguments about the economic strength of Britain. "Everyone
recognises that finance is one of the great factors in Defence."
Sir John recalled that the Prime Minister, when he was
Chancellor of the Exchequer, had reached the conclusion that
£1,500m. was the maximum sum Britain could afford. Now
they had to tell the country that the figure must be increased to
£1,650m. In the middle of February the Cabinet decided that
was the absolute maximum. The Cabinet was now being asked
to increase it. There was a second question, Sir John Simon
said—what was the best method of meeting this very dangerous
situation? He spoke further on the subject, but without ventur-

[1] Cab. 23. 63, p. 124

ing far on the merits of the appeasement policy so soon after the invasion of Austria. Mr Duff Cooper argued that the country was in danger of getting three defence Services, all of them inadequate. Lord Winterton, Chancellor of the Duchy of Lancaster, pointed out that the main pressure from the House of Commons upon the Prime Minister was to know how the expansion of the Royal Air Force was to be implemented. Mr Chamberlain replied that the air programme was "a very difficult question for decision by the whole Cabinet", and could be more usefully investigated by a smaller body. The Cabinet agreed that the Prime Minister, the Chancellor of the Exchequer, the Minister for Co-ordination of Defence and the Secretary of State for Air should prepare written recommendations to be read by the Cabinet at their next regular weekly meeting. Lord Swinton was thus deprived of such support as he had in the full Cabinet for further discussion of R.A.F. schemes for acceleration and expansion of air strength.

About the time that these discussions on air power were occupying the Cabinet, a potent figure, Sir Warren Fisher, Permanent Under-Secretary in the Treasury and Head of the Civil Service, passed a minute to the Prime Minister marked *Air*. He attached to it an Air Comparison as at April 2nd, showing that Germany possessed some 5,000 first line aircraft and Britain only 1,630, some obsolete; that German output was 6,100 for 1938 and British output at most 2,250. To these "appalling facts from reliable sources", Sir Warren added the comment that "for some years we have had from the Air Ministry soothing-syrup and incompetence in equal measure. For the first time in centuries our country is (and must continue to be) at the mercy of a foreign power."

This drew a terse rejoinder from Sir Maurice Hankey that he did not agree where the blame lay. He forwarded the minute to the Prime Minister. Sir Warren updated his minute with a long memorandum to the Prime Minister on October 1st 1938, coincident with the Munich crisis, in which he took pains to recall how over the years "you and I" . . . "have done much to prepare in the Air", and placing responsibility for muddle and delay on incompetence and indifference in the Air Staff. He knew of "one—and only one—Crown Servant of first-rate ability in the Air Ministry, Sir Arthur Street"; he called for the key posts to be filled by the right men; and for the Defence Requirements Sub-Committee to be reorganised. Sir Warren sent a copy of his October document to Sir Kingsley Wood, who had meanwhile become Secretary of State for Air, and it elicited from him some corrective information relevant to the period in question. "At the beginning of the period of German rearmament our Secret Service opinion was necessarily scanty, but we were fortunate enough to secure in 1934 a copy of the plan on which the German Air Force was being rebuilt. All the information which has reached the Air Staff, Foreign Office or Secret Service has been correlated and placed periodically before the Cabinet and the Committee of Imperial Defence." "The Germans had the advantage of setting the pace. It would have been provocative in 1933 to have laid down a policy giving Britain absolute supremacy in the air and would have given the Germans the incentive to even larger programmes. It was inevitable that the Air Ministry should produce a series of programmes comparable with that at which the Germans were aiming." In November 1934, Kingsley Wood reminded the Prime Minister, the Treasury had opposed acceleration of aircraft production. By the summer of 1937, German intentions were abundantly clear, and in October 1937 a plan had been submitted by the Air Ministry to the Plans Committee of the Committee of Imperial Defence, but the Cabinet in December 1937 had "accepted the principle of financial limitations and . . . rejection of the Air Ministry proposals. . . . Indeed on March 12th, the same day that the Cabinet instructed my predecessor to put forward new proposals, Lord Swinton received a letter suggesting a quota for the Air Ministry which might well have meant the establishment, for at any rate some considerable time, of a position of air inferiority as compared with Germany."[1] The Kingsley Wood Memorandum thus laid the blame back at the Treasury door.

In the Cabinet of Wednesday, April 13th, Lord Swinton reported that the Committee of Four were not yet in a position to submit a new programme for aircraft production. Recruitment of labour was still a difficulty. The Cabinet thereupon agreed to a procedure whereby the Air Ministry would put its requirements for personnel to the Treasury "to receive

[1] Premier 1. 252 (see also C.P. 219. 38)

authority for recruitment". The Treasury would also scrutinise the Air Ministry's works and buildings programme. Meanwhile a small Air Ministry mission would visit the United States to see what were the possibilities of purchases there. On the following Monday the Cabinet met to approve the Budget, and on April 27th to discuss British efforts to induce talks between the Czechoslovak Government and the Sudeten German minority. They reviewed as well the prospect of future talks with Germany. Lord Halifax restated his policy of caution and his reasons for "thinking the present moment not suitable for setting up a Danubian anti-German bloc", as intended by France on the basis of taking up the exports of Central European countries. He proposed "to take the line in Berlin on future relations with Germany that Britain was anxious to resume the interrupted negotiations, but that the present moment did not appear opportune."[1]

The Cabinet then discussed the impending meeting in London of Mr Chamberlain and Lord Halifax with M. Daladier and M. Bonnet. Proposals for Military Staff conversations with France would have to be discussed. The Prime Minister recalled that the Cabinet recently had been in favour of Staff talks with France, but that the War Office General Staff now had misgivings that such talks would "come as a severe shock", when the very limited amount of military assistance that Britain could give was revealed to the French Government. "Our maximum Army contribution, if we gave one at all, could not exceed two Divisions at the outset of a war. He thought it would be difficult to refuse if the French wanted to have conversations as to how that force could be used. . . ." "To refuse a request for conversations would seem rather churlish," said Chamberlain. He therefore supported the request of Lord Halifax for some latitude during the talks with the French. Sir John Simon pointed out "the risk of coming so near to the point of a commitment to send two divisions that it would be assumed by the French as a definite undertaking. . . ."[2]

[1] Cab. 23. 93, p. 195
[2] Cab. 23. 93, p. 19. Throughout these minutes the original draft contains the phrase *two divisions and a mobile division*. The words *and a mobile division*, contained in the previous communication to France on proposed assistance, are deleted throughout in red ink.

"There was a distinction between saying that the maximum force that could be sent, if any were sent, would be limited to two divisions, and saying that in certain circumstances we would be willing to send a force of this size."

Lord Halifax summed up that "everyone wanted to avoid commitments". It was important, he agreed, to make plain that we could not commit ourselves to send troops to the Continent. "But it was also important not to say that in no circumstances would Britain ever send any troops . . . France must prepare her plans on alternative assumptions."

The Prime Minister concluded that if he and Lord Halifax were asked to say to Daladier that in no circumstances would they allow any Staff conversations "there might be an uncomfortable jar". Lord Maugham talked of a risk that such conversations, together with the British air mission to America, might stimulate Hitler into action against Czechoslovakia. Mr Chamberlain doubted whether there was any risk of a coup against Czechoslovakia as a consequence to these events, "but even an increase of ill-will might be very dangerous".

The Cabinet agreed that the Prime Minister and the Foreign Secretary should have latitude to agree to extend the existing Air Staff conversations with France to the Army Staffs as well, and that Lord Halifax should consider a communication to the German Government to deter them from attaching an exaggerated importance to Anglo-French Staff Conversations".[1] The Cabinet passed on to considering a proposal for exchange of economic information with France and Belgium for the purpose of collaboration in the event of war. Several Cabinet Ministers "expressed apprehension" as to the effect of these proposals coming on top of military talks, but others asked how indeed Staff talks could be accepted and economic talks refused. The matter was left to the discretion of the Prime Minister, though Sir Kingsley Wood urged that "we must not drift back into the old position of consenting to all that France asks while refusing all German requests".

When the Cabinet next met on May 4th 1938, Lord Halifax gave an account of the meeting of Mr Chamberlain and himself with M. Daladier and M. Bonnet. "They had used the latitude which the Cabinet had given them and had accepted

[1] Cab. 23. 93, p. 203

the proposal for Military Staff conversations with all cautions and reserves." The French had pressed strongly for naval conversations too. The Cabinet were apprised of a dispatch from Sir Nevile Henderson[1] warning that Germany might take Anglo-French Naval talks as a pretext to denounce the Anglo-German Naval Agreement. Mr Duff Cooper said that he really was not moved by this prospect, as the Germans would denounce the Anglo-German Naval treaty whenever it suited them to do so. Mr Chamberlain told the Cabinet that by lunch-time on the second day of the French visit to London, the whole Conference with Daladier would have been threatened by any further resistance on this subject, whereupon he and Lord Halifax had conceded that Anglo-French naval talks should also take place.

Lord Halifax was questioned about policy commitments by Cabinet Ministers and declared that they had avoided "any-thing that might be construed as a commitment over Czecho-slovakia". At a subsequent meeting on May 11th the Cabinet discussed the danger that France might start a "preventive war" over Czechoslovakia, but the Prime Minister said that he was "quite satisfied after his conversations with M. Daladier and M. Bonnet that public opinion in France generally would be opposed to any policy of military adventure". It is note-worthy, however, that Mr Chamberlain did not expose even partly to his Cabinet colleagues the impassioned and strongly argued case that M. Daladier had put (for a joint diplomacy), nor yet the views of M. Bonnet that a crisis was much closer than the British supposed. The French arguments were not widely discussed after the visit of M. Daladier to London in May 1938. As recorded in the Foreign Office Archives[2] a whole range of subjects was raised, beginning with relations with Italy, and only reaching the heart of their problems, Central Europe, at the third meeting. M. Daladier then spoke at con-siderable length, pointing out that it had been no warmonger but M. Aristide Briand, the apostle of peace, who had assumed the first commitments to Czechoslovakia. Daladier affirmed that the Czechs had already made large concessions to their German

[1] Dispatch 381, April 20th 1938
[2] F.O. 371. 21591, also Documents on British Foreign Policy, Third Series, Vol. II

minority, but that Herr Henlein in his Karlsbad speech had
plainly revealed his intention of dismembering the Czechoslovak State. The whole tendency of Daladier's remarks was to
rally Chamberlain to a common policy, but the British Prime
Minister was not to be drawn. Coldly he cited the Committee of
Imperial Defence opinion that Czechoslovakia could not be
saved in a military sense by anything that Britain and France
might do. "He asked himself whether the picture was as black
as M. Daladier had painted it, and whether Herr Hitler really
intended to destroy the Czechoslovak State or rather *a* Czechoslovak state. He doubted whether at the present moment Hitler
intended to bring about an *Anschluss* of the Sudeten territories
with Germany." There was some contradiction between these
reflections and his attitude a few minutes earlier, when Mr
Chamberlain had given what was probably a more genuine
version of his thoughts, in attempting to assess whether, in a
situation similar to the invasion of Austria, the moment would
be opportune to declare war on Germany.

"It made his blood boil," said Mr Chamberlain, "to see
Germany getting away with it time after time and increasing
her domination over free peoples. But such sentimental considerations were dangerous, and he must remember, as M.
Daladier would also have to remember, the forces with which
we were playing. . . ." Were Britain and France "sufficiently
powerful to make victory certain? Frankly, he did not think
they were."

In the course of this conversation Mr Chamberlain described
thus the proposition of an open Anglo-French declaration on
Czechoslovakia. "He considered that this was what the
Americans in their card games called bluff. It amounted to
advancing a certain declaration in the hope that declaration
would prevent the events we did not wish to occur. But it was
not a certainty that such action would be successful. It might be
true that the chances against war were 100–1, but so long as
that one chance existed we must consider carefully what our
attitude must be, and how we should be prepared to act in the
event of war."

M. Bonnet objected that Quai d'Orsay information did not
support the views of Mr Chamberlain that Hitler would be
satisfied with a Czechoslovak state on a federal basis. There

might perhaps within the next month be an act of force by Germany "removing Czechoslovakia from the map of Europe". "If solidarity existed between France and Great Britain they could ensure the success of their views. . . . Such solidarity should be reached in advance. . . . His view was that we could only succeed if we agreed in advance upon our policy in the face of German intentions that were publicly announced to every traveller who passed through that country."[1]

Lord Halifax replied that "it would not be safe to rely on the use of force. It would represent a gamble." Daladier spoke with emotion at seeing his friends in the last war killed around him on the Somme battlefield. He was not in favour of a preventive war, he said. Nor did he intend to bluff. But German policy had certainly hitherto been that of bluff. He feared that time was not on the Allied side. "If we allowed Germany a new success every month or three months till she achieved a hegemony, she would turn on the West. If there were no signs of a determined policy and a common agreement between the British and French Governments, they would have sealed the fate of Europe."

Lord Halifax after lunch on April 29th simply repeated that there could be no fresh commitments. Not even, he told M. Bonnet, if Czechoslovakia made reasonable concessions could Britain accept an obligation towards her, and the recorded agreement did not go beyond promising a British *démarche* to be taken in Berlin in the interests of a pacific solution and a joint Anglo-French *démarche* for concessions in Prague to the German minority.

The Cabinet on May 11th did not return to Air Ministry affairs after the deadlock between Lord Swinton and the Treasury. This urgent question was still absent from the agenda or the Cabinet on May 18th, as was also Lord Swinton himself, his place as Secretary of State for Air having been filled by Sir Kingsley Wood, whose place as Minister of Health was filled by Mr Walter Elliott, while a new recruit to the Cabinet, Mr John Colville, became Secretary of State for Scotland. No word from Mr Chamberlain in explanation of these changes is recorded in

[1] This will have been an oblique reference to a remark made earlier by Mr Chamberlain that "friends of mine" visiting the Sudeten German districts found everybody in favour of territorial *Anschluss* with Germany.

the minutes of the Cabinet of May 18th, other than briefly to welcome Mr Colville to the Cabinet.

"The Prime Minister asked me to go and see him," recalled Lord Swinton, "and I went over from the Air Ministry. Neville Chamberlain said to me: 'I want you to go.' He gave me no reason, but the row over air strength was going on in Parliament. He wanted a quiet political life and he didn't believe the war was coming. He offered me any other job in the Cabinet from Lord President downwards, but I told him that this Air Ministry job was the best I had ever done and I would not take any other."[1]

Lord Swinton had been a powerful and clear-spoken member of the Conservative Government, many times a Minister, with a long and competent record in previous governments. He owned at Masham a stately house, where there was lavish entertainment, and his grouse moors, the best in Yorkshire, were shot regularly by his Conservative friends in politics. It may well be supposed that the abrupt dismissal of this political magnate, who was in no way to blame for the deficiencies in British air strength, had a chilling effect on the remainder of those Ministers who had argued in Cabinet for accelerated rearmament. They were soon to be roused from the dismal reflection that nobody was really safe these days, by the first full-scale crisis over Czechoslovakia.

[1] To the author, February 1970

CHAPTER XI

The May Crisis

MUCH HAS BEEN written about the crisis of September 1938 and the Munich Four Power Conference, but much less is remembered of the preceding crisis of May 19th–22nd, at which Hitler was warned against aggression and consequently took decisions that sealed the fate of Czechoslovakia and ultimately that of the Third Reich.

It may be that rather more was spoken between Daladier and Chamberlain, when they met in London in late April, than was committed to the Foreign Office secret transcript of their conversations on the 28th and 29th. For there were intervals for lunch and informal occasions, as well as the recorded sessions. There was also at this time from Sir George Ogilvie-Forbes, the British Minister in Berlin, a report to Sir Robert Vansittart that Hitler had given undertakings to the German General Staff not to embark on any immediate action against Czechoslovakia that would involve defiance of the Western powers. He would not assume that there would be no risk of military intervention by France. The western fortifications of Germany, Hitler was reminded, were still non-existent and the only General Staff contingency plan for operations against Czechoslovakia, *Fall Grün*, was of a secondary character and unsuited to conditions prevailing in May 1938. It seems fairly certain, however, that despite assurances given that he would not expose Germany to the danger of a war on two fronts, Hitler was playing with the idea of fomenting disorders inside Czechoslovakia and making movements of para-military forces. There was also some activity among German troops in frontier regions. The Conservative elements in the German General Staff viewed this policy momentum with misgivings, involving as it did S.S. and National Socialist Motorised Corps units not under Army control.

It has been sometimes asserted that the British and French reached a secret entente in April 1938 to challenge the behaviour of Germany, though I find no Cabinet record of any such arrangement. M. Bonnet even went so far as to assert that at their London meeting Chamberlain consented to try out a common political strategy. As we have seen at the Anglo-French talks in London, as far as open diplomacy over Czecho-slovakia was concerned, joint moves were resisted in favour of solo British diplomatic moves in Berlin and joint diplomacy in Prague. Nevertheless, Bonnet relates that after the French had insisted that a firm Anglo-French front would deter Hitler from aggressive action against Czechoslovakia, Chamberlain rejoined: "We are prepared to try this experiment with you."[1] This sort of language was unusual in the Chamberlain vocabulary.

The success of any common policy would depend very much on the circumstances of the trial of strength. For the Committee of Imperial Defence, having reached the conclusion that Czechoslovakia was indefensible, there could be no serious idea of Britain going to the aid of Czechoslovakia if a warning to Hitler was rejected or ignored and military action followed.

A sharp increase in the violence of German press and radio attacks on Czechoslovakia was noticeable on May 18th and 19th after a visit by Hitler to Rome. Reports to British and French newspapers spoke of German troop movements, especially by General von Reichenau's Army Group IV near the Czecho-slovak border. Local elections on Sunday in Czechoslovakia gave a pretext for clashes between the Sudeten German Party and the Czech police. On the night of Friday, May 20th, President Beneš and the Czechoslovak Cabinet decided that the situation was alarming enough to warrant a mobilisation of one class of Army reservists, which was announced on Saturday. With a regularity not usually associated with the English week-end, the entire British cabinet of twenty-two Ministers met at 10 Downing Street at 5 p.m. on Sunday, May 22nd.

It is stated in the preamble to the Cabinet record that according to War Office intelligence, units of eleven German divisions had been traced moving towards the frontier in Bavaria and Saxony and one class of recruits had been called up in Leipzig. This information was embodied in a Summary presented to the Sunday Cabinet, which met, as was customary in emergency, with "No Agenda Paper Issued". The Summary[2] contained

[1] P. Bonnet, Quai d'Orsay, p. 169   [2] Cab. 23. 93. 325

reports from the British consuls in Dresden and Munich that German troops were concentrating in northern Austria and southern areas of Silesia, and that German Army leave had been suspended for May 22nd, the date of communal elections in Czechoslovakia. Lord Halifax reported that Sir Nevile Henderson had been instructed to make inquiries on May 20th and had been told by General Keitel that these reports were nonsense. In Prague Mr Newton was told on the Saturday that the reports were "substantially accurate", and that consequently Czechoslovak reservists were being called up. Early on May 21st, two Sudeten Germans on bicycles in a frontier area failed to stop when challenged by Czechoslovak sentries and were shot dead. This incident had further inflamed the situation. Herr von Ribbentrop "made a very unpleasant and threatening communication" to the Czechoslovak Minister in Berlin at 7 p.m. on May 20th, even before this incident, and after it told Henderson that "the patience of Germany is almost at an end". Lord Halifax said that he had repeated to the German Ambassador in London warnings already given through Sir Nevile Henderson in Berlin, "as to the dangers of precipitate action which might lead to a general conflagration". "The Cabinet discussed the matter at some length," and were told by the Foreign Secretary of the steps that he would take to restore calm both in the House of Commons and in a meeting with the British press. At the same time Sir Eric Phipps was being instructed by cypher telegram to warn the French Government that though Britain would still stand by France if she was the victim of unprovoked aggression, British statements did not warrant the assumption "that his Majesty's Government would at once take military action with the French Government to preserve Czechoslovakia against German aggression".[1]

The Meeting of Ministers on May 22nd was singular in that the Minutes record practically no discussion.[2] The Ministers heard a long statement from Lord Halifax, and the impression is of a formality—perhaps designed to impress the Germans, like the ordering of a railway coach from the Reichsbahn in

[1] Cab. 23. 93, p. 334
[2] Duff Cooper noted in his biography (p. 221) that in the mood of the Cabinet, annoyance with Czechoslovakia and sympathetic concern for Germany seemed to predominate.

E

Berlin at the height of the crisis to carry British diplomats and
their families away from what might be hostile territory. The
German leaders were startled at the whole phase of activity that
Britain developed, but later incredulous, suspecting that they
had been the victims of nerve warfare. It is therefore of some
interest to examine the account of these Cabinet proceedings.

Lord Halifax admitted when the Cabinet met again on the
25th May that he was somewhat concerned to read that the
press attributed the restored situation to British and French
firmness.[1] (Sir Nevile Henderson was convinced that French
suggestions that Hitler had "climbed down" were "a damned
awful show".) The Foreign Secretary then imparted to the
Cabinet his thoughts on the future.

"If we had turned the first corner successfully we should be
getting ready for the second. The French obligation to Czechoslovakia dated from a time when Germany was disarmed. In
present circumstances it was desirable, if possible, to obtain a
release for the French from their obligations. He did not think
that Britain could support any particular solution to the
Sudeten question in Czechoslovakia as the British Government
were not equipped with the necessary knowledge. He doubted
whether a strong demand for a plebiscite could be resisted. He
did not feel that we could ask the French, Czechoslovak or
Russian Governments to denounce their Alliances. He would
like, however, to see the Czechoslovak State move into a
position of neutrality, like Switzerland. Under such a system the
Alliances would automatically disappear."

The Cabinet discussed "and commended" a cantonal system
for Czechoslovakia, but expressed doubts about the feasibility
of a "plebiscite". Mr Chamberlain spoke his approval of the
views of Lord Halifax. "His own mind had moved in the same
direction . . . it might be possible to get a settlement in Europe."
To a question in Cabinet whether the French themselves had

[1] Of the May crisis Professor Henderson Braddick, Professor of International Relations, Lehigh University, U.S.A., has made a monograph
study entitled *Germany, Czechoslovakia and the Grand Alliance 1938*. He writes:
"It is clear that just before the crisis . . . Hitler was preoccupied with the
problem of reducing Czechoslovakia without general war, and had rejected
a strategic surprise attack as too risky. Hitler's preparations had in fact not
matured, either in terms of military planning or of subversive preparation
in Czechoslovakia itself."

put forward any idea for escaping from their dilemma, Lord Halifax said that they had communicated nothing to him, but he thought that M. Bonnet would be glad of any suggestions. . . . "We were living in a shifting situation which could not endure long unless something was done."

Evidently, after the elation of a diplomatic success there was a period of caution again, for the Cabinet passed on to discussing the extent to which it would be prudent to extend the Staff conversations that had been agreed with France and considered a memorandum from the Ministry for Co-ordination of Defence. British Ministers were concerned to see it made clear that "His Majesty's Government were not committed to send even two divisions on the outbreak of war" . . . "the discussions would be on a technical basis . . . wholly hypothetical. . . . The Chiefs of Staff had made clear the limited scope of the conversations". The British Military Attaché in Paris was to make clear "that only two Divisions could be available for dispatch to the Continent if circumstances elsewhere permitted . . . no commitment to send them could be taken in advance".

On May 28th the *Führer* summoned his closest advisers, having realised that he had been the victim of a game of bluff. His adjutant, Captain Fritz Wiedemann, remembered a two hours' harangue at the Chancellery, in which Hitler exclaimed: "It is my unshakeable determination that Czechoslovakia shall be wiped off the map. We will deal with the situation in the East only. Then I will give you three or four years' time and we will take on the situation in the West." This was confirmed by an order to the Supreme Command of the Wehrmacht on May 30th 1938: "It is my unalterable decision to smash Czechoslovakia by military action in the near future." Hitler made up his mind then for a general mobilisation in the month of September.

At the following Cabinet on June 1st 1938, Sir John Simon had some news for the Cabinet that prompted him to unusually strong language. An instalment of interest on the Austrian Loan was due that very day, and the German Government had intimated that they would not pay a dividend. He described this decision as "outrageous" and said that the matter would be taken up with Germany after the Whitsun holidays.[1]

[1] Cab. 27. 623, p. 205

Sir John's indignation may have been rooted in the recollection that he had advised the Bank of England in March that there was no good reason to refuse a transfer to Germany of £3m. in gold held before the *Anschluss* in deposit for the National Bank of Austria.

The Foreign Affairs Committee of the Cabinet, which had in March 1938 met and discussed at considerable length British policy towards Czechoslovakia, was on April 6th already studying ethnic maps of Czechoslovak territory. It seems not to have met at all in May 1938. Its first meeting in June was devoted to a memorandum on "British Influence in Central and South Eastern Europe" which set forth proposals to check the process of German economic domination in the Balkans by increasing British trade and investment. The Prime Minister was dubious whether an economic front could succeed where there was no military front, and asked whether, if Germany's economic life were strengthened, might that not lead to quietude? After much discussion the Committee agreed to set up an Inter-departmental Committee to strengthen British political influence in S.E. Europe by economic methods. Similar support for China was next debated, which raised apprehensions of violent reaction from Japan. A memorandum on "Chinese Request for Financial Assistance" set forth the advantages to British policy in the Far East of supporting China and mentioned the recent completion of the Burma Supply Road, but it was decided that financial assistance could not include a Government loan or guarantee, and that the Chinese Nationalist Government must see what terms it could make for itself in the City of London, without sponsorship from Downing Street.

Reflecting on the events of May 1938, Mr Chamberlain wrote to his sister that "I cannot doubt in my own mind that the German government made all the preparations for a coup, that in the end they decided after getting our warnings the risks were too great. But the incident shows how utterly untrustworthy and dishonest the German Government is."[1] Yet he became at once more cautious in his attitude and mistrustful of the Czechs.

On June 3rd an article in *The Times* urged the view that the Sudeten Germans "ought to be allowed by plebiscite or

[1] Feiling, *The Life of Neville Chamberlain*

otherwise to decide their own future, even if it should mean their secession from Czechoslovakia to the Reich". "I wish *The Times* would keep off it," wrote Vansittart in a minute to Lord Halifax on June 14th. "They are at it again in their leader today. I have heard again from Henlein that he really does not want it" (incorporation in the Reich). Sir Robert reported on a visit to London by Herr Henlein that "he promised us not to break off negotiations with the Czechoslovak Government". He also referred to the necessity "to put Henlein back in the collar" if he strayed from his promise, but although the Vansittart reports on Henlein and his negotiations were full and frequent, they become less confident and soon he took up Sir Nevile Henderson sharply for reporting that the Reich Germans were exerting no authority over the Sudeten Germans.

Vansittart had drawn the main conclusion from the events of May 19th–22nd that Hitler could be brought to reason only by firmness. He pressed a memorandum on the Prime Minister on the need for a larger and better co-ordinated propaganda apparatus. Either remorse that he had gone quite so far on May 21st, or annoyance at Vansittart's frequent use of the first person singular and his somewhat grand language, caused Mr Chamberlain to minute this paper to Sir Warren Fisher, Head of the Treasury, that "I have never read such an extraordinary document from a Civil Servant".[1] The Treasury influence in policy, invisible but persistent, is well illustrated in its criticism of the Vansittart proposals. Sir Warren endorsed the opinion of Mr E. Hale of the Treasury, who submitted in a commentary that "I do not believe that in the long run it will be possible to combine the policy of appeasement with a forward policy in propaganda. Armaments may be infinitely more expensive, but they at least have the virtue of being dumb and do not cause the same ill will." The Treasury memorandum recalled that Britain's diplomatic efforts on May 21st had been "read as implying that the Germans were on the point of aggression . . . and bitterly resented (by them). . . . From the point of view of appeasement the propaganda race seems to me the more serious danger."

There was a final meeting of the Cabinet Committee on Foreign Affairs on June 16th to take note that previous attempts

---

[1] Premier 1. 272

at a solution with Herr Henlein had come to nothing. The Sudeten German leader had made a show of moderation privately that summer in talks with Sir Robert Vansittart and Mr Churchill, but that illusion was over. It remained for Lord Halifax to propose to the Committee "a distinguished mediator" between the Czechs and the Sudeten Germans.[1] The Foreign Policy Committee then ceased to meet between June and November 14th 1938, an extraordinary gap, by which time the Czechoslovak Republic in its previous viable form had ceased to exist.

[1] Viscount Runciman, former President of the Board of Trade, was chosen.

CHAPTER XII

"Our Ultimate Attitude"

THE CABINET CONTINUED to hold its Wednesday meetings throughout June and July 1938, the discussion of foreign affairs being given to the Spanish Civil War, to Japan's war on China, and to brief situation reports by Lord Halifax on progress in the search for a solution to the Sudeten German problem. He mentioned again the idea of mediation, but noted that the Czechoslovak Government "might not accept it, if told, as she must be told, that Britain could not be committed to guarantee the result of a mediation". Herr Konrad Henlein, who through Vansittart continued regular contact, was apparently optimistic and still describing himself as free from interference by Hitler. On July 20th, in the absence of Lord Halifax, who was in attendance on King George VI in France, there was an event of note. Mr Chamberlain gave the Cabinet an account of a visit to London by Captain Fritz Wiedemann, Hitler's Adjutant, and a meeting with Lord Halifax at his London home. Mr Chamberlain spoke of a *"most binding assurance"* which Captain Wiedemann had been authorised to give that in present circumstances the German Government were planning no kind of forcible action and that *his Government might be able to give an assurance of the kind suggested limited to a definite period* . . . "though it was not in the Foreign Secretary's written notes, he gathered that the period contemplated might be one of a year".

The Prime Minister also informed the Cabinet that a visit to London by Field-Marshal Goering might take place in the autumn for conversations on "all questions outstanding between the two countries, which would include Colonies". The Cabinet appeared to welcome "anything which made for delay in the risk of a war".

An account of his two-hour conversation with Captain Wiedemann had been circulated by Lord Halifax to the Cabinet and has since been published in the Documents on British Foreign Policy.[1] It makes plain that Hitler was offering links

[1] Third Series, Vol. I, p. 584

of a personal character, even circumventing his own Foreign
Minister, Herr von Ribbentrop. After giving instances of setbacks to Anglo-German relations, the Goering visit was
mentioned by Captain Wiedemann and the assurances given
of "no kind of forcible action . . . so far as one could see into
the future". The most notable aspect in Cabinet discussion of
the Wiedemann visit is the importance that the Prime Minister
attributed to this mission, and the lack of enthusiasm of other
Ministers.[1]

Sir Kingsley Wood told the Cabinet of progress towards the
development of an aircraft construction industry in Canada.
The Prime Minister felt bound to emphasise that he regarded
this as an expansion of Britain's war potential rather than of her
present production of aircraft, as the cost of each aeroplane built
in Canada would be 25 per cent higher than in home factories.

The Minister for Co-ordination of Defence then presented to
the Cabinet a memorandum on the proposed new naval standard of strength and after a preamble on the financial aspects,
described it as "impossible of attainment within existing financial limits". The Prime Minister, as he had done in the case of
Lord Swinton's proposals for R.A.F. Scheme K, proposed a
small Committee of Ministers to see what sum could be
afforded. Mr Duff Cooper then spoke at length and with great
firmness, saying that to ration the Defence Departments over a
long period of years was a mistake. . . . If the country was in
danger it was difficult to defend the maintenance of all the
Social Services and ration the Armed Services. An Appendix
to the memorandum submitted by the Board of Admiralty,[2]
as he pointed out, showed Britain to be "in a position of numeri-

---

[1] There is some discrepancy between Mr Chamberlain's idea of a "most
binding assurance" and the record of his visit to Halifax on July 18th made
by Captain Wiedemann . . . "Again and again (the question from Halifax):
Could it be possible that Germany would give a declaration saying that we
did not contemplate solutions by force? To this I said: I am in no way
authorised to say anything official about this. To make such a declaration
for an indefinite period or for any circumstances (massacre) would be
impossible. But I know enough of the intentions of the Führer to be able to
say that for the foreseeable future (about one year) there is no thought of
force. Nevertheless in some way the Sudeten German problem must be
solved one day. . . ." Documents on German Foreign Policy, Series D, Vol.
VII. p. 628.

[2] C.P. 170 (38)

cal inferiority to Japan, except in capital ships. Over Germany we only showed a small margin . . . Italy was left out of the calculation." He urged that the new naval standard of strength be adopted and that naval estimates should be dealt with on a yearly basis as in the past. Sir John Simon, as he had already done in arguing against increased Air estimates, stressed that "this was a matter for the responsibility of the whole Cabinet". The Prime Minister ingeniously suggested that it was "unnecessary to discard the New Standard Programme and say that it would never be adopted, but that was not the same as saying that it must be adopted now". The Cabinet agreed that the new Naval standard could not be adopted in present circumstances, but that the Minister for Co-ordination of Defence, the Chancellor of the Exchequer and the First Lord of the Admiralty should seek agreement on the total sum to be allocated to the Admiralty for the remainder of the five-year period.

That evening the Cabinet met again to consider problems of finance in relation to the Indian Army and the Prime Minister announced that the Parliamentary recess would begin on July 29th. At the following Cabinet on July 27th, Lord Halifax, back from the royal visit to France, reported that on his return to London "he had found a deadlock setting in over Czechoslovakia. After consulting the Prime Minister he had sent a telegram to the Czechoslovak Government containing the suggestion of a British mediator. He was glad that the Prime Minister in his speech at the House of Commons on the previous day had made it clear that Lord Runciman would be acting on his own responsibility and not under instructions from His Majesty's Government, or any other Government. That was a matter of some concern to Lord Runciman himself who had suggested that 'this was putting me out on a dinghy in mid-Atlantic'.

"The Foreign Secretary continued that he thought the Cabinet would be interested to know that some of his advisers, who had been inclined to take rather a grave view of the outlook over Czechoslovakia, now thought that the war party in Germany had received a check at the end of May, and perhaps were receiving a further check by what was happening now, and for that reason there might be a better prospect of a peaceful issue to the affair."

The Cabinet passed on to a discussion of the question of sharing defence costs in the Suez Canal zone with the Egyptian Government and reports from the High Commission in Palestine on a growth of communal strife and violence. Ministers were told that as a result of talks after the previous Cabinet, the total sum to be allocated to the Royal Navy for the next three years had been increased from £355 to £410m. "for all purposes". This would help towards the new standard of naval strength, though that would not be achieved by any particular date, the Prime Minister emphasised. The Ministers met again on July 28th to deal with outstanding business before the recess and to say farewell to Sir Maurice Hankey, who had acted for a quarter of a century as Secretary to the Cabinet. His place was to be taken by Mr E. E. Bridges, a Treasury official and son of the Poet Laureate, Robert Bridges. The Prime Minister presented Sir Maurice with a clock inscribed with the names of Ministers and said a few appropriate words. Sir Maurice then addressed the Cabinet for the first and last time. He told them that he had served seven Prime Ministers and fourteen Governments in 1,100 meetings of the Cabinet, and took leave of them with affectionate thanks. The Cabinet dispersed into the English summer with no forebodings recorded in the last Minutes by this old Cabinet servant.

The holiday interval was short lived. Available Ministers met again a month later in a much less hopeful mood. For meanwhile warnings had reached Downing Street, from Germans of still undefined Opposition groups, that there was a critical time ahead. These groups were emerging in the aristocracy, where monarchist tendencies were still latent, in cells of the Diplomatic Service, in the Military Counter-Intelligence (Abwehr) and in the higher ranks of the Army itself. The extreme vigilance of the Gestapo made any open display of opposition to Hitler's policy impossible, but in the middle of August 1938, Ewald von Kleist-Schmenzin, a Prussian monarchist travelling with a passport provided by Admiral Canaris, Chief of German Intelligence, arrived in London in a conspiratorial role. His purpose was at the same time to ascertain that the British knew the extent to which Germany was already committed to large-scale military action against Czechoslovakia in the autumn, and to seek proof that Britain and France would not remain inactive. There is of necessity little documentary record of some initiatives ascribed since to the secret German Opposition, but a report was made by Sir Robert Vansittart to Mr Chamberlain on the mission of Herr von Kleist. Mr Chamberlain's sceptical comments exist in the Documents on British Foreign Policy,[1] as do some dispatches from the British Embassy in Berlin containing similar warnings from German sources of an impending crisis.

After intimating to Sir Robert on August 17th that September 27th would be the latest date at which Hitler could be stopped from invading Czechoslovakia, Herr von Kleist urged that it should be made clear to Hitler that the attitude of Britain and France taken up on May 21st was not bluff and that they would really intervene. "His first remedy, as you will remember," wrote Vansittart to the Prime Minister, "is the same as that which I have been reporting to you as being the desire and the almost open request of a number of other German moderates who have been in communication with me during these past weeks."

From Chequers Mr Chamberlain wrote to Lord Halifax on August 19th about recent reports from Central Europe, and said of this visitor: "I take it that Von Kleist is violently anti-Hitler and is extremely anxious to stir up his friends in Germany to make an attempt at his overthrow. He reminds me of the Jacobites at the Court of France in King William's time and I think we must discount a good deal of what he says. . . . Nevertheless I confess to some feeling of uneasiness and I don't feel sure that we ought not to do something," but he rejected the idea of an open warning. The same rejection, for the same reason, was attached by the British Ambassador in Berlin to similar advice from a German source reporting to his Military Attaché, Colonel F. N. Mason-Macfarlane. A Herr X told him of a general mobilisation in process and that "if by firm action abroad Hitler can be forced at the eleventh hour to renounce his present intentions, he will be unable to survive the blow". Sir Nevile wrote: "We know Herr X's attitude (hostile to Hitler) and his pronouncements are clearly biased, though his information should be taken seriously."

Sir John Simon was asked by Mr Chamberlain and Lord

[1] Third Series, Vol. II, p. 683

Halifax to make a speech at Lanark on August 27th, which would add a fresh note of alarm to the previous Chamberlain warnings of March 24th. The Lanark speech did not, however, provide the unmistakable open warning required if any deterrent action was to be attempted inside Germany by opponents of Hitler.

The volume of alarming intelligence from Germany could be ignored no longer and a Meeting of Ministers was called. It is noteworthy that Mr Chamberlain did not achieve a full meeting of the Cabinet on Tuesday, August 30th. It was therefore described as a Meeting of Ministers and no agenda was issued. Eighteen Ministers were present, and Sir Nevile Henderson had been summoned from Berlin to attend. Four Ministers were beyond easy recall, the Marquess of Zetland, Lord Hailsham, Mr Burgin and Lord Stanley of Alderley.[1] The Prime Minister began by saying that he had been unwilling to break into the holidays of his colleagues, but the situation was so grave that Members of the Cabinet should know how matters stood. Lord Halifax then reported the wide extent of the German military manœuvres, confirmed "by a number of apparently independent sources", with purchases of oil reserves by Germany, stoppage of leave, and conscription of labour for work on fortifications. This had prompted the Prime Minister and himself to address a Memorandum to Hitler in the form of "an appeal in regard to German military measures". Hitler had sent the memorandum back to the German Foreign Ministry and the reply of Herr von Ribbentrop had been entirely unhelpful. On August 20th "the German Ministers in Yugoslavia and Roumania had given a warning that Germany was prepared to intervene if necessary to obtain a satisfactory solution to the Sudeten problem. . . . A somewhat similar communication appeared to have been made in Moscow". . . . "One view—and there was a great deal of evidence in support of it—was that Hitler, against the advice of the Army and of the moderate party, was determined to intervene by force. It was suggested that this policy was based on an estimate that France could not achieve much if she were to intervene and that we should do our best to prevent French

[1] Lord Stanley had taken over the Dominions Office from Mr Ormsby-Gore.

intervention. . . . The second view, that Hitler had not yet made up his mind to use force, but was determined to have everything ready, using a mixture of bluff and force, was the view of the British Ambassador too. It was impossible to say which view was correct. He therefore proposed to examine both possibilities."

Lord Halifax "did not think it much use to repeat what the Chancellor of the Exchequer had said so well at Lanark. The only deterrent which would be likely to be effective would be an announcement that if Germany invaded Czechoslovakia we should declare war upon her. He thought that this might well prove an effective deterrent.

"Against this it was necessary to take into account what would be the results of making such a declaration. It was clear that a declaration in this sense could not be kept secret. He thought that it would probably have the result of dividing public opinion both in this country and the Empire. He was not too certain what effect it would produce on the Czechoslovak Government. He would feel extremely uneasy, in making any threat, if he was not absolutely certain that the country would carry it out. His colleagues would have to think most carefully whether they were prepared to give effect to such a threat. . . ."

The Foreign Secretary drew a gloomy picture of the prospects of saving Czechoslovakia by military action. "He agreed that there was much more in the present crisis than the attempt to defend Czechoslovakia against Germany. But he asked himself whether it was justifiable to fight a certain war now in order to forestall a possible war later."[1]

Assuming next that Hitler had not yet made up his mind to use force, Lord Halifax said "that there was not much we could do except to continue to act on the basis of the Prime Minister's speech of March 24th and the Chancellor of the Exchequer's speech of August 27th at Lanark. In effect we should try to keep Herr Hitler guessing. The fact that the present meeting was being held and the recall of our Ambassador from Berlin would all be helpful." . . . "He had in the preceding week considered the possibility of asking the First Lord of the Admiralty to take some rather dramatic action with the Fleet. He had not done so, partly because he felt that action on these

[1] Cab. 23. 94, p. 291

lines was not quite on all fours with other action that we were taking.

"The Foreign Secretary added that many moderate Germans were pressing us to go even further than the Prime Minister's speech of March 24th, and had said that, if we did so, there would be no attempt to coerce Czechoslovakia, and the Hitler regime would crack. For his part he received these messages with some reserve. Further he did not believe that the internal regime of one country was destroyed as the result of action taken by some other countries. He therefore came to the conclusion that the two lines to pursue were, first to keep Germany guessing as to our intention, and secondly to do all we could to forward the success of the Runciman Mission. There was no guarantee that this policy would be successful, but the only alternative was to make a direct threat to Germany. He wished it to be clearly understood that if this policy failed, the Government would be told that if only they had the courage of their convictions, they could have stopped the trouble. They would also be accused of deserting the principle of collective security and so forth. But these criticisms left him unmoved."

Mr Chamberlain described this statement as "full and masterly. . . . A decision must be reached at the present meeting, he said, as to how far we were prepared to go. Many people in this country and in Germany took the view that if we made it clear now that if Germany used force, we should come in on the side of Czechoslovakia, there would be no war. Many people of this way of thinking thought that such a statement would probably be followed by a revolution which would upset Herr Hitler." He then read extracts from a letter from Mr Robert Boothby, M.P., giving a forecast of German action against Czechoslovakia in September and advocating firmness.

The Prime Minister said that he had gone over in his mind very carefully the case for an immediate statement, "but he always came back to the same conclusion as that reached by the Foreign Secretary. No State, certainly no democratic State, ought to make a threat of war unless it was both ready to carry it out and prepared to do so. This was a sound maxim. . . . Although it was possible that such a statement, if made now, might avert war, it was not certain that it would do so. Herr Hitler was withdrawn from his Ministers and lived in a state of exaltation. He might well take the view that the statement was bluff. If he did, we should then have to choose between being shown up as bluffers and going to war. . . . War in present conditions was not a prospect which the Defence Ministers would view with great confidence. . . . If we were right up against war, public opinion might well change suddenly. . . . What line would be taken by South Africa? The policy of an immediate declaration or threat might well result in disunity in this country and in the Empire."

Several senior Ministers then spoke without a dissenting opinion. Sir Nevile Henderson sketched out the future developments of German policy towards Czechoslovakia, concluding that in his view Hitler had probably not decided to use force. His view was that if "a threat" was made by Britain to Hitler "that would not be the end. Hitler would press on with his rearmaments. . . . He thought the views expressed to Mr Robert Boothby by his German friends were to some extent fostered by their desires."[1]

Mr Duff Cooper then made a lengthy statement, remarkable in that he differed in his assessment from all that had been said by the Prime Minister and the Foreign Secretary. "The rumours were all to the same effect," he said, "namely that only strong action by Britain would stop Germany from attacking Czechoslovakia.

"There was a story going round that the German Generals had told Hitler that they were not ready for war. Herr Hitler's reply had been that he was banking on a swift invasion of Czechoslovakia which would break down the primary defences within five days before we had time to complete mobilisation. Hitler then proposed to hold his hand and offer to make peace, and he reckoned that this manœuvre was likely to come off. The Generals who had been strongly opposed to war against Czechoslovakia had gone away from the meeting saying that perhaps the *Führer* was right again.

[1] It is relevant to the advice given in Cabinet by Sir Nevile Henderson at this meeting, against an open warning to Hitler, that during his visit to London, Henderson was privily told of a plan in the mind of Mr Chamberlain to fly to Germany and negotiate with Herr Hitler. Chamberlain first discussed this plan in an upstairs room at 10 Downing Street with only Wilson, Henderson and one secretary present. Sir Horace Wilson does not recall the date, but has told me that it was either August 29th or 30th.

"The First Lord did not agree with the view that if this *coup* against Czechoslovakia was made, it would weaken Germany. On the contrary he thought that it would enormously strengthen her, at any rate for the time being. . . . He thought that if war came, the Czechoslovaks would fight well and bravely and the French would go to their assistance. . . . In his view the position was that if there was a European war, we should inevitably be involved in it. . . . He thought that we ought to show that we were thinking of the possibilities of using force. He had discussed the matter that morning with the First Sea Lord from the point of view of what action we should take if we were contemplating immediate war. The Fleet was going to the North Sea in fourteen days' time. This time could be advanced by four or five days." He suggested bringing H.M.S. *Repulse* back from the Mediterranean and other measures as an answer to the announced German naval manœuvres, which would have an advantageous effect on public opinion.

Sir Kingsley Wood disagreed and spoke of the "terrible retaliation" that bombing of Germany would bring. Mr Hore-Belisha thought that "a threat of war could only be made if there was an overwhelming public demand first". Earl De La Warr retorted that at least "it should not go out that the Cabinet had virtually decided to take no action if Hitler marched into Czechoslovakia".

Other Ministers did not speak in favour of what were by this time described as "threats" to Germany. For the words "open warning" or "warning" had been discarded by the supporters of the Chamberlain line. A few opinions were given in favour of some show of resolution, but Lord Halifax thought that even an announcement that the date of the naval manœuvres was being put forward would be "playing Germany's game". He did not wish to repeat the diplomatic action of May 21st.

The Prime Minister summed up. "The Cabinet," he said, "was unanimous in the view that we should not utter a threat to Herr Hitler, that if he went into Czechoslovakia, we should declare war upon him. It was of the utmost importance that this decision should be kept secret. He asked Ministers to bear this in mind in private conversations. . . ."

"There remained the hypothetical case that, in spite of all our efforts to bring about a settlement, Herr Hitler might brush everything aside and have recourse to force. What we should do in that event could not be decided today. He thought that if some such situation did arise it would probably be found to be very different from the situation as it was envisaged today, and the Cabinet would of course be called together at once to consider the position."

A communiqué was issued that did no more than announce that the Ministers had met to hear a full statement on the international situation. The conclusions recorded as Secret were that no warning declaration was to be made to the German Government; that policy on Czechoslovakia would remain unchanged; and that Britain "should try to keep Germany guessing as to our ultimate attitude".

CHAPTER XIII

Prime Minister's Rule

THREE CROWDED WEEKS began on September 8th with the Prime Minister's plan to fly to Berchtesgaden and ended with the Munich Agreement on the 30th. It has been generally assumed to have been, but was it originally the Prime Minister's plan? A draft telegram by Sir Alexander Cadogan to Sir Eric Phipps on September 14th reveals that "we have moreover during past weeks had several suggestions from various quarters in Germany that a direct communication from the Prime Minister to Herr Hitler, still better a personal interview— might be the best means of reaching agreement. . . . The Prime Minister hopes that the French Government will trust him never to lose sight of the common aims and policies of the two Governments, French and British."[1] This was in reality the same idea of a meeting that Hitler had put to Baldwin and which Baldwin had been prudent enough and comparatively strong enough to disregard.

As to Cabinet responsibility at this time, a new volume appears on the Cabinet Office shelves, as if in proof of a change. In it are bound up the Notes of Informal Meetings of Ministers during the Czechoslovak crisis, 1938.[2] The dates extend from September 12th to October 2nd 1938, with never more than four Ministers present, the Prime Minister, Lord Halifax, Sir John Simon and Sir Samuel Hoare. Their advisers were Sir Alexander Cadogan, Sir Horace Wilson and, sometimes, Sir Robert Vansittart. From the point of view of convention, though not a constitutional point, it is difficult to see why this urgent work was not entrusted to the Cabinet Foreign Affairs Committee, but in practice the Prime Minister with only three Ministers had a safer consensus than he would have received in the older Committee.

The Notes in this volume are sparse and the two first such meetings are omitted altogether, so that the diary of Sir Alexander Cadogan is the best reminder of what happened

[1] F.O. 371. 21737. p. 244 (c. 708)   [2] Cab. 27. 646

on September 8th and 9th. He noted on September 6th that "Horace Wilson came over and told me that he had been visited by Herr Kordt who had said that he put conscience before loyalty and told him that Hitler was preparing to act against Czechoslovakia on September 20th". Cadogan and Wilson decided that "Vansittart should get Neville Chamberlain down from Scotland". Herr Theo Kordt was not, like Herr von Kleist, a reminder of the Jacobites, but the accredited Counsellor in the German Embassy, and his advice to Lord Halifax, when Kordt returned to 10 Downing Street, again by the garden gate, on September 7th was that there should be a British declaration "that could not be clear and unmistakable enough".[1] This created a dilemma for Mr Chamberlain, for it added another and more authoritative voice to the many reaching him out of the shadows, whose reasoning he and Lord Halifax had dismissed already in the Meeting of Ministers on August 30th. His mind being firmly made up on the dangers of an open warning to Hitler, he did not call a Cabinet meeting immediately, but announced it for September 12th, a few hours before Hitler was to speak at the Nuremberg Party Congress.

Meanwhile, he set about the problem with those Ministers who were closest to him. Since there is no official record of the first two meetings on September 8th and 9th, I refer to the Cadogan Diary for events before the Notes of Informal Meetings of Ministers were started.

Chamberlain had bidden Lord Halifax, Sir John Simon and Sir Alexander Cadogan to the Cabinet room at 11 a.m. on September 8th. "The Prime Minister thought a warning not a good idea," noted Sir Alexander, "and mentioned that he wanted to visit Hitler." Lord Halifax said that "he thought they should call for Van". The Chief Diplomatic Adviser was then called in, "was consulted about the proposal of the Prime Minister to visit Hitler and spoke strongly against anything of the sort. He mentioned the word Canossa. . . . While Vansittart spoke, Neville Chamberlain put his elbows on the Cabinet table and his head between his hands and never said a word."[2]

On September 9th there was another meeting of the three Ministers, at which a carefully worded warning was drafted.

[1] Erich Kordt, *Nicht Aus Den Akten*   [2] *The Cadogan Diary*

Of this meeting there is also no official record, but Cadogan noted on September 9th, "Van wants a warning. I want to prevent Hitler committing himself irretrievably." Others who feared that a public warning might irritate Hitler were Sir Nevile Henderson in Nuremberg, Mr Basil Newton in Prague, and Lord Runciman, whose opinions were sought as a counterweight to Vansittart.

A private warning was, however, drafted in insistent language and sent via Mr Ivone Kirkpatrick, who was directed to send it on to Sir Nevile in Nuremberg. This *démarche* was to be made to Herr von Ribbentrop, he was told, and the text of the note shown to Herr Hitler. Its language went further than anything so far, in that it declared that once France was involved in war on behalf of Czechoslovakia "it seems to His Majesty's Government inevitable that the sequence of events must result in a general conflict from which Great Britain could not stand aside".[1] The word inevitable was new in the vocabulary of British warnings.

On September 10th, Sir Samuel Hoare looked into the Cabinet room to give the Prime Minister some news from Balmoral, where he had been in audience with the King. Chamberlain again tried out his idea of a visit to Hitler and Sir Samuel was favourable.[2] The Prime Minister, therefore, asked him to stay when Simon and Halifax entered to discuss again the question of the private warning to Hitler before his Nuremberg speech. Thus the four Ministers came together on whose support Chamberlain would rely.

The outcome of this cabal on the 10th was that a telegram was sent by Lord Halifax excusing Sir Nevile Henderson "in view of strong opinion in your communication" from presenting the firm British note even to Herr von Ribbentrop. "I think it right," wrote Cadogan. "Van furious."[3] On the 10th the four

[1] F.O. Telegram 354. Documents of British Foreign Policy, Third Series, Vol. II

[2] Hoare, *Nine Troubled Years*

[3] Sir Nevile's two letters, scrawled from his Nuremberg railway coach on September 8th and 10th, appear neither in tone nor in content to provide convincing reasons for cancelling the *démarche*. "For Heaven's sake", he wrote on September 8th, "send no more instructions as on May 21st. Hitler's position is that of a man who is bluffing with a full house in his hand." On September 10th he added: "A second 21st May will push him

Ministers also agreed further about the visit of Chamberlain to
Berchtesgaden, saying that it would require Cabinet approval.
On the 11th the same Ministers decided against any further
defensive preparations by the Royal Navy as liable to cause
irritation. There is no official record of any of these decisions.
To the full Cabinet when it met on the 12th, Mr Chamberlain
said: "This Cabinet meeting, announced in advance, will assist
in keeping public opinion steady." He then invited Lord Halifax
to relate what had happened since the Ministers last met on
August 30th, and a summary of events followed.

France had called up reservists and manned the Maginot
Line, began Lord Halifax. He related that new proposals, put
to the Sudeten Germans by the Czechs, were considered
satisfactory by Lord Runciman. *The Times* on September 7th
had published "an unhappy leading article advocating consideration of the secession of certain fringe areas". On September 8th, M. Daladier had stated to Sir Eric Phipps that if
Germany entered Czechoslovakia, France would declare war.
On September 9th, Sir Nevile Henderson had repeated to Herr
von Ribbentrop in Nuremberg a warning in "clear and strong
language". The Prime Minister, the Foreign Secretary and the
Chancellor of the Exchequer had met that same day to consider "a further formal warning". He reminded them that
Ministers had been against such a warning on August 30th.
Since then information had been received that "Hitler had
decided to march into Czechoslovakia on some date between
the 18th and 29th September". However, Sir Nevile Henderson,
on receiving instructions to deliver the further formal warning
to Hitler at Nuremberg, "had urged with all the force at his
command that he should not be instructed to make the official
démarche—Sir Nevile reported that the moderate elements in
Germany in particular were most strongly against what they
termed the 'repetition of 21st May'.[1] It had, therefore, been

over the edge, if not of actual madness, of mad action ... I've been running
around here like a lunatic myself. I do not believe Hitler is planning
recourse to force *now*. Other sources may think they know better and Heaven
knows how easily I may be wrong. But even if I am, another warning will
not help. If he has decided, that will not alter his decision. If he has not
decided, that will help him to do so, that is all" (C. P. 196 (38)).

[1] It is significant that Mr Bridges' Minutes in the Standard Cabinet file
contained first the words that "*the moderate elements in the Nazi Party*, in

decided to telegraph to Sir Nevile (who lacked any cypher facilities) that provided he had conveyed the substance and our meaning and intentions were fully understood by Germany, the official *démarche* need not be delivered."

Lord Halifax went on to say that British warships had been brought out of reserve, as announced on September 10th, and the crews of the Seventh Destroyer Flotilla brought to full complement. The Prime Minister and the Foreign Secretary had seen Mr Winston Churchill on September 11th and he had told them that in his opinion Britain would incur no added risk in telling Germany "that if she set foot in Czechoslovakia we should at once be at war with her". The Foreign Secretary claimed that Mr Eden was in complete agreement with the line taken by the Government, though another visitor, Lord Lloyd of Dolobran, had been concerned whether Sir Nevile Henderson had made the meaning of the Cabinet quite plain. Lord Halifax thought that Hitler was "possibly or even probably mad" . . . "If he made up his mind to attack, there was nothing that we could do to stop him. . . . Any serious prospect of getting Herr Hitler back to a sane outlook would probably be irretrievably destroyed by any action on our part . . . involving him in a public humiliation. . . . This view of the situation was supported by all who were in a position to judge the facts. . . .[1] The wise course was to await Hitler's speech and then review the situation."

Sir Thomas Inskip asked what was the impression that Sir Nevile Henderson was satisfied that he had conveyed to the German leaders. Lord Halifax read in reply from telegram No. 354, the message that Sir Nevile had declined to deliver, which contained the warning that "France having become involved, it seems to His Majesty's Government inevitable that the sequence of events must result in a general conflict from which Great Britain could not stand aside". Mr Chamberlain commented that this "represented the probable sequence of

particular, were most strongly against what they termed a 'repetition of May 21st'". In red ink the word *Germany* has been inserted and *the Nazi Party* crossed out. C.P. 196 (38). The previous version would have been intelligible, but as Lord Halifax had previously told the Meeting of Ministers on August 30th, the moderates in Germany were in growing favour of a repeated warning, and Herr Kordt, whose advice he omitted from this summary to the Cabinet, was one of them.

[1] Sir Robert Vansittart's differing views were also not mentioned.

events rather than a definite commitment", to which Mr Duff Cooper remarked that this could not be described as "a warning ultimatum". He thought it was an admirable statement of the position which ought not to upset Herr Hitler.[1] Duff Cooper complained that "We have not taken the course of an official *démarche* on the advice of Sir Nevile Henderson only" . . . "It seemed that the solution which Sir Nevile contemplated would result in a complete surrender on the part of the Czechs." He suggested that a formal warning should now be considered by the Cabinet. The Prime Minister replied that "all his advice suggested that the formal warning would not stop Hitler, if determined upon that course, and if not yet decided upon it, might drive him to adopt the course that the Cabinet were anxious to avoid".

They passed on to discussing the importance of "neither applying the brake nor the accelerator to France". Indeed it seemed that British policy had been applied to keeping France guessing as well as Germany. It was said that any reply to M. Bonnet was to avoid precise statements on future British action. Meanwhile the Chiefs of Staff were to prepare an appreciation of the likely course of events if there should be immediate hostilities.

Hitler made a thunderous speech to his Party masses at Nuremberg that afternoon, but the Prime Minister let a day pass before he called the Cabinet again. Meanwhile, according to the Notes of Informal Meetings, on September 13th, at 3 p.m., he met in the Cabinet room with Sir John Simon, Lord Halifax and Sir Samuel Hoare. Vansittart, Cadogan and Wilson were in attendance. They appraised the Hitler speech in advance of the Cabinet meeting. Mr Bridges notes that Items 9 and 10 at this small meeting related to:

(9) The Z Plan. (The Prime Minister's visit to Herr Hitler.)
(10) Publicity for Z Plan.

There is no record of what was said on these items, which may well have been carried forward to a second meeting at 10 p.m., at which Vansittart was not present.

[1] In his diary Duff Cooper records that he criticised the time chosen for this Cabinet meeting as too late to deliver a warning to Hitler and too early to draw any conclusions from his speech.

At the first meeting it is noteworthy that the idea of a
Four Power Conference[1] was first discussed and that it was
thought to be "not in any way attractive to Germany, except in
so far as it involved the exclusion of Russia. Generally not
considered likely to do any good."[2] At the second meeting at
10 p.m. "the Prime Minister and the Secretary of State further
discussed the position. It was agreed that the proposed message
should be dispatched (Plan Z), but that in view of the lateness
of the hour Sir Nevile Henderson should not attempt to get in
touch with Herr von Ribbentrop until early on the morning of
September 14th."[3]

Mr Chamberlain was now ready to face his next full Cabinet
meeting on September 14th. He told the Ministers that an
examination of Hitler's Nuremberg speech "showed that the
action we have taken was justified, in as much as Hitler has
not done anything irrevocable". The Prime Minister then
discussed the difficulties of a plebiscite, and though he admitted that Hitler had not asked for one, emphasised that "it
would be difficult for the democratic countries to go to war to
prevent the Sudeten Germans from saying what form of Government they wanted to have". He then passed on to discussing
"a plan which had occurred to me as one which might be put
into force at a moment's notice. . . . The plan was that as soon
as it became clear that a solution could be reached in no other
way, the Prime Minister should go to Germany himself and see
Herr Hitler."

The Prime Minister referred to his proposal as Plan Z. A
succession of incidents in the Sudeten areas and "a remarkable
communication" on the afternoon of September 13th from Sir
Eric Phipps, who had seen M. Bonnet and described the
Foreign Minister as "in a state of collapse" and "thoroughly
cowed" had led Mr Chamberlain to consider the time ripe for
Plan Z. M. Daladier had wished to speak to the Prime Minister
later on the same day, but the Prime Minister had avoided a
telephone conversation and Sir Eric Phipps had seen the French

[1] Britain, Germany, France, Italy

[2] Sir Robert Vansittart wrote on September 13th a strong minute to
Lord Halifax against any Four Power Meeting that excluded Russia, as
this would "ultimately drive Russia into the arms of Germany".

[3] Cab. 27. 646

Prime Minister instead. He had found him "a very different person from what he had been on September 8th" and "saying that some way must be found out". M. Daladier had said that at all costs Germany must be prevented from invading Czechoslovakia, because in that case France would be faced with her obligations. The Prime Minister thought that this language was significant. He mentioned that Henlein had also broken off negotiations with the Czechoslovak Government.

After this preparation the Prime Minister came to a point of some delicacy. He revealed to the Cabinet that he and Lord Halifax with the advice of the Chancellor of the Exchequer and the Home Secretary—two former Foreign Secretaries, as he was careful to point out—had already sent a dispatch to Sir Nevile Henderson putting Plan Z into operation. "He hoped that the Cabinet would feel that he had not gone beyond his proper duty in taking this action on the advice of those of his colleagues whom he had mentioned but without consulting the full Cabinet." He then enlarged on Plan Z. "Herr Hitler liked to see Heads of State, and it might be agreeable to his vanity that the British Prime Minister should take so unprecedented a step. . . . You could say more to a man face to face than you could put in a letter . . . The right course was to open by an appeal to Herr Hitler on the grounds that he had a great chance of obtaining fame for himself by making peace in Europe and thereafter establishing good relations with Great Britain . . . He had in mind to propose Lord Runciman as the final arbitrator. But he felt that Herr Hitler might now accept nothing less than a plebiscite . . . That would be achieved only with 'enormous difficulties' . . . The Czechs might prefer to die fighting than accept a solution that would rob them of their natural frontiers . . . He might even, most unwillingly, have to accept a new liability and join in guaranteeing the frontiers of a new Czechoslovakia." By way of comfort he added that "Once this question is out of the way, Field-Marshal Goering has intimated that 'Germany would be surprisingly moderate'".

Lord Hailsham asked what would happen if other minorities asked for a plebiscite. The Prime Minister replied that "he did not expect any such demand to be made". This startled Lord Halifax, who put in a cautionary remark that the idea of a plebiscite might be "infectious". The Ministers spoke then in turn, some in praise of the idea and others pointing out difficulties, but none in absolute opposition to the idea of the journey. Many of them welcomed an added idea of Sir John Simon that there should be a deferred plebiscite in six months' time or later. Mr Duff Cooper is recorded as saying that he had come to the Cabinet prepared to recommend a mobilisation of the Fleet, but "this was now out of the question and he much preferred Plan Z". He is, however, recorded further as saying that "the choice is not between war and a plebiscite, but between war now and war later". Sir John Simon, who had saved his observations to the last, welcomed "the brilliant proposal" of the Prime Minister and "asked the Cabinet to record their unanimous approval, to express their confidence and trust in the Prime Minister. . . ."

"His absence from this country, if only for a short time, is a grievous matter, but if he comes back with the seeds of peace with honour, he will be immediately acclaimed as having carried out the greatest achievement of the last twenty years." Mr Chamberlain "was much touched by the confidence placed in him. It was impossible to lay down precise limitations, he said, but he would do his very best in the light of the discussion."

The conclusions of the Cabinet approved the action that he had already taken, authorised him "to confer with Herr Hitler on the general lines indicated" and deferred consideration of a mobilisation of the Fleet.

There is a published record by Herr Schmidt, the German official interpreter, of the meeting on September 15th, between Mr Chamberlain and Adolf Hitler. The text was accepted afterwards by Sir Nevile Henderson. Not everything said in so long an interview will have been included. A version of this discussion was printed in the *British Blue Book* after the outbreak of war. What I have sought to add from the Chamberlain narrative in Cabinet is the Prime Minister's assessment and presentation of his case to his colleagues, made without reflection or hindsight.

He told his story at some length on Saturday, September 17th, in the Cabinet room, not sparing them a description of the journey to Berchtesgaden. Duff Cooper, who described the effect as "frightful", noted in his diary that Chamberlain described Hitler as "the commonest little dog you ever saw", though the Prime Minister appeared also flattered that Hitler was described as referring to him, Chamberlain, as "a man". The Cabinet record is more discreet. "On a first view Hitler was unimpressive. There was nothing out of the common in his features," noted Mr Bridges.

After tea and "talking platitudes for about half an hour", Herr Hitler asked Chamberlain "what was to be the next stage? Would he like two or three of each side to be present?" The Prime Minister had said that "he would prefer a private talk with Herr Hitler alone". About 5.20 p.m., therefore, the Prime Minister and Herr Hitler went off with Dr Schmidt (the interpreter) to Herr Hitler's room. The conversation lasted until 8.15 p.m. The Prime Minister said that "he had no idea that this conversation would last anything approaching so long a time". "He had in mind to open about a new understanding between Britain and Germany . . . Herr Hitler had replied that there was something else of greater urgency, namely the Sudeten German question. . . .

"The Prime Minister saw no signs of insanity but many of excitement . . . Occasionally Hitler would lose the thread of what he was saying and go off into a tirade. It was impossible not to be impressed with the power of the man. He was extremely determined and would not brook opposition beyond a certain point. Further, and this was a point of considerable importance, the Prime Minister had formed the opinion that Herr Hitler's objectives were strictly limited."

Mr Chamberlain then described Hitler as saying that if there was to be no understanding with England, then he might as well denounce the naval agreement.

The Prime Minister had at once interrupted and asked, Did the *Führer* mean that he would denounce the Anglo-German Naval Treaty before we went to war with him? The *Führer* answered in the affirmative. He had signed it on the assumption that the British had renounced all idea of war with Germany. Mr Chamberlain had said he would like to deal with this point at once. "There would be just grounds for complaint if we let it be thought that in no circumstances would we go to war with Germany." Hitler passed on to saying that he did not want the Czechs—he was only concerned with those of German race. As to the difficulties in incorporating the majority areas of the Sudeten Germans in the Reich, "these were academic". Hitler became excited in his manner. It had quietened him, and the conversation went better, after Mr Chamberlain said that he wondered whether he was wasting his time and had not better go home. If the British could not accept the principle of self-determination there was no point, retorted Hitler, in pursuing the negotiations. Chamberlain said that he then told Hitler "as his personal opinion, looking at the question as one of principle . . . it was immaterial to me whether the Sudeten Germans stayed in Czechoslovakia or were incorporated in the Reich. What the British people wanted was a peaceful and just settlement."

They had parted with a grudging assurance from Hitler that "he would not set the machine in motion" pending the resumption of negotiation, if he could help it.

The Prime Minister may have noted consternation on the faces of some of his colleagues at this narrative. For he then explained that "he had gone to Germany in a situation of desperate urgency. If he had not gone, hostilities would by now have started."

"It was now important to lose no time. There had been no opportunity for him to put smaller points" . . . "He was uncertain what impression he personally had made on Herr Hitler, but information from other sources had been that the *Führer* was most favourably impressed" . . . "The Prime Minister thought it was not possible to deal with a man like Hitler by attaching conditions. If the principle of self-determination was accepted, he thought that Hitler would not prove too difficult."

The record of discussion is surprisingly brief at this point. "Some Ministers" expressed concern that the path on which they were then embarked might end with the dismemberment of Czechoslovakia, but it was nearing lunch-time and Mr Chamberlain was happy to have an adjournment without seeking a consensus of approval for his handling of the Berchtesgaden visit. For even the Cabinet Minutes make it plain that he had the worst of the encounter with Hitler.

Lord Maugham opened after lunch that Saturday with some

sonorous observations on the precepts of Canning and Disraeli in foreign policy. "Before we intervene British interests have to be seriously affected and we should only intervene from overwhelming force." British interests, the Lord Chancellor concluded, were not involved.

Mr Duff Cooper retorted that "it was a primary interest of Britain to prevent any single power dominating Europe. We were now faced with the most formidable power for a century.[1] It was of the utmost importance to pacify Germany and he would go to almost any length to attain this end. But what chance was there of achieving this? Hitler's promises were quite unreliable. He hoped that the Prime Minister would attach conditions to a plebiscite when he next saw Hitler, with careful inquiry on the application of the principle of self-determination.

Sir Thomas Inskip "doubted whether there was any essential difference between the conclusion of the First Lord and that of the Prime Minister". Duff Cooper rejoined that "he hoped this was so". The Prime Minister soon made plain that it was not. For he reaffirmed that "to deal satisfactorily with Hitler we must accept the principle of self-determination unconditionally and talk about conditions later".

Earl De La Warr, Lord Privy Seal, then spoke strongly for firmness—"he was prepared to face war in order to free the world from the continual threat of ultimatums".

Lord Hailsham rallied to the Prime Minister, saying that one power did already dominate Europe and "we have no alternative but to submit to humiliation". This led Earl Winterton to comment that in pursuit of this argument the British might acquiesce "in the invasion of Kent or the surrender of the Isle of Wight" . . . "There was hard fibre in the British people, who did not like to be told that unless they acquiesced it was all up with them."

The Foreign Secretary spoke long and thoughtfully, advancing all his previous arguments about the impossibility of defending Czechoslovakia. As to the view that "if we did not have war

[1] In his own version of this statement Duff Cooper repeated the point that as Britain did not possess overwhelming force at that time and was unlikely to attain it, it would follow from the Lord Chancellor's remarks that she could never again intervene in Europe. "We were in fact finished." Duff Cooper Diary.

now, we should have it later on, that was really the argument for a preventive war". That theory meant "that we should have a bad war every twenty years to prevent a war from occurring five years later". He thought that we should accept the principle of "the transfer of these peoples". Mr Oliver Stanley objected that "this question was almost as direct an attack upon us as an attack on the Isle of Wight". He agreed with the First Lord of the Admiralty—"if the choice for the Government in the next four days is between surrender and fighting, we ought to fight". He was less hopeful than before the Berchtesgaden interview and felt that we were virtually faced with an ultimatum. When the Prime Minister met Herr Hitler again, he would have to start negotiating conditions. Mr W. S. Morrison drew the attention of the Cabinet to the fact that Hitler had not once in his Nuremberg speech or his conversations with Mr Chamberlain used the word "plebiscite". After some cautious words by Mr Hore-Belisha and Sir Kingsley Wood, approving the Chamberlain line, Duff Cooper restated Lord Hailsham's words that the position was that "we should submit to a humiliation. . . . He thought we should make it plain to France that we would rather fight than agree to an abject surrender and support the French rather than put a brake on their actions."

Mr Chamberlain then began quietly to assert his position. He said that "his colleagues had accepted the principle of self-determination and given him the support he had asked for". As he saw it, Earl De La Warr and not the First Lord of the Admiralty had been the first who contemplated actual hostilities. Modern war, he reminded them, affected the whole population. He wished he could show them some of the many letters reaching him from all over the country. Acceptance of the principle of self-determination was not "abject surrender".

"In the account of his conversations with Herr Hitler he could not repeat every word which had passed. It might be thought that he (the Prime Minister) should have used some rather different language, but he had agreed to the principle of self-determination and so secured the only condition on which negotiations could be carried on. It had never entered his head that he should go to Germany and say to Herr Hitler that he could have self-determination on any terms he wanted. As to the arrangements to be made, he agreed with the Foreign Secretary in disliking a guarantee to a distant country. It was not to be excluded, but could be considered when the time came, and could be discussed with the French Ministers at a meeting arranged for 11 a.m. on Sunday morning." Once more the Cabinet adjourned without an expression of confidence in Mr Chamberlain.

After a very difficult Sunday morning with the French, the four British Ministers entertained them to lunch and then withdrew to consider their own position, but without summoning the Cabinet. The British foursome "agreed that Great Britain should offer to join France in a guarantee of Czechoslovakia against aggression, conditional upon

(a) the Czech Government agreeing to accepting a position of neutrality.
(b) accepting to act on our advice on issues of peace and war."

The Notes continue that "It was agreed that Czechoslovakia herself would place no confidence in such a guarantee. Nevertheless, there would be no harm in us having the guarantee."[1]

The idea of getting Germany and Russia to join in a guarantee was discussed. It might be impossible to get both, Mr Bridges noted, it might be a question of choosing one or the other power. As for Dr Beneš, Lord Halifax "thought it should be stated pretty bluntly that if he did not leave himself in our hands, we should wash our hands of him". The four British Ministers then "agreed that it should be made quite clear to Dr Beneš that unless he gave a prompt acceptance of the present proposals the French and British would not hold themselves responsible for the consequences. There was no time to be lost."

Armed with these resolutions, the British Ministers met the French again at 3.30 p.m., and soon after 5 p.m. a verbal message to be delivered to President Beneš was drafted and amended, and dispatched that night to Prague.

At the Cabinet of Monday, September 19th, the Prime Minister first acquainted his colleagues with the Sunday discussions with M. Daladier and M. Bonnet. He said that these had lasted all day and had turned on whether, if the French

[1] Cab. 27. 646

accepted the principle of secession, Britain would join some
form of international guarantee for the new Czechoslovakia.
The French thought that secession of the Sudeten areas might
have to come, but that a plebiscite would plunge Europe into
chaos.

There had finally been agreement on a joint Anglo-French
message to President Beneš stating their view that in the interests
of Czechoslovakia herself and European peace, the Sudeten
German areas should be "transferred to the Reich". Mr Chamberlain said that he had "felt considerable misgivings about the
guarantee that would have to accompany this proposal, but
delay in reaching agreement with the French would have been
'disastrous' and under the terms of such a guarantee there
would be 'neutralisation of Czechoslovak foreign policy' ". The
import of the above record is that Mr Chamberlain had once
more committed the Cabinet to a major act of foreign policy
before seeking its approval.

The Minister most unhappy with this account appeared to be
Mr Hore-Belisha, whose unprepared Army might thus be
saddled with a new Continental commitment. To his objections
about the strategically unsound position of a truncated Czechoslovakia, Mr Chamberlain replied with disarming frankness
that "it was not right to assume that the guarantee committed
us to maintaining the existing boundaries of Czechoslovakia.
The guarantee merely related to unprovoked aggression. He
appreciated the difficulty of seeing how we would implement
the guarantee. Its main value would be in its deterrent effect."[1]

In view of the French attitude, the Cabinet submerged its
previous misgivings and in its conclusions endorsed the attitude
which the Prime Minister had taken up in his discussions with
Herr Hitler on Thursday, September 15th. It endorsed the
sending of a joint message (already sent) to President Beneš
and authorised the Prime Minister to continue his negotiations
with Herr Hitler.

Events followed fast, as the German Army moved towards its
zero day, September 28th 1938. The Anglo-French verbal
démarche was conveyed to President Beneš in Prague on Tuesday
September 20th, advising him that if the partition recommended
in the Anglo-French plan was not accepted, Czechoslovakia

[1] Cab. 23. 95, p. 126

The Chamberlain Cabinet waves goodbye to the Prime Minister before he enters his plane at Heston, September 29th 1938

Hitler and Chamberlain at Bad Godesberg, September, 1938

would be solely responsible for the ensuing war and France would not fulfil her treaty obligations. President Beneš received the diplomats at the extraordinary hour of 2 a.m. and described their message as "a kind of ultimatum". The upshot was that as soon as the Hodza Government accepted these terms, it fell. On September 21st, General Syrovy, a veteran of the Czech Legion, became Prime Minister.

When the British Cabinet met at 3 p.m. on the 21st, Duff Cooper noted,[1] Mr Chamberlain was "a little stiffer". Some Ministers spoke up for "a decent interval" before Germany occupied the Sudeten area. The First Sea Lord himself urged that the Prime Minister should tell Hitler that he had reached the limit of his concessions and rather than retreat further would, if necessary, risk war. "I think what I said produced an effect—nobody contested it."[2]

The Cabinet set out agreed guidelines for the Prime Minister at his second meeting with Herr Hitler, among which were:

(1) That if Hitler would not reach a settlement without including the Hungarian and Polish minorities, the Prime Minister should say that he must return home to consult his colleagues.
(2) Regarding the proposed guarantee to the new boundaries of Czechoslovakia, the Prime Minister should proceed on the basis that France, Great Britain and Russia are the joint guarantors.[3]

The second encounter between Chamberlain and Hitler, at Bad Godesberg on the Rhineland, lasted from September 22nd to 24th. It was brusquely interrupted, as they had feared, by Hitler, who responded to the Anglo-French proposals with, "I am sorry, but all that is no use any more."

He objected to the timing as too dilatory[4] and now raised the claims of the Poles, the Hungarians and the Slovaks, the "infectious" danger against which Halifax had cautioned his Prime Minister. These claims would have effectively disembowelled Czechoslovakia. Mr Chamberlain withdrew to his hotel and resorted to an exchange of letters. On Friday, he

[1] Duff Cooper Diary   [2] Ibid.
[3] The name of Russia was never mentioned to Hitler, as events turned out.
[4] November had been suggested for the plebiscite.
F

coldly took leave of Hitler, offering to convey his new terms to Czechoslovakia, but saying that he could not recommend their acceptance.

Once more Chamberlain repeated his now established practice of meeting his chosen Ministers before the full Cabinet. He invited Sir John Simon, Lord Halifax and Sir Samuel Hoare to the Cabinet room at 3.30 p.m. on Saturday, September 24th, to review events. The advisers present were Vansittart, Wilson, Cadogan and Strang. Neville Chamberlain related his Bad Godesberg experiences and the minutes then record his state of mind as follows:

> Did Hitler mean to go further? The Prime Minister was satisfied that Herr Hitler was speaking the truth when he said that he regarded this as a racial question. He thought he had established some degree of personal influence over Herr Hitler. The latter had said to him: "You are the first man in many years who has got any concessions out of me." Herr Hitler had said that if we got this question out of the way without conflict, it would be a turning point in Anglo-German relations. That, to the Prime Minister, was the big thing of the present issue. He was also satisfied that Herr Hitler would not go back on his word once he had given it.

The full Cabinet met at 7.30 p.m. and Mr Chamberlain explained Herr Hitler's change of attitude as "due to his great mistrust of the Czechs" . . . "He had written two letters to Herr Hitler in an attempt to clarify the position, only to be told that his suggestions were of 'no value'." He had accordingly crossed the Rhine a second time to take leave of Herr Hitler about 10.30 p.m., when Hitler had presented him with an "outrageous" document demanding withdrawal of the Czech forces to new ethnic boundaries beginning on September 26th. The Prime Minister went on to say that "on the first day at Bad Godesberg he had felt indignant. . . . After further conversation with Herr Hitler, he had modified his views. . . . It was necessary to appreciate their motives and see how their minds worked in order to understand people's actions. In his view, Herr Hitler had certain standards. Herr Hitler had a narrow mind and was violently prejudiced on certain subjects: but he would not deliberately deceive a man whom he respected and with whom he had been in negotiation, and he was sure that Herr Hitler now felt some respect for him." . . . "He had also said that once the present issue was settled, he had no more territorial ambitions in Europe" . . . "The Prime Minister said that it would be a great tragedy if we lost this opportunity of reaching an understanding with Germany on all points of difference between the two countries." He then repeated at length his detestation of war.

Mr Duff Cooper cut sharply across these reflections with the proposal that "our right course was to order a general mobilisation which might yet result in deterring the Germans from war".

This provoked considerable discussion, with Chamberlain advising postponement of any such measures. The Cabinet agreed to postpone decisions on defence at least until a proper conclusion had been reached on Hitler's proposals for an immediate German entry into Czechoslovakia.[1]

Meanwhile the Czechoslovak Government was told that Britain could no longer advise her against mobilisation measures.

On the morning of Sunday, September 25th, there was a full Cabinet meeting to discuss the Bad Godesberg rupture. Lord Halifax surprised many Ministers by confessing that there might now be some divergence between him and the Prime Minister. He made this hesitantly plain after hearing other Ministers object to any further concessions to Hitler.

Lord Halifax, in telling the Meeting of Ministers on August 30th about the nature of the crisis that was now upon them, had begun by saying that almost all warnings from Germany had been accompanied by the advice that a firm attitude towards Hitler would lead to a check for his regime and might prove an effective deterrent. In rejecting that advice, which the Government then felt unable to take, the Foreign Secretary had said that any subsequent criticism that Britain should have stood firm to avert a crisis and all its consequences would, in the light of their full deliberations, "leave him unmoved". He was, however, on this subsequent date obviously moved at the straits into which their policy of compromise with Hitler had brought them and perhaps saw that Britain and France had lost or were about to lose the last chance of checking Hitler other than by almost complete surrender to his demands. Lord

[1] Cab. 23. 95, p. 190

Halifax, as Duff Cooper noted in his diary, spoke with much
emotion.

The Foreign Secretary "had found his opinion changing
somewhat in the last day or so. . . . Even now he was not too
certain of his view. Yesterday he had felt that the difference
between last Sunday's proposals (for an orderly transfer)
and the scheme now put forward (for immediate transfer of
minority territories) did not involve a new acceptance of
principle. He was not quite sure, however, that he still held
that view. . . . He could not rid his mind of the fact that Herr
Hitler had given us nothing and that he was dictating terms. . . .
So long as Nazism lasted, peace would be uncertain. For this
reason he did not feel that it would be right to put pressure on
Czechoslovakia to accept the German demands."

He referred to the possibility that Hitler was gaining his
way by a bluff of words—"if he was driven to war, the result
might be to help to bring down the Nazi *regime*" . . . "The
Foreign Secretary concluded by saying that he had worked
most closely with the Prime Minister throughout the long crisis.
He was not quite sure that their minds were still altogether at
one. Nevertheless he thought it right to expose his hesitations
with complete frankness."[1]

Lord Maugham came to the rescue of Chamberlain. Indignation was a bad guide, said the Lord Chancellor. Czechoslovakia
ought to be told that France, Great Britain and Russia could
not prevent her being overrun and destroyed.

Lord Zetland "wondered what sort of regime would exist in
Germany after a world war. Might it not be even more dangerous to us than the Nazi *regime*?" Other Ministers spoke their
indignation over the "outrageous" demands of Germany, but
wanted the door to Hitler to be kept open, as Mr MacDonald
suggested, for "some more genial agreement later".

That afternoon, talk turned again in Cabinet to Czechoslovakia's other treaty power, Russia. Sir Samuel Hoare
"thought it was of the utmost importance that the countries
involved (Great Britain, France and Russia) should examine
the military position as impartially as possible. We should not
take a final decision until we knew how we should stand with
the Dominions."

[1] Cab. 23. 95

When Mr Chamberlain summed up he detected a much greater diversity of opinion in the Cabinet, but he was able to point out that these outrageous demands were not put to Britain, but to the Czechs. There could be no question of forcing Dr Beneš to accept them. The Cabinet reached the conclusion that Britain would not commit herself "either to make war or not to make war", if a refusal by President Beneš led to a conflict with Germany.

The Cabinet had been restive. M. Daladier was angry and resentful at the cross-examination manner of Sir John Simon when inquiring as to French military intentions. General Gamelin, the French Commander-in-Chief, had produced a written appreciation of French military intentions in the event of war, showing that he would commence a cautious offensive against the German West Wall five days after the outbreak of war, having already twenty-three French divisions in position in face of eight German divisions. He would begin by attacking industrial targets in the frontier region and would hope to take pressure off the Czechs.

Mr Chamberlain had a formula both for his Cabinet and the French. He would send an emissary to Hitler, to make plain the new Anglo-French determination to resist. He named Sir Horace Wilson and showed M. Daladier the message that Sir Horace would carry.

Sir Horace Wilson arrived in Berlin on September 26th, the day of a mass meeting at the Sports Palace, at which Hitler was expected to deliver a final challenge, much as he had done in Nuremberg, to President Beneš.

In the pocket of Sir Horace was a letter from Mr Chamberlain to Hitler presenting Sir Horace as his representative, also a short memorandum.

The French Government has informed us that if the Czechs reject the (German) memorandum and Germany attacks Czechoslovakia, they will fulfil their obligations to Czechoslovakia. Should the forces of France in consequence become engaged in active hostilities against Germany, we shall feel obliged to support them.

Sir Horace, in the mood of fury in which he found Hitler

[1] Cab. 23. 95, p. 248

before his speech, deemed it prudent not to present this memorandum. Hitler spoke on the 26th with even less restraint than at Nuremberg. On the morning of the 27th Sir Horace saw Hitler again before his departure to London, read him the message slowly and then answered Hitler's questions. Sir Horace told the Cabinet that "Herr Hitler had taken this message very quietly".

Indeed, to the practised German eye the Chamberlain message contained gaps that M. Daladier had perhaps not perceived. How active would the French have to be before Britain supported them? What support would she give? If she declared war, would she attack Germany? This kind of question from Hitler to Wilson at once robbed the Chamberlain message of any value. Much more effective, though belated, was an announcement on the night of September 27th that the British Fleet was being mobilised. Another steadying factor was a British Foreign Office communiqué, emanating from the News Department on September 26th, that spoke for the first time of Britain *and Russia* being bound to go to the aid of France if she became involved in a war over Czechoslovakia.

The climax came on September 28th, in the House of Commons, when Mr Chamberlain was describing his efforts for a settlement. He had on the previous day quietly taken up with Signor Mussolini the plan for a Four Power Conference that had already been discussed by the Inner Cabinet on September 13th, the conference from which Russia would be excluded.

His inquiry in Rome bore fruit conveniently on September 28th. A note passed along the benches to Mr Chamberlain as he spoke to a crowded House of Commons, informed all that Hitler agreed to a Four Power Conference. The Munich conference seemed to many who heard him speak a chance for the salvation of peace.

What emerges from the Cabinet papers is that the real decisions were taken before the Cabinet meetings. A few Ministers only had access to the Intelligence reports. The Prime Minister sought their agreement to his policy first in an Inner Cabinet. Both the decision to go to Berchtesgaden and the ultimatum to President Beneš were related to the Cabinet only after action had been taken. The public proposal for a firm warning to Hitler was explained to the Cabinet as having already been rejected by "all those in possession of the facts".

It was presented as no longer an open question. The Cabinet was allowed to debate, but asked to endorse and approve actions taken. The real Cabinet may be said at this time to have consisted of the Prime Minister acting as his own Foreign Secretary, the Foreign Secretary proper, and two previous Foreign Secretaries.

I have said that the Ministers did not have access to the Intelligence reports. These cannot be seen today and some Cabinet papers containing references to them are still withheld for security reasons by the Lord Chancellor's rulings. To what degree they offered solid prospects of action against Hitler within Germany must remain for the time being an unsolved question.

There is a story from serious sources that Sir Robert Vansittart had established a link with General Ludwig Beck, Chief of the German Army Staff, and was endeavouring to persuade Chamberlain, in view of the likelihood of real opposition to Hitler, to take a firmer line with Hitler. Sir Winston Churchill, in his memoirs, repeats the story of General Franz Halder, Beck's successor, that a Generals' plot to overthrow Hitler was hourly imminent on September 14th, the day that the message from Chamberlain was received in Berlin, giving Hitler room for manœuvre. This is of further interest when we reflect that the message was sent as the result of a decision outside the Cabinet, which Sir Alexander Cadogan described afterwards[1] as "quite unconstitutional". Mr. Oliver Harvey, private secretary to Lord Halifax, dining with Miss Marjorie Maxse of the Conservative Central Office twelve days after Munich, "discussed frankly the P.M.'s dictatorship in the Cabinet"[1]

During the crisis Cabinet responsibility had been reduced to a formality. It had not been called upon to take any real decision. The conclusion may be that the Cabinet was far from being, as Churchill had described it, "twenty-two men of blameless party character sitting round an overcrowded table, each having a voice". In reality they were deprived of secret Intelligence, unsure of what had been said, done and written, and unconsulted until the essential and irrevocable lines of policy had been devised by Chamberlain and accepted in the Prime Minister's foursome meetings. It was Prime Minister's rule.

[1] To the author   [2] The Diplomatic Diaries of Oliver Harvey

CHAPTER XIV

Munich: the Aftermath

MR CHAMBERLAIN TWICE flourished in public the declaration that he and Hitler signed in Munich, once at Heston airport and again from the windows of Downing Street, saying; "This is the second time in our history that there has come back from Germany to Downing Street peace with honour. I believe it is peace in our time."[1] Mr Churchill contrasted this assertion with a remark made to Lord Halifax by the Prime Minister as they drove in from Heston that "all this will be over in three months". Churchill assumed that these words expressed the Prime Minister's doubts on the solidity of his achievement. Lord Halifax sharply corrects this interpretation, saying that Chamberlain was referring solely to the popular excitement.[2] It seems that Mr Chamberlain really believed that he had brought back a lasting achievement. This is shown by repetitions in private of the words that he spoke in public. On October 3rd he sought the support of Lord Swinton in the House of Lords. His dismissed Secretary of State for Air was still a powerful man in the Conservative Party, and he told Chamberlain privately: "I will support you, Prime Minister, provided that you are clear that you have been buying time for rearmament." Neville Chamberlain produced the paper for a third time, exclaiming: "But don't you see, I have brought back peace."[3]

There is no Cabinet paper containing the thoughts and reservations of Mr Chamberlain after Munich. His remarks in Cabinet are, however, also a significant record of his frame of mind and we have to trace in subsequent Cabinet meetings his tenacious belief in his policy.

The Cabinet met at 7.30 p.m. on Friday, 30th September, immediately after the return of Mr Chamberlain from Munich. There was no agenda and no copy yet of the Munich Agreement to study. Later an annex of three short paragraphs was attached

[1] Feiling, *The Life of Neville Chamberlain*   [2] Halifax, *Fulness of Days*
[3] Lord Swinton to author

to the minutes, the joint Anglo-German declaration signed at
Munich that morning, affirming the resolve of the British and
German peoples "never to go to war with one another again"
and to use instead "the method of consultation".

Sir John Simon expressed "on behalf of the whole Cabinet"
their "profound admiration and pride in the Prime Minister".
Mr Chamberlain thanked them—"as things had turned out, he
felt that they could safely regard the crisis as ended". He then
described the discussions that began on the 29th and 30th, salt-
ing his narrative with the ominous detail that "when the time had
come to sign the final Agreements, it had been found that the
ink pot into which Herr Hitler had dipped his pen was empty".
He described the terms obtained as a real improvement.

Hitler's Bad Godesberg memorandum had been in fact an
ultimatum with a time limit of six days, the Prime Minister
explained, whereas under the Munich Agreement, the evacuation of territory would be carried out in five clearly defined
stages between 1st and 10th October. The final boundary line
would be fixed by an International Commission. The Hitler
line had disappeared. The plebiscite areas beyond those
occupied in the first phase were to be supervised by an international force. He continued to enumerate concessions obtained
from Hitler and said that he thought the Munich Agreement
"a vast improvement . . . a triumph for diplomacy". The Prime
Minister answered a number of questions and was then asked
about the paper that he had signed that morning with Herr
Hitler. The Prime Minister read it out to the Cabinet. He
informed them that he had also discussed limitation of armaments with Hitler, as well as Spain and south-east Europe.

Mr Duff Cooper said that he realised that the differences
between the Bad Godesberg terms and those in the Munich
Agreement were greater than he had previously recognised.
He was prepared to defer a final statement of his position until
he had studied the Agreement more closely. Nevertheless, he
had come to the Cabinet prepared to resign and still felt that it
was his duty to offer his resignation. Mr Chamberlain answered
that this was a matter that should be discussed between the
two of them, nor did he miss the opportunity to accept it.
The Cabinet adjourned over the weekend, meeting again on
Monday, October 3rd, when it was faced with a nasty bill for

breakages. Czechoslovakia had asked for a loan of £30m. On this Sir John Simon argued that "it was not the case that Czechoslovakia had any legitimate grievance against us. A world war had been averted and thereby Czechoslovakia had been saved." He spoke in favour of a small immediate advance to tide over currency difficulties, and the Prime Minister mentioned the figure of £10m. As for a proposal to open a public fund, "the Prime Minister was rather afraid that the opening of a Fund might have a bad effect upon public opinion in Germany".[1] The Foreign Secretary was authorised to discourage the Lord Mayor of London from adopting the proposal, though in fact a Lord Mayor's fund was nevertheless started.

The Cabinet met that morning without Mr Duff Cooper, who explained his resignation to the House of Commons in a ringing speech. Mr Walter Elliot, Minister of Health, another of the doubters, asked "whether the Prime Minister was in a position to give any guidance as to the line which his colleagues should take in any speeches on the possibility of limitation of armaments. . . . One view . . . strongly held . . . was that we must never again allow ourselves to be got into the position in which we had been for the last few weeks, and that every effort should be made to intensify our rearmament programme." Lord Halifax supported this view, saying that "he hoped nothing would be said that would preclude proper consideration of the need for such intensification".

The reply of Mr Chamberlain explains very much his entire thinking. He did not dissent from the views expressed, the Prime Minister said, but he would like to make his own position clear. Ever since he had been Chancellor of the Exchequer he had been oppressed with the sense that the burden of armaments might break our backs. This had led him to try to resolve the causes responsible for the armaments race. We were now in a more hopeful position, he thought. The contacts established with the Dictator Powers opened up the possibility that we might be able to reach some agreement with them that would stop the armaments race. It was clear, however, that it would be madness for the country to stop rearming until we were convinced that other countries would act in the same way. For the time being, therefore, we should relax no particle

[1] Cab. 23. 95, p. 301

of effort until our deficiencies had been made good. That, however, was not the same as saying that we would embark on a great increase in our armaments programme as a thank offering for the present *détente*.[1]

At the tail of this Cabinet, Lord Winterton made an appeal of importance. "We must not allow Germany to maintain her superiority over this country in the air." Sir Kingsley Wood also offered to show his colleagues the latest Air Ministry estimates of German air strength.

Over the weekend of October 1st and 2nd there had been more informal meetings of Sir John Simon and Lord Halifax at 10 Downing Street to discuss the question of a guarantee to Czechoslovakia and the proposed loan. Sir Horace Wilson confirmed to them that Russia had not been mentioned at the Munich Conference and the assumption was that she would not be a guarantor. General Lord Gort attended on October 1st. The Chief of the Imperial Staff reported that six battalions of British troops, four of them Guards battalions, had been chosen to enter the Sudeten territories, "led by Colonel Thorne, former Military Attaché in Berlin, who is *persona grata* to Hitler". The Germans would make the requisite dispositions for their movement via Hamburg and Aachen to participate in the plebiscite arrangements. Lord Gort said that there were also a thousand British Legion men available for the plebiscite areas, armed only with ash sticks. Lord Halifax commented that he foresaw "an embarrassment in British troops following up the German Army through Sudeten areas".[2] These arrangements, a little known curiosity in the annals of the British Army, never came into effect, as the International Commission set up by the Munich Agreement to supervise the plebiscite quickly collapsed. That the Munich Agreement was thought a difficult subject to justify is clear from Sir Horace Wilson's remarks on October 2nd to Sir John Simon and Lord Halifax at the last of their Informal Meetings. The Prime Minister would not, he said, invite extensive discussion in Parliament of the conditions of the Munich Agreement.

[1] Cab. 23. 95, p. 305
[2] Cab. 27. 646. Sir Frederick Maurice had also pleaded that on no account were his British Legion men to mingle with the French contingent of *Anciens Combatants*.

The Notes of Informal Meetings on the Czechoslovak Crisis 1938, a leather-bound foolscap volume, thus ends abruptly on October 2nd. Thereafter the Cabinet chronicles return to their orthodox books, among them the papers of the Committee of Imperial Defence, which met on October 6th to discuss a subject that Mr Chamberlain had carefully postponed for so long in expectation of better things. That subject was "Acceleration in Rearmament". The Services Departments were asked to report on the extent to which already approved programmes would be completed by August 1939, and what steps could be taken to improve their performance. As soon as these reports were received there would be a review of proposals to accelerate defence. The Cabinet decided to leave it to the Prime Minister to settle the procedure for dealing with these reports, and he set up a Cabinet Committee of seven Ministers for this purpose.[1] In view of the Prime Minister's own remarks on his return from Munich, acceleration was an acceptable policy, but not expansion.

The Cabinet on October 26th discussed Mr Churchill's idea of a Ministry of Supply, which the Prime Minister thought "unnecessary at the present time, though it might be discussed later". He concluded on the 31st that the Minister for Co-ordination of Defence was sufficiently able to co-ordinate supplies for defence as well.

Czechoslovakia had meanwhile fallen into the lap of the British Cabinet, an orphan state requiring as much time on the agenda as had in the past been occupied by Spain. There was also the Anglo-Italian Agreement to be implemented, of which Lord Halifax told the Cabinet on October 26th that "it is important that we should do all we can to liberate Signor Mussolini by degrees from the pressures to which he is subjected by Berlin". The argument used in favour of putting the Agreement into force was that "Spain has now ceased to be a menace to the peace of Europe".[2]

Hitler was not long satisfied with his Munich gains, soon realising how little the Western Allies had been prepared to make war. He delivered a truculent speech in Saarbruecken on October 9th, asserting that soon the British warmongers might well take over from the peaceable elements. No doubt

[1] Cab. 23. 96, p. 60   [2] Cab. 23. 96, p. 47

Mr Chamberlain had this speech in mind when he summed up to the Cabinet on October 31st his ideas on foreign policy and defence.

Our foreign policy is one of appeasement. We must aim at establishing relations with the Dictator Powers which will lead to a settlement in Europe and a sense of stability. A good deal of false emphasis has been placed . . . in the country and in the Press . . . on rearmament, as though one result of the Munich Agreement has been that it will be necessary to add to our rearmament programmes. [He proposed] to make it clear that our rearmament is directed to securing our own safety and not for purposes of aggression. [He hoped] that it may be possible to take active steps and to follow up the Munich Agreement by other measures. He also hoped that one day we shall be able to secure limitation of armaments, though it is too soon to say when this will prove possible.

Sir Kingsley Wood ventured to say that British weakness in the air might provoke aggression, and Lord Halifax thought it necessary to balance two factors—"our diplomacy is dependent on our strength, and secondly at present the dictators are in a jumpy frame of mind".[1]

The next Cabinet, on November 2nd, agreed that it was necessary to set up the manufacture of toxic gas which would be used in case of war only as a retaliatory measure after a Cabinet decision. In the Cabinet of November 7th the Services defence proposals came up for consideration. Extracts circulated to them of a meeting of the Committee of Imperial Defence on October 6th, directly after Munich, showed that the Air Staff were still at variance with the politicians. The former postulated that parity in the air with Germany meant that Britain must command a force of equal striking weight to the *Luftwaffe*. Sir Thomas Inskip and Sir Kingsley Wood did not accept this definition as correct. Sir Thomas defined air equality as an "effective deterrent strength" not necessarily of equal weight. It is noteworthy that in the Committee of Imperial Defence Sir Warren Fisher was still resisting arguments for greater arms production, and laying down the principle of

[1] Cab. 23. 96

economic strength: "if we withstood the first blow of war, it would be necessary to be in a position to outlast our enemies; if our export trade was ruined, this might not be possible". Sir Kingsley Wood finally formulated his view of a correct air strength as that it should be "sufficient to protect this country and to act as a deterrent, so that whatever the strength of the German air force, Germany itself would risk destruction if they attacked us".[1]

Sir Kingsley Wood on November 7th presented the case to the Cabinet "that in the view of the Committee of Imperial Defence, the country could not be considered safe until the Royal Air Force and the anti-aircraft defences had been increased and its passive defence arrangements substantially improved". The first line Metropolitan strength would by April 1939 have slightly exceeded the expected numbers, though not all aircraft would be of the latest types. The decisions taken by the Cabinet envisaged delivery of 12,000 aircraft by April 1942, but his figures showed that at present Britain, with 1,606 first line aircraft, had only half the German first line strength of 3,200 and in August 1939 would have only 1,890 compared with a German first line strength of 4,030.[2] Acceleration was thus plainly required.

Sir John Simon warned that acceleration would mean more borrowing of money. He pleaded that the emphasis should be laid on the fighter part of the programme. Mr Chamberlain, in a quiet conversation in Hitler's flat on September 30th, before they had signed the joint resolve never to go to war again, had appealed for abolition of the bombing aircraft.[3] The Prime Minister now backed Sir John. He "thought that it was rather difficult to represent this part of our force (bomber strength) as in any way defensive. . . . It was a very nice act to keep these two steeds in step. He felt very uneasy about the (Air Staff) proposal that we should concentrate on the type of very heavy bomber now proposed." He recalled the satisfaction which greeted the first building of Dreadnoughts. . . . "Before long other countries had started to build Dreadnoughts. He could not help wondering whether the proposal to concentrate on building Manchester and Halifax bombers would not result in Germany producing a super Halifax. These heavy bombers

[1] C.I.D. 1472. B   [2] C.P. 218 (38)   [3] C.P. 214 (38)

cost as much as four fighters." This intervention was decisive
in postponing the heavy bomber programme.

An Admiralty programme of escort vessels, minesweepers,
and air defence for naval establishments was approved, to which
was appended a curious order for "2,200 tons of armour plate
to be placed in Czechoslovakia". The War Office programme,
passed on November 7th, was solely for anti-aircraft equipment.
The decision on R.A.F. requirements approved that orders for
half of an additional programme of 3,700 fighters should be
placed, aiming at a maximum production of fighters by March
1940, instead of 1942. The Secretary of State for Air was to
"consider further the heavy bomber policy". Meanwhile
sufficient orders would be placed for bombers to avoid "substantial dismissals in the aircraft factories concerned".

There was in November after the Munich Agreement a
savage pogrom against Jews in Germany. This impelled the
Cabinet on November 16th to consider once more the question
of a national home or an area of refuge for the Jewish
communities in British African territories. Again the Cabinet
came back to the awkward question of the guarantee for
Czechoslovakia. It had still not been finally decided what states
were to assume this obligation, and the Foreign Secretary thought
this a problem that could be conveniently passed on to the
long dormant Foreign Affairs Committee of the Cabinet, the
Chiefs of Staff Committee advising on strategic aspects of such
an obligation.

The Prime Minister told the Cabinet on November 22nd
that he meant to tell the French Government at their next
meeting quite firmly about the limits of British military assistance on land. He proposed at the same time to ask for some
reassurance about a previous pledge by M. Delbos of French
aid if Britain were the victim of German aggression. If this
pledge still held good, he proposed to ask what steps would
France take in support of Britain. "He had been assured that
France was not proposing to sign a non-aggression pact with
Germany that would rule out help to this country."[1]

As to the final boundary agreements between Germany and
Czechoslovakia, under which 30,000 more Czechs and 6,000
Sudeten Germans passed under German rule, "the result was

[1] Cab. 23. 96, p. 247

to be deplored but there was nothing that we could do in the matter".

On November 30th Mr Chamberlain told his colleagues that at Munich Signor Mussolini had discussed with him a visit to Rome. Since prospects of appeasement were not bright in Berlin, said Chamberlain, it might now be useful for him to visit Rome. Indeed, not bright at all—for the Cabinet of December 14th was told by the new First Lord of the Admiralty, Earl Stanhope, that Germany had notified her intention to construct submarines up to 100 per cent of British submarine strength and to convert two six-inch gun cruisers into eight-inch gun cruisers. He "feared that public opinion might take the view that Germany was definitely against us and that there was no hope of any real appeasement".

In the last Cabinet of 1938, on December 21st, Lord Halifax spoke of the Prime Minister's visit to Rome, at which Britain should work on the principle of "Nothing for Nothing", making no concession to Mussolini "unless he will help us to obtain the *détente* which the object of our policy".

"The Prime Minister said that he did not disagree with the principle of 'Nothing for Nothing', but its complement was 'Something for Something'. Signor Mussolini should be used to help bring the war in Spain to an end. We must of course make plain that we could not support Italian claims to French territory. The Prime Minister "was also undertaking the visit with the definite purpose of securing Signor Mussolini's good offices in Berlin. For some time past it had been impossible for Great Britain to take any useful action in Berlin. . . . He hoped that Signor Mussolini could be persuaded to prevent Herr Hitler from carrying out 'some mad dog act' ."

CHAPTER XV

A Review of 1939

MR CHAMBERLAIN AND Lord Halifax duly made their pilgrimage to Rome, being absent from January 11th–14th, 1939, but the Prime Minister had to confess to his Cabinet colleagues on January 18th, when he gave them an account of the visit, that he had failed to engage Mussolini in any confidential discussion of Herr Hitler. The Berlin–Rome Axis remained unshaken.

"The Prime Minister said that he was convinced that Signor Mussolini and Herr Hitler could not be very sympathetic to each other, and that though they had some interests in common, their interests were not identical. Further, he rather doubted whether Signor Mussolini was aware of Herr Hitler's plans. Accordingly he had on several occasions given Mussolini a chance to express his real feelings about Herr Hitler. The Duce had never taken the opportunity offered to him, but had remained throughout absolutely loyal to Herr Hitler. The Prime Minister said that at the time this attitude had somewhat disappointed him, but on reflection he thought that it reflected credit on Signor Mussolini's character."[1]

Lord Halifax had nothing of significance to add to the picaresque account of their Roman triumph, given by Mr Chamberlain. The Prime Minister appeared to attach much importance to the exuberant welcome given to him and dwelled upon this enthusiasm, as he had upon the acclamations of the German populace after the signing of the Munich Agreement in the previous year. Mr Chamberlain went as far as to say that the Duce, who "looked fit and well . . . had . . . at no time during the visit . . . shown the slightest sign of jealousy at the great reception given to the Foreign Secretary and the Prime Minister", a welcome which Mr Chamberlain described as "heartfelt, spontaneous and universal". Lord Halifax added, by way of explaining that they had in fact returned empty-handed, that "he had always thought that the main purpose of the visit was to allow Italian opinion an opportunity to make

[1] Cab. 23. 97, p. 6

itself articulate". He agreed with the Prime Minister that the broad instinct of Signor Mussolini was for peace.

The Cabinet passed on to a discussion of dispatches from the British Embassy in Berlin and from Intelligence sources which expressed concern at evidence of German aggressive intentions towards Holland. These were referred to the Foreign Policy Committee of the Cabinet for study. The Cabinet had also to consider the question of credits to be extended to friendly countries in Europe, financial assistance for China, increasing Arab terrorist activity in Palestine and finally a Most Secret statement on currency legislation by the Chancellor of the Exchequer, which showed the damaging effect of the policy of appeasement in 1938 upon the pound sterling. Sir John Simon made a statement in pessimistic language which contrasted with the pleasant descriptives of Mr Chamberlain about his visit to Rome.[1] Sir John said that:

> for a considerable period up to about a year ago, there was a great flow of capital funds towards London, mainly from people in European countries who were afraid to leave their money there. The £800 millions worth of gold which we held last April (1938) represented in considerable measure refugee money of this kind and gave our financial position an appearance of strength which was in part misleading.
>
> Since last April anxieties on the part of foreigners as to the fate of this country, in the war which they regard as impending, has led to a great efflux of these funds, chiefly to America, which is regarded as a safe depository. A return which we have recently made shows that some £150 millions of gold was lost between April 1st and September 30th 1938.
>
> One would have hoped that with the Munich Settlement, the drain on the pound would have subsided, but that is not what has occurred. It appears only too evident that the view continues to be persistently held abroad that war is coming and that this country may not be ready for it . . . Lying behind that anxiety is the further anxiety created by the worsening of our financial position, by the heavy increase in our adverse balance of trade and by the growth of armament expenditure.

[1] This Treasury statement, classified as Most Secret, was attached in a sealed envelope to the Standard file of Cabinet Minutes and given no circulation.

Sir John described measures taken at the end of 1938 to replenish the gold in the Exchange Equalisation Account, from which he hoped to see a good effect.[1] "The Chancellor was glad to be able to say that the drain we had suffered was so far an external one, and there was as yet little or no evidence of a flight from the pound by British nationals." He foreshadowed an increase in the note issue above the normal statutory figure related to gold coverage, and this would make immediate legislation necessary when Parliament met.[2]

Troubles did not come singly. On top of the ferment between Arabs and Jews in Palestine, there had been a letter to the Home Office in the form of an ultimatum from the Irish Republican Army, menacing Great Britain with retaliatory action if British troops were not withdrawn from Ireland by January 16th. Sir Samuel Hoare said that this letter had been forwarded to the Dominions Office, "which had not taken the threat seriously," and had not brought it to the attention of Scotland Yard until after the 16th, when bomb explosions had taken place in the United Kingdom. The police had then made some successful raids on the homes of members of the Irish Republican Association and seized quantities of arms and explosives.

At their next Wednesday meeting on January 25th, Lord Halifax addressed the Cabinet on a series of disturbing Intelligence reports from Germany describing Hitler as highly dissatisfied with the restraints placed upon him by the Munich Agreement. The mood and economic stresses in Germany were tending towards an explosive risk of war in the near future. These reports had been considered by the Foreign Policy Committee of the Cabinet on January 23rd.

"However disturbing the possibilities may be," began Lord Halifax, "there is no ground for extreme pessimism or for a belief that we shall in the near future inevitably be the victims of a German attack. While they would certainly welcome an easy victory, the German people as a whole do not want a prolonged war." He then referred to "a curious unaminity" in

[1] On January 7th 1939, London newspapers had published an announcement of a transfer of £350m. in gold from the Bank of England to the Exchange Equalisation Fund.

[2] Cab. 1. 39 (9) Currency Legislation

British Intelligence reports that Hitler had been both encouraged and infuriated by the Munich Agreement, encouraged
by his strategic gains but infuriated at having to forgo a quick
war. A steadily worsening economic situation might tempt him
to seek forcible access to those raw materials that he could not
obtain by any other means.

Until the end of the year 1938 "there was no evidence that
such an explosion would occur elsewhere than in the East",
said Lord Halifax. "Unfortunately ... during the present month
we began to receive reports that the minds of the rulers of
Germany were moving in a different, and for us more sinister
direction." Hitler had referred to the British as "arrogant
apes who think that they can rule the world for ever with
fifteen battleships". Germany had been pressing to convert the
anti-Comintern pact with Italy and Japan into a defence pact,
and in the inner circles of the Nazi party, war was expected in
March or April. A highly placed German had informed the
British that "a plan for a completely surprise air attack on
London was being studied". The Finance Minister, Count von
Schwerin-Krosigk, had described the internal economic situation to Hitler as desperate. Hitler had asked the General Staff
to provide him with plans of attack both in the East and in the
West, the latter for invasion of Holland and Switzerland, involving simultaneous action against Britain and France. He
intended to terrorise Western countries by troop concentrations
on his Swiss and Netherlands frontiers. Dr Schacht had been
removed from the Reichsbank and another partisan of peace,
Captain Fritz Wiedemann, Hitler's adjutant, had been "exiled"
to the Consulate General in San Francisco.

Such was the review of prospects in 1939, an exercise customary to the Foreign Secretary in the January Cabinets. "I
conclude my summary of these disturbing reports as I began it,"
said Lord Halifax. "We have very definite indications that
Herr Hitler may be contemplating an attack on the West
during the coming spring . . .; but we have no proof that the
Führer has definitely committed himself to such action. All
that can be said with practical certainty is that an 'explosion'
of Germany is likely to come in the comparatively near future
and that it is necessary for us to take immediate measures to
guard against the possibility of it being directed against us."

Lord Halifax outlined certain steps being taken in consultative diplomacy with the United States, France, Belgium and Holland. His analysis was then subjected to the cold drip of the Chamberlain mind. The Prime Minister first explained to his Cabinet colleagues why the "extremely confidential" intelligence reports, upon which the assessment of Lord Halifax was based, had to be kept within the "smallest possible limits". There was no intention to withhold information from the Cabinet. He agreed with the Foreign Secretary that the indications of Germany's possible attitude could not be ignored . . . "We might be dealing with a man whose actions were not rational."

"At the same time," the Prime Minister said, "he was a long way from accepting all this information. Some allowance must be made for the rather disturbing atmosphere in which those who received these secret reports necessarily worked. Again, while many of the forecasts received from these sources had proved correct in the past, this was not always the case."

The Prime Minister appeared puzzled by the suggestions that Hitler was irritated by the Munich Agreement. He proceeded to cite assurances reaching him personally that some minds in Germany were concentrated on activities other than war, such as trade and economic reform.

"The Prime Minister thought that if Germany attacked Holland, we should be bound to intervene, but . . . if we made an immediate statement to this effect we should enter into a binding commitment which, in certain circumstances, might prove embarrassing . . . A rather similar issue had arisen in regard to France . . . France had undertaken to come to our assistance if we were attacked . . . but . . . France might be attacked from more than one quarter, whereas we were only liable to be attacked by Germany . . . Obligations of mutual assistance in the event of attack could not therefore be equal . . . He would deprecate any attempt to define the position more narrowly."[1]

The Cabinet discussed at length the uncertainties of the future and the difficulty of achieving any effective military action. They agreed:

[1] Cab. 23. 97, p. 57

That while there was little scope for acceleration of the Defence Programmes over the next two or three months, it was important to take all practicable steps to put the Defence Services into a state of readiness to meet the contingency of a possible emergency in the near future.

The Foreign Policy Committee of the Cabinet met next day, January 26th, at 3 p.m., with the Chief of Naval Staff, the Chief of Air Staff and the Deputy Chief of Imperial General Staff in attendance. The practical outcome of their discussions was that no approach was to be made to Dr Colijn, the Prime Minister of the Netherlands, in view of the fact that neither France nor Belgium would be prepared to go to the aid of Holland. British Staff talks with France and Belgium, when they took place, were to be extended to the Mediterranean and the Middle East. However, the Prime Minister explained to the next full Cabinet on February 1st that despite the lack of a military commitment at present, "it was difficult to see how either of these countries, France and Belgium, could keep out of war if Germany invaded Holland".[1]

The Foreign Policy Committee had studied the opinions of the Chiefs of Staff that a failure to intervene if Germany attacked Holland would have more disastrous effects than the risks of a conflict. The Committee had endorsed these conclusions, said Mr Chamberlain, and stated that a German invasion of Holland would constitute a *casus belli*. However, the Prime Minister interpreted that decision thus: "It would give rise to a situation which would justify our going to war with Germany, but that did not mean that we should necessarily have to go to war forthwith without taking into account other considerations." . . . "One such was the possibility that Holland would not resist invasion."

The Cabinet was seized of the Chiefs of Staff appreciation of Britain's predicament that "if we were compelled to enter such a war in the near future, we should be confronted with a position more serious than the Empire had ever faced before. The ultimate outcome of the conflict might well depend upon the intervention of other Powers, in particular of the United States of America".[2]

[1] Cab. 23. 97, p. 100   [2] C.O.S. Report 25.1.39. F.P. (36) 77

Seldom did the Cabinet meet again on Thursday after its regular Wednesday meeting, but on February 2nd it did so to consider the position of Belgium and the state of preparedness of the British Army. Mr Hore-Belisha reminded his colleagues that a year previously his task had been to equip the Army for service overseas, but not for a Continental role. "The General Staff were now greatly perturbed lest some situation might arise, committing British troops to undue and unnecessary risks as at present equipped." He presented a paper that proposed to equip four divisions of the Regular Army and two mobile divisions on the Continental scale and similarly to equip four Territorial divisions.

Mr Chamberlain was plainly disconcerted. He described this as "rather a new conception". The Secretary of State for War had described his proposals as "modest" but the total cost amounted to £81m. "An unanswerable case," said Mr Chamberlain, "can be made for increased armaments in every Service, if the financial aspect is ignored, but finance can not be ignored since our financial strength is one of our strongest weapons in any war that is not over in a short time." He feared also lest the coming talks with the French should expose the British to demands for an increased contribution to Continental defence. Sir John Simon echoed the Prime Minister's misgivings—"he was gravely disturbed lest our financial strength might be slipping away". Lord Halifax pointed out that here were "two sharply conflicting necessities" and urged that there should be no delay longer than a week in coming to a decision about them. The Cabinet agreed to furnish a full scale of training equipment for all twelve Territorial divisions, but deferred the plans for equipping the Regular Army in a Continental scale, to be discussed later. In the subsequent Cabinet of February 8th a timetable for developing Staff talks with France, and later with Belgium, was laid down, to be followed afterwards by tentative discussions with Holland. Mr Chamberlain tended to the view that the Dutch would be more likely to resist an attack if they knew that the British were concerned for their survival, but he still resisted the idea of an open declaration. The Foreign Policy Committee met on February 8th to consider economic aid to friendly countries in South East Europe. It was not convened again until March

27th, after a decisive event had taken place, the German march into Prague.

On February 22nd the Prime Minister told the Cabinet of progress achieved in meetings between himself, Lord Chatfield, the new Minister for Co-ordination of Defence, the Chancellor of the Exchequer and the Secretary of State for War on the equipping of four Regular and four Territorial divisions and preparedness of the Army for a Continental role. The first echelon of two (regular) Contingents would be put on a footing to embark twenty-one days after outbreak of war, the second echelon sixty days after the outbreak of war, and four Territorial Infantry divisions six months after the outbreak of war. Mr Chamberlain said that he preferred this timetable for the Territorials to an alternative of readiness within four months of war as "this would reduce the cost by some £3 to £4 millions", and he recommended no final decision on dates for the first and second echelons to embark for service abroad until the Staff conversations had been held with the French. He saw this as a new and serious liability to which there was no alternative. The Cabinet agreed on plans to move non-essential Government Departments into the provinces, but to maintain Government Departments in the central area at the outbreak of a war, with a plan in reserve to remove the Government machine as a whole to the provinces if necessary. The Cabinet in March 1939 was occupied with growing demands for a Ministry of Supply, with the guidelines for staff talks with the French, with complaints from the Palestine Arabs and counter demands from the Jewish community.

Finally, there was another report from a visitor to Germany. Mr Frank Ashton-Gwatkin, a Foreign Office official who had been active with the Runciman Mission to Czechoslovakia during the previous summer, had made a visit to Berlin in early March 1939. He had seen Herr von Ribbentrop, Dr Funk and Field-Marshal Goering, as Lord Halifax told the Cabinet, in a "very friendly atmosphere". Mr Ashton-Gwatkin "had gained the impression that no immediate adventures of a large type were contemplated. This, however, did not rule out the possibility of further pressure being brought to bear on Czechoslovakia."

Upon the nature that these pressures might assume the

Cabinet forebore to inquire, and proceeded to discuss arrangements for the Duke of Norfolk to represent King George VI
at the coronation of Pope Pius XII. There was no more
mention of Czechoslovakia, except on March 12th, when Mr
Chamberlain answered a question in the House about the
British guarantee against aggression with the cryptic comment
that no such aggression had yet taken place. Sir Samuel Hoare
spoke to his London constituents in Fulham on March 10th
about "the golden age" that might spring from peace and
commerce, if the leaders of the four European powers willed it.

His speech was recalled afterwards in a storm of public
indignation and derision, and Sir Samuel, having twice
stumbled in foreign affairs, "felt that my part in Government
was finished and that I had better retire from public life".[1]
Yet most of what Hoare said in Cabinet has stood up to the
test of time, and although the British Government had practically no warning in advance of the march into Prague, he was
not to be counted among the optimists. He gives an interesting
explanation of the miscalculation in his Fulham speech. "As
I wished to allude to foreign affairs, I consulted Chamberlain
on the line that I had better take. His comment was that I
should discourage the view that war was inevitable." And
Chamberlain then himself sketched out the allusion to the
golden age.

Precisely on the day of the Fulham speech, Lord Halifax
wrote to the Prime Minister at Chequers a long letter of rebuke[2]
for having accorded to Lobby Correspondents a general review
of foreign affairs without consulting the Foreign Secretary, and
for making the forecast that there would be a disarmament
conference before the end of the year. Events soon proved that
the complaint of Halifax was justified.

In the night hours of March 14th, previous to the next meeting of the British Cabinet on the 15th, Marshal Goering and
Herr von Ribbentrop were pursuing President Hacha and
Dr Chvalkovsky round a table in the Berlin Chancellery,
forcing them to sign a document which extinguished the
independence of Czechoslovakia and established for Bohemia
and Moravia a German Protectorate.

[1] Hoare, *Nine Troubled Years*, p. 328
[2] Feiling, *The Life of Neville Chamberlain*, p. 396

Lord Halifax read out to the Cabinet at 11 a.m. the "agreement" signed by the Czechs, and the Prime Minister said that the fundamental fact was that the State whose frontiers we had undertaken to guarantee against unprovoked aggression had now completely broken up".... "He thought it would be wise to take an early opportunity of saying that in the circumstances which had arisen, our guarantee had come to an end." He comforted himself with the observation that "our guarantee was not a guarantee against the exercise of moral pressure" ... "German action had all been taken under the guise of agreement with the Czechoslovak Government. The Germans were therefore in a position to give plausible answers."

Lord Halifax suggested that this was an occasion on which "pious and futile lectures" should be avoided. The Cabinet agreed that there was no case at the moment for recalling the British Ambassador,[1] but that a visit which Mr Oliver Stanley, President of the Board of Trade, was to have made to Germany with a view to reducing friction between the two countries in the world export market should now be postponed. It was left to the Prime Minister and the Foreign Secretary to settle upon the words in which the former would acquaint the House of Commons with his views and attitude. Mr Chamberlain in his statement laid blame on the Slovak Diet which had just previously declared Slovakia a separate State and precipitated the crisis. This was a more convenient argument than that which first occurred to him in Cabinet—that the Czechs had simply yielded to German pressures. He told the House that the British obligation to Czechoslovakia no longer existed. "It is natural that I should bitterly regret what has now occurred, but do not let us on that account be deflected from our course. Let us remember that the desire of all the peoples of the world still remains concentrated on the hopes of peace."

This dry assessment was soon to be followed by stronger words from the lips of Chamberlain.

[1] Sir Nevile Henderson was, however, recalled two days later, in line with the withdrawal of the American Ambassador in Berlin.

CHAPTER XVI

A Rather Troubled Period

Mr Chamberlain in a speech at Birmingham on Friday, March 17th came suddenly out of the trance of appeasement. It was as if he had never spoken those chill obituary words in the House of Commons over the raw corpse of Czechoslovakia. Some of his colleagues are said to have impressed on him that he had missed the true mood of the country. Keith Feiling relates that strong representations from the House, the public and the Dominions decided him to speak out, and that he was informed by fuller knowledge. It is difficult to see from the Cabinet papers what this fuller knowledge can have been, other than that the Services Chiefs, the Foreign Office and members of his own Party and Cabinet saw the destruction of Czechoslovakia in a more serious light than he did. Lord Halifax had as early as a week after the Munich Agreement written to him on the advantages of broadening his Cabinet, perhaps taking back Eden and inviting in Churchill to the advantage of his own policy. Chamberlain had not in the least desired that in October 1938, but if he were to withstand Party pressures to broaden his Cabinet in March 1939, he must speak with a different voice.

Mr Chamberlain said in Birmingham: "Who can fail to feel his heart go out in sympathy to the proud, brave people who have suddenly been subjected to this invasion, whose liberties are curtailed, whose national independence is gone? Now we are told that this seizure of territory has been necessitated by disturbances in Czechoslovakia. If these were disorders, were they not fermented from without? Is this the last attack upon a small state, or is it to be followed by another? Is this in fact a step in the direction of an attempt to dominate the world by force?" . . . If so Britain would resist it to the utmost of her power.

Something had now to be done in earnest, since time was slipping away fast. Mr Chamberlain called a Cabinet meeting at the unwonted hour of 6 p.m. on Saturday, March 18th, after his emphatic speech in Birmingham. He apologised to his colleagues for transgressing against the English weekend, "but it seems that we are entering upon another rather troubled period". Lord Halifax informed the Cabinet of the reason for this sudden meeting: a message from the Roumanian Minister in London, Mr V. V. Tilea, which suggested that Germany had demanded a monopoly of the exports of Roumania in exchange for a German guarantee of her frontiers, proposals that were described as taking the form of an ultimatum. Plainly the object of such a German demand would be the production of the Roumanian oilfields. The Roumanian Minister for Foreign Affairs, M. Gafencu, had denied that there was any truth in the report of a German ultimatum, but the possibility should nevertheless be studied by the Cabinet. Lord Chatfield thought that the economic domination of Roumania by Germany seemed likely to lead to very serious consequences. He thought that the views of the General Staff would be that if Poland and Russia would be prepared to help us, we should join them in resisting German aggression. Mr Chamberlain then spoke.

"The Prime Minister said that up till a week ago we had proceeded on the assumption that we should be able to continue our policy of getting on to better terms with the Dictator Powers, and that although those Powers had aims, those aims were limited. We had all along had at the back of our minds the reservation that this might not prove to be the case, but we had felt that it was right to try out the possibilities of this course.

"On the previous Wednesday, German action in Czechoslovakia had only just taken place. Neither he nor any of his colleagues had had time to give the matter proper consideration. It had been unfortunate that owing to the Opposition's demands, it had been necessary to have a debate in the House of Commons immediately on the heel of these events. He had now come definitely to the conclusion that Herr Hitler's attitude made it impossible to continue to negotiate on the old basis with the Nazi regime. This did not mean that negotiations with the German people were impossible. No reliance could be placed on any of the assurances given by the Nazi leaders. On the basis of this conclusion and after consultation with the Foreign Secretary and other colleagues, he had made his speech at Birmingham."[1]

[1] Cab. 23. 98, p. 50

After a warm show of approval from the Cabinet, Mr Chamberlain concluded that "our next course is to ascertain what friends we have who will join us in resisting aggression. Lord Halifax said that "it was no doubt highly desirable to have France, Poland, Turkey and the U.S.S.R. as allies". The Cabinet discussed the possibility of "German public opinion" preventing a war from starting. They were told that the Dominions approved of Mr Chamberlain's speech. They agreed on the importance in a war of compelling Germany to fight on two fronts; that no time should be lost in making the necessary approaches to other countries; and that no other country than Great Britain was in a position to organise resistance to German aggression. Mr Hore-Belisha favoured "frank and open alliances" with Poland and Russia and "steps vastly to increase our military strength" . . . "Germany had just seized in Czechoslovakia the complete equipment of 38 infantry and 8 mobile divisions".

The Prime Minister "thought that Poland was very likely the key to the situation. . . . Our communication to Poland should probably go somewhat further than to other countries. We should not merely ask what attitude Poland would adopt, but explain how we envisaged the situation and that we thought the time had now come for those threatened immediately or ultimately by German aggression to get together."

Mr Walter Elliot thought it "most important to get into touch with Russia" . . . "On the whole an attack in the West was more likely than an attack in the East."

The Cabinet agreed to set up a Committee to consider Acceleration of Defence Programmes; to approve the new line of policy proposed by the Prime Minister; to make a public announcement on resisting German aggression, provided that satisfactory assurances could be obtained from others; and to authorise telegrams to be drafted immediately to those countries likely to respond to the call to resist aggression.

These urgent measures arose both out of the German occupation of Prague and the subsequent message from M. Tilea, against which Sir Reginald Hoare, British Ambassador in Bucharest, vainly protested to the Foreign Office as "an enormous blunder"—a blunder, as events soon proved, scarcely distinguishable from the truth.

After this excitement had subsided, Lord Halifax realised that practical diplomatic steps could not be rushed, and that it would be appropriate to limit approaches first to France, Russia and Poland and obtain some statement on a four power basis. He explained to his colleagues on Monday, March 20th, the difficulties of drafting a declaration to which all interested Powers could subscribe. The formula stuck fast on what would constitute the kind of threat on which the Powers would seek consultation.

The Prime Minister referred to the draft declaration before the Cabinet as "aimed at avoiding specific commitments", though "public opinion would certainly attach importance to such a declaration signed by the four Powers". . . . "The real issue was that if Germany showed signs that she intended to proceed with her march for world domination, we must take steps to stop her by attacking her on two fronts. We should attack Germany not in order to save a particular victim but in order to pull down the bully."[1]

Mr Chamberlain said that he favoured an approach to the three big Powers rather than lining up small states. Lord Chatfield pointed out that any declaration was bound to be scrutinised by Allies afterwards and promises exacted, which would amount to commitments. The Cabinet entered into considerable discussion of the draft declaration, which emerged in this final form:

> We the undersigned hereby declare that inasmuch as peace and security in Europe are matters of common interest and concern, and since European peace and security may be affected by any action which constitutes a threat to any European state, we have pledged ourselves immediately to consult together if it appears that any such action is being taken.

Not a very heroic formula, as Lord Halifax observed in the drafting of it, and the Cabinet was much exercised as to whether it was "too free" and lacking in emphasis.

Lord Chatfield asked whether it was proposed to extend the staff conversations with France to Poland and Rusisa as well, and the Prime Minister said that "if we were envisaging a

[1] Cab. 23. 98, p. 96

war on two fronts he thought that we should be wise to have staff conversations". He proceeded to say that he was considering a private letter to Signor Mussolini as "probably the only person who could put the brake on Herr Hitler", a move to which the Cabinet assented with the proviso that Lord Halifax should have a hand in drafting it.

On March 22nd Lord Halifax told the Cabinet that he had somewhat stiffened the draft declaration to "consultation on joint resistance". M. Charles Corbin, the French Ambassador, had expressed to him the fear that Colonel Joszef Beck would respond unfavourably to anything less. The Polish Foreign Minister had not replied, and when he did, Colonel Beck described the declaration as being in conflict with the Polish–German Agreement. King Carol of Roumania had denied that a German ultimatum had been put to him, and M. Litvinoff "seemed somewhat perturbed" that the British had not been more enthusiastic about a Russian proposal for a conference of Russia, Britain, France, Poland, Roumania and Turkey in Bucharest. The Egyptian Ambassador had mentioned, said Lord Halifax, that in his view a front of Great Britain, France, the Soviet Union and the Balkan states, even without Poland, would be enough to halt Hitler.

This was a shrewd assessment, but before the next Cabinet meeting on March 29th, the Inner Cabinet had taken decisions which were crucial for the course of subsequent diplomacy. There is no record of the conversations on Sunday, March 26th, between Mr Chamberlain and Lord Halifax, but they had been in consultation with the French Foreign Minister, M. Georges Bonnet, on March 23rd. He had emphasised the value of Poland to a Western alliance.

The key to this drift in British foreign policy is a meeting of the Cabinet Committee on Foreign Policy held by the Prime Minister in his room in the House of Commons on Monday, March 27th, at 5 p.m. It was attended by Sir John Simon, Lord Halifax, Sir Samuel Hoare, Lord Chatfield, Sir Thomas Inskip, Mr W. S. Morrison and Mr Oliver Stanley. Mr R. A. Butler, Sir Horace Wilson and Sir Alexander Cadogan were also present, but not Sir Robert Vansittart, the Chief Diplomatic Adviser, whose views on the necessity of Soviet Russia to any alliance capable of stopping Hitler were well known to Mr

Chamberlain. Certain conclusions had been provisionally reached on the previous day (Sunday), said Lord Halifax to the Committee, and Mr Chamberlain then expounded his line. In view of Polish reluctance to participate in a Four Power declaration with Russia, he saw as the best alternative:

(1) A public declaration by Great Britain, France and Russia.
(2) A secret bilateral understanding between Great Britain and Poland.
(3) Existing Franco-Polish obligations to be linked with this framework.

Our efforts to build up a front against German aggression were likely to be frustrated, said the Prime Minister, if Russia was closely associated with the present scheme. Poland and Roumania objected to any such public association. Similar objections had been received from Finland, Yugoslavia, Italy, Spain and Portugal.[1]

At some recent point evidently Mr Chamberlain had been deflected from his first resolution not to be distracted by the compunctions of small states, and the British proposals had been spread to the above countries, all of whom were in some degree dependent upon Germany either politically or economically, and none of whom could have been expected to entertain any thought of entering an alliance or declaration of intent if Russia was a participant.

"In these circumstances," pursued Mr Chamberlain, "we must abandon the policy of the Four Power declaration and concentrate on the country likely to be the next victim of aggression, Roumania." He proceeded to enlarge on the importance of Roumania strategically both for her oil and as shielding the flank of Poland herself. He adumbrated a mutual arrangement between Britain and France, Poland and Roumania which would offer reciprocal aid if Hitler attacked anywhere in the West. Roumania was needed because "control of that country by Germany would go far to neutralize an effective naval blockade. . . . Poland was vital in the scheme, because the weak point of Germany was her present inability

[1] Cab. 27. 624, p. 200

We, the German Führer and Chancellor and the
British Prime Minister, have had a further
meeting today and are agreed in recognising that
the question of Anglo-German relations is of the
first importance for the two countries and for
Europe.

We regard the agreement signed last night
and the Anglo-German Naval Agreement as symbolic
of the desire of our two peoples never to go to
war with one another again.

We are resolved that the method of
consultation shall be the method adopted to deal
with any other questions that may concern our two
countries, and we are determined to continue our
efforts to remove possible sources of difference
and thus to contribute to assure the peace of
Europe.

[signature of Hitler]

Neville Chamberlain

September 30. 1938.

Anglo-German naval agreement, signed by Hitler and Chamberlain

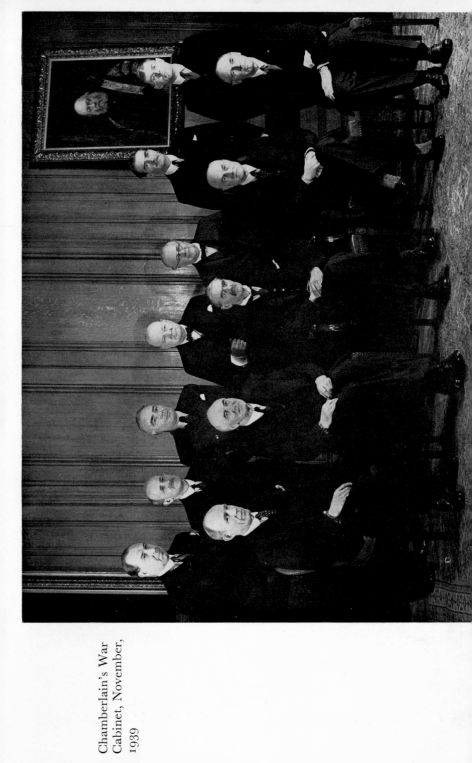

Chamberlain's War
Cabinet, November,
1939

to conduct war on two fronts, and unless Poland was with us, Germany would be able to avoid this contingency."[1]

"It would be observed that this plan left Soviet Russia out of the picture. . . . We should have to explain to her that the objections to her open inclusion come not from ourselves but from other quarters. . . .

"The Prime Minister emphasised the necessity for urgent and immediate action. He had not thought it expedient to summon an emergency meeting of the Cabinet to consider the new proposals first 'as this might have caused undue publicity'. If the Foreign Policy Committee approved the course now proposed, the draft telegrams which the Meeting was to consider could be despatched that evening in the form adopted by the Committee."[2]

It is noteworthy that Sir Samuel Hoare, who had evidently not been party to the Sunday talks, objected in Committee that "in effect the new proposals involve the dropping out of Soviet Russia from the scheme. I fully realise the dilemma with which we are faced, but it must not be overlooked that the dropping out of Russia will be regarded in many quarters as a considerable defeat for our policy."

Lord Halifax's reply was that besides Poland, "Portugal, Spain and Italy would be against us if we entered into any pact which included Russia". Thus once more an irrevocable step was being taken after an unrecorded Sunday meeting, at which the critical argument had been whether to build upon Russia, or upon the assortment of states that lay between her and Germany. Once more the decision had been taken by very few minds, had been presented to the Foreign Policy Committee as an adopted plan, and would be told to the Cabinet when finalised. When the full Cabinet met on March 29th, Lord Halifax reported that France had accepted the draft declaration against aggression, that Russia had agreed to sign it if Poland would, but that Poland had made a very hesitant reply. "It was clear that too close an association of Russia with the proposed declaration made difficulties for a number of countries."[3]

Poland was anxious that any arrangement made between

[1] Cab. 27. 624, p. 202   [2] Cab. 27. 624, p. 205
[3] Cab. 23. 68, p. 97

G

Britain and Poland should be of a secret nature, explained Lord Halifax. Sir Samuel Hoare and Mr Walter Elliot both emphasised the importance of Russia, the latter saying that "it would be less provocative if this country were to associate herself with Russia at the present state rather than to wait until such a contingency as . . . an attack on the Ukraine . . . had taken place". Lord Halifax . . . replied "that he and the Prime Minister had in mind the point of view expressed by the Home Secretary and the Minister of Health. . . . He agreed that it was desirable that we should get as much assistance from Russia as was practicable. The essential point was to manage matters so as to secure the support of Poland. At the same time he would take what steps were possible to keep in with Russia."[1]

These negotiations were taking a long time, the Foreign Secretary admitted, but he thought that Germany would think twice before involving herself in a major war, and meanwhile it was significant that Colonel Beck had not altered his arrangements to visit London in the following week.

While the choice of an alliance thus hung in the balance, Oliver Harvey noted in his diary for March 29th an event that helped the Prime Minister to make up his mind. "Colvin, Berlin correspondent of *News Chronicle* called on Halifax today and made great impression. He said he was convinced Hitler would attack Poland very shortly unless it was made quite certain that we would then attack him. There would then be a good chance that German generals would stop him or revolt. Generals had been prepared to revolt in September if we had stood up to Hitler. H. took him over to P.M. and as a result it may be decided to announce at once, i.e. tomorrow, our decision to fight for Poland without waiting for Beck's reply."

Next day the Cabinet was summoned again, with no agenda issued, at the request of Lord Halifax, who apologised but

[1] This view of the greater importance of Poland was already implicit in a telegram from the Foreign Office to Sir Howard Kennard in Warsaw and Sir Reginald Hoare in Bucharest on March 27th stating that "it is becoming clear that our attempts to consolidate the situation will be frustrated if the Soviet Union is openly associated with the initiation of the scheme". It "would tend to excite anxiety among a number of friendly Governments". This telegram acknowledged the importance of not increasing the tendency of Russia towards isolation, but announced the British intention first to reach an understanding with Poland and Roumania.

explained that on the previous day information had been received disclosing a possible German intention to execute a *coup de main* against Poland after the recent seizure of the port of Memel.

"The Foreign Secretary said that he had also had an interview with the Berlin correspondent of the *News Chronicle*, who . . . had come over to London especially to give information which had reached him from various contacts in Germany to the effect that Poland was next on the German programme of aggression. This thesis was supported by a good deal of information, including the statement of a local industrialist that he had orders to accumulate rations opposite Bromberg by March 28th." Mr Ian Colvin had also quoted a despatch from the Military Attaché in Berlin to the effect that he would be glad to see Britain at war with Germany within three months, for unless this happened Germany would have absorbed Poland.[1] The Foreign Secretary explained that his own anxiety was lest Herr Hitler should make some immediate move. He thought that we should consider whether we could take some prior action to forestall Hitler's next step. The proposal that he wished to put before his colleagues was that we should make a clear declaration of our intention to support Poland, if Poland was attacked by Germany. There was the objection that such a declaration would be very provocative to Germany, "but the Foreign Secretary had no particular objection to a provocative statement, provided that it did not land us in an unpleasant situation."

Mr Chamberlain commented that under the proposals approved by the Cabinet on the previous day we were seeking an agreement between Poland, Roumania, France and ourselves. The Foreign Secretary's proposals amounted to no more than an anticipation of action which it was intended to take in certain events. At the same time, it was a serious step and was the actual crossing of the stream. It was right that all his colleagues should consider the matter carefully before they took any

[1] Colonel F. N. Mason-Macfarlane's dispatch was forwarded from the British Embassy in Berlin on March 29th 1939, and did in fact recommend preventive war "to bring Germany *quickly* to heel by our one effective weapon—Blockade". Documents on British Foreign Policy, Third Series, Vol. IV, p. 264.

irrevocable step. The Prime Minister thought "it was important to secure that the publication of the draft statement will not bring us up against a tremendous decision on some point which does not affect the independence of Poland. . . . We are faced with a dilemma. If we take no action, there is a risk that we shall find that Poland has been over-run. On the other hand, if we utter a warning such as is now proposed, we shall be committed to intervention if Germany persists in aggression."

Lord Chatfield gave the views of the Chiefs of Staff that they had come to the fairly definite conclusion that, if we did have to fight Germany, it would be better to do so with Poland as an ally, rather than allow her to be absorbed and dominated by Germany. Poland would be likely to be over-run within two or three months. Nevertheless Germany would suffer heavy casualties in the process. In a report circulated to the Cabinet through the Minister for Co-ordination of Defence, the Chiefs of Staff urged that a reciprocal guarantee be obtained from Poland, as otherwise it could not be ensured that any war would be on two fronts. They also asked that steps be taken to deny Roumanian oil to Germany in case of war.

The Ministers offered their views but without any fundamental objection. The Prime Minister said that he thought the declaration should end up on "a somewhat less defiant note . . . and should indicate the desirability of settling differences not by force but by discussion". Lord Halifax was "a little averse from indicating our willingness to enter into discussions between Germany and Poland" . . . "To be an effective deterrent the statement would have to be made publicly." The Prime Minister revealed that in answer to a question on Friday about the rumours of a German attack on Poland, he would answer that without attaching any credence to these rumours, "if any action resulted which clearly threatened Polish independence and the Polish Government felt accordingly obliged to resist, H.M. Government and the French Government would give the Polish Government all the support in their power".

The Cabinet authorised telegrams to Warsaw and Paris informing the French and Polish governments of this policy. It authorised the Foreign Policy Committee to draft that afternoon the Prime Minister's Friday statement, and to send telegrams to the Dominions explaining the position.

In the Policy Committee that afternoon, Sir Horace Wilson argued that German military dispositions did not support the theory of an immediate military coup against Poland. Above their normal complement of divisions on both sides of the Polish corridor, the Germans had in the area those fourteen divisions, four of them mobile, which had been used in the invasion of Czechoslovakia. The Prime Minister agreed with his interpretation. Should Germany be warned that a warning was on the way? The Committee considered the proposal "as a matter of courtesy", but deferred a decision on this point, agreeing instead that it would be desirable to send a communication in the form of a personal letter from the Prime Minister to Signor Mussolini.

The Prime Minister's statement, as finally approved for Friday, March 31st, read:

> In the present case I trust (and believe) that the rumours referred to are unfounded, but I feel bound to add on behalf of His Majesty's Government that, pending the conclusion of the consultations now proceeding with other Governments, in the event of any action which clearly threatened Polish independence and which the Polish Government accordingly considered it vital to resist with their national forces, His Majesty's Government would feel themselves bound at once to lend the Polish Government all support in their power. They have given the Polish Government an assurance to this effect. The French Government have authorised me to make plain that they stand in the same position.

Meeting early on March 31st with the Foreign Policy Committee, Mr Chamberlain explained how he had resisted attempts by the Opposition leaders to make him include a reference to Russia in his statement. He had assured Mr Greenwood and Sir Archibald Sinclair that the omission was based on expediency and not on ideological grounds, and that this arrangement was intended only to cover an interim period. Lord Halifax would shortly see M. Ivan Maisky, the Russian Ambassador.

The statement was duly read by Mr Chamberlain and accepted by Colonel Beck, who gave a reciprocal assurance. This action was greeted with relief in Europe, many seeing some respite from the new technique of aggression and weekly alarms, but by Easter the Berlin–Rome Axis had moved in another direction, and when the Cabinet met on April 5th it was to consider the invasion by Italy of the kingdom of Albania.

Nor was it all plain sailing towards a defensive alliance with Poland. For evidently even Halifax was having second thoughts about his own boldness and said to Oliver Harvey, his private secretary, that he wanted to gain time, because every month produced 600 more British military aircraft. Harvey took these thoughts seriously enough to make them the subject of a note to his Minister advising that "I do find it very difficult to decide in my own mind whether delay really does benefit us." For he feared that procrastination would "encourage the view of the forward school in Germany and Italy that we don't really mean business".[1]

[1] Oliver Harvey Diaries, p. 278

CHAPTER XVII

The Inadmissible Soviet

To a question in the House of Commons on April 6th, whether Britain had any interest in Albania, Mr Chamberlain replied "no direct interest, but we have a general interest in the peace of the world". Heavier cares than the fate of Albania were his, and troubles came thick and fast after every British diplomatic step taken. Colonel Beck was now refusing a mutual guarantee to Roumania, and Roumania was asking whether Britain would guarantee Roumania if Poland did not! Mr Chamberlain suggested to his Cabinet colleagues that withholding a British guarantee "might in itself encourage Poland to agree to render such assistance". Colonel Beck was also drawing distinctions between military action in common with such countries in the West as Holland, Switzerland or Belgium, and aiding countries in the south-east, such as Roumania and Yugoslavia, against aggression. The Foreign Policy Committee had to consider whether Turkey and Bulgaria could be lined up against aggression, and whether Greece would be useful as an ally, if it became necessary "to smash Italy". The Committee agreed on April 10th to extend a guarantee to Greece and to consult with Turkey, which had been assessed as an important power by the Strategical Defence Committee of the Cabinet. Lord Halifax reported from an interview that day that M. Ivan Maisky had been "suspicious and inquisitorial". The Soviet Ambassador had told him that Britain exaggerated the importance of Polish and Roumanian objections to Russian participation and that when giving guarantees to those countries, Soviet Russia could have been brought into the mutual assistance pact.

The British made proposals through the British Ambassador in Moscow, Sir William Seeds, that all that was required of Russia at the moment was to give a public promise of assistance to any neighbour in eastern Europe that might be the victim of aggression, if that assistance was desired. To this Maxim Litvinov delivered a reply on April 18th that was perhaps calculated to take their breath away.

The Litvinov proposal of April 18th, under eight headings, asked for a pact of mutual military assistance between the U.S.S.R., France and Britain extending over five or ten years with an undertaking after the outbreak of hostilities "not to enter into negotiations of any kind whatsoever and not to conclude peace with aggressors separately from one another and without common consent of the three Powers". The British Government was to explain to Poland that this would apply exclusively to assistance against aggression on the part of Germany.

Sir Alexander Cadogan studied Telegram No. 69 from Moscow, containing these proposals, with Mr R. A. Butler, Parliamentary Under Secretary in the Foreign Office, on the morning of April 19th. He had to prepare in haste a minute for the Cabinet Committee on Foreign Policy that afternoon comprising his views on this development.

"This Russian proposal is extremely inconvenient," he commented. "We have to balance the advantage of a paper commitment by Russia to join in a war on one side against the disadvantage of associating ourselves openly with Russia. The advantage is, to say the least, problematical." He spoke of the limited military usefulness of Russia outside her own frontiers. Poland had just refused to be associated in a four power declaration with Russia and "in order to placate our left wing in England, rather than to obtain any solid military advantage, we have since asked the Soviet whether they would declare that in the event of any act of aggression against any European neighbour of the Soviet Union, which was resisted by the country concerned, the assistance of the Soviet Government would be available, if desired, in such manner as would be found most convenient. The Soviet Government now confront us with this proposal. If we are attacked by Germany, Poland under our mutual guarantee will come to our assistance, i.e.: make war on Germany. If the Soviet are bound to do the same, how can they fulfil that obligation without sending troops through or aircraft over Polish territory. That is exactly what frightens the Poles."[1]

This was a solitary minute written on a Moscow telegram which had not yet been circulated for the comments of others

[1] F.O. 371. 22969

in the Foreign Office. In the haste of preparation it fell short of correct usage by referring to "the Soviet", an abbreviation that pervades the subsequent minutes of the Cabinet Foreign Policy Committee in a curious way. It is to be remarked that the instinctive objections of Sir Alexander Cadogan were first that Russia would not honour her obligation, and that if she did honour it, that action would anyway be unwelcome to an ally. Upon this minute the minds of the Cabinet Committee would form their own views.

Mr Chamberlain on April 19th reminded his colleagues in the Cabinet Committee of his assurance already given to the Leaders of the Opposition that he had no ideological objection to an agreement with Russia. They must then consider what was the military value of Russia? The Chiefs of Staff, the Cabinet was told, had done no more than hastily consider this aspect on March 18th, when asked as a matter of urgency to advise on the subject of the alleged German ultimatum to Roumania.

The Chiefs of Staff[1] had on that date averred that "if the U.S.S.R. were on our side and Poland neutral, the position would alter in our favour. It should however be noted that the U.S.S.R. is today militarily an uncertain quantity and the Chiefs of Staff were unable to form any considered opinion as to the extent of her military intervention in the Allied Cause. . . . It would not be possible with Poland neutral for Russia to exert any considerable pressure upon Germany by air action. Moreover it is unlikely that any use could be made of Russian manpower to assist us in theatres of war outside the Soviet Union." On March 10th a dispatch from the British Embassy in Moscow had described the Russian Army as "greatly weakened by purges, of small offensive value, but expected to show good defensive qualities". This military appreciation was also discouraging about Russian air strength.

Lord Chatfield said that he thought that if Russia were an ally, the Soviet Navy might contain the German Navy in the Baltic, a role of some importance, though not a major role. Mr Chamberlain remarked that all his information from other Prime Ministers went to bear out the view that the Russian fighting services were of little use for offensive purposes.

[1] C.O.S. 283rd Meeting, March 18th 1939

Sir Samuel Hoare then interposed that he was not happy about the prospects in eastern Europe. His opinions throughout this controversy show realism and prescience, but Sir Samuel had lost political poise at the time of the Hoare–Laval pact with Italy and since then could assert no decisive weight in Cabinet. In his judgment, he said, Poland would be able to offer little military resistance to German invasion and would soon come to the end of her munitions. We should be in no position to supply her and Russia was the only possible source for munitions for Poland and other countries of Eastern Europe. He thought it essential that the Chiefs of Staff should be asked to produce a report on the military value of Russian assistance. Mr Butler countered this argument by pointing out a passage in a Foreign Office telegram to Moscow on April 14th which explained the guarantees to Poland and Roumania. It had been suggested that "it would therefore seem to be in complete accord with this policy were the Soviet Government now to make a public declaration on their own initiative in which . . . they would repeat that in the event of any act of aggression against any European neighbour of the Soviet Union, which was resisted by the country concerned, the assistance of the Soviet Government would be available if desired, and would be afforded in such a manner as would be found most convenient". This formula, Mr Butler said, was intended to deal with the very question of supplies of munitions.

The Prime Minister added that the Committee was considering "the Soviet's present proposal for a definite military alliance between England, France and Russia. It could not be pretended that such an alliance was necessary in order that the smaller countries of Eastern Europe should be furnished with munitions."[1]

Sir Thomas Inskip, who had been translated from Defence Co-ordination to the Dominions office, asked his colleagues "to consider the probable motives behind the Russian approach. It is very likely that it is a mere attempt to entangle us. If it is not a machination of this kind, and if the Soviet were sincerely desirous of restraining German aggression, they would presumably supply munitions to Eastern Europe whether the military alliance existed or not. On the other hand, it must be admitted

[1] Cab. 27. 624, pp. 298–9

that so large a Power as Russia, provided she means business, would be of some considerable military value."

The Committee on Foreign Policy had on this important occasion the appearance of having been trimmed to the Prime Minister's line of thinking. Sir Robert Vansittart, the friend of Ivan Maisky and the Russian line, had been dropped out; Sir Alexander Cadogan, Head of the Foreign Office was not present; Sir Thomas Inskip had been kept in; Sir Horace Wilson and Mr R. A. Butler were there; and Mr W. S. Morrison, another intimate, was the first Chancellor of the Duchy of Lancaster to be offered regular attendance of this committee on foreign affairs. The Duchy's opinion, carefully cast at the appropriate moment, was that the Russian approach was not sincerely helpful "since Mr Litvinoff must be as aware as we of the effect of this proposal on our potential friends".

The Prime Minister picked up this cue from Mr Morrison— Colonel Beck during his visit to London, he reminded the Committee, had described public association with Russia as "an unnecessary provocation to Germany and one that ought to be avoided". His subsequent reasoning is underscored in the standard file of Committee minutes. . . . "We should have to convey to the Soviet in diplomatic language the importance which we attached to maintaining the morale of Poland. . . . Anything tending to shake Polish confidence was most undesirable. . . . Meanwhile the Soviet could very greatly help by supplying munitions to the smaller Eastern European countries. . . . While therefore not turning down the Russian proposal, we should endeavour to convey the impression that the time for a military alliance was not yet ripe. At present there were very serious difficulties in the way. . . . Colonel Beck had indicated that he could not accept the idea of Russian troops being invited on to Polish soil." The Committee then mused on the meaning of the sudden recall of M. Maisky to Moscow.

Mr Morrison came again to the aid of the Prime Minister . . . "He was in complete agreement. Our policy at the present stage must confine itself to making arrangements for the States directly menaced. Only after this stage should we able to make defensive arrangements with States like Russia. . . .

Nothing must deflect us from our task of erecting the first essential barrier against aggression."

Mr Butler was anxious lest it should become "public property" that Britain and France were rejecting a Russian proposal for an alliance. The Prime Minister, who had made Mr Attlee and Mr Greenwood aware of his attitude in this matter, replied that "he would do his best to inculcate in to them a sense of responsibility".

Lord Chatfield suggested that "the general view appeared to be that the political arguments against a military alliance . . . between this country, France and Russia were irresistible and such as to outweigh any military advantages. For this reason in asking the Chiefs of Staff for an appreciation we must give them strictly limited terms of reference," relating to the actual military capability of the Soviet armed forces.

The Committee summarised its conclusions thus: "They were not, as at present advised, disposed to accept the Soviet proposal. The views of the French Government should be invited. The Chiefs of Staff sub-committee should prepare an appreciation of Russia's military strength, but this should not take the form of a review of the military arguments for or against accepting the Russian proposal." The Prime Minister was to warn the Leaders of the Labour Opposition to secrecy.

The French Government quickly put its finger on the lack of reciprocity evident in the British proposals to Russia. This could be overcome, Sir Eric Phipps informed the Foreign Office, and he transmitted a new French formula.

> If France and Britain found themselves at war with Germany as a result of existing engagements taken by them to prevent all changes by force of the status quo in Central or Eastern Europe, Russia would immediately assist them. If as a result of help given by Russia to France and Great Britain in the above conditions Russia found herself at war with Germany, they would immediately assist her.

At the Foreign Policy Committee of April 25th, Lord Halifax and Mr Chamberlain expressed their dislike of these proposals. Armed with the Chiefs of Staff report on Russia, the Prime Minister felt able to say that "the new French proposals might have some slight political value but would involve very grave discouragement of all our potential friends and allies in Eastern Europe and in return we should not obtain any accretion of strength of any great military value."

Into the meeting on April 24th, which discussed the Chiefs of Staff report, Sir Alexander Cadogan and Mr William Strang had been drawn, but the Chiefs of Staff were not themselves present or otherwise represented than by the Minister for Co-ordination of Defence. Lord Chatfield read and gave his interpretation of their report.

"Their views might be summarised as follows. Russia, although a great Power for other purposes, was only a Power of medium rank for military purposes. On the other hand the Chiefs of Staff could not deny that Russia's assistance in war would be of advantage to her allies. Her assistance would be of considerable, though not of great, military value and the side on which she participated in the war would undoubtedly fight the better for her help." After enlarging on the Chiefs of Staff argument that despite a strength of 130 divisions she would not be able to maintain in the field more than 30 divisions, Lord Chatfield concluded that "the military assistance that Russia could bring to bear was not nearly so great as certain quarters represented it to be".[1]

The discussion recorded is surprisingly brief. Mr Malcolm Macdonald said that nevertheless it would be important in war to have Russia on the Allied Side and not neutral, or siding with Germany. Lord Halifax concluded that "we ought to play for time".

"The Prime Minister thought that the Committee were in agreement that our first task must be to erect a barrier against aggression in Eastern Europe on behalf of states directly menaced by Germany. Until that barrier had been erected it was clear that we ought to do nothing to impair the confidence of those states." The Committee invited Lord Halifax to report to the full Cabinet at 6 p.m. on the tenor of these discussions, and to reply to the French proposals for a tripartite agreement that had been designed to satisfy the Russian demands for reciprocity.

Since the Chiefs of Staff soon produced a very different

[1] Cab. 27. 624, p. 320

document, their "Report on the Military Value of Russia" is worth studying in summarised form.

It was a foolscap document[1] of twelve pages, signed by Air Chief Marshal Sir Cyril Newall, General Lord Gort and Admiral Sir Andrew Cunningham, Deputy Chief of Naval Staff. Its conclusions were presented in the order of seniority of the British fighting Services rather than the importance of each Russian Arm. Thus it was the contribution of the Russian Navy in the Baltic, Black Sea and Far East that was first evaluated, then the contribution of the Russian army and thirdly the value of the Russian Air Force.

In a preamble the adverse effect of purges and Communist political control were estimated, and the "almost insurmountable difficulties" of maintaining such large forces as Russia could muster in the field. In the fifth paragraph of this preamble the military men dwelled on the unwillingness of various countries to allow deployment to the Russian forces and of the reluctance of Russians to expose their forces to a bourgeois environment. "This deep seated hostility to Communism and vice-versa may well nullify the value of many of the military advantages we put forward in support of Russian co-operation."[2]

The Chiefs of Staff report made it plain that the Russian Baltic Fleet could contain considerable enemy naval forces and interrupt to some extent supplies of Swedish iron ore to Germany. The Russian Army could mobilise on the Western Front in the first three months of war 100 infantry divisions and 30 cavalry divisions, largely horsed, but comprising 9,000 tanks of high quality. Russian artillery fire power was low and communications by road and rail in a deplorable condition. Under the heading of Economic Aspects, it was stated that Russia would be "unable to switch over to manufacture of such types of armaments as might be required by Poland and Roumania".

In paragraphs 24 and 25, the Chiefs of Staff stated that:

"Even if the war went so badly for the Allies as to result in Poland and Roumania being overrun, the Russians would still contain very substantial German forces on the Eastern front. We should perhaps draw attention to the very grave military dangers inherent in the possibility of any agreement between Germany and Russia."

[1] F.P. (36) 82 of 24.4.(39) see Cab. 27. 627   [2] Cab. 27. 627, p. 273

In the summary of conclusions, it was stated that:

The Russian Navy: would contain considerable German Naval strength in the Baltic and would be an added deterrent to Japan in the Far East.

The Russian Army: would not be in a position to afford material support to Poland,
would not be able to maintain a military effort of material size in Roumania or Turkey,
is likely to resist a German advance through the Baltic states,
would contain substantial German forces in the East in the event of Poland and Roumania being overrun.

The Russian Air Force: could produce a limited threat to Germany and Italy, if allowed to operate from neighbouring countries,
could contain more German air defence units in the East,
could be of some assistance in strengthening the air defences of Poland.

Russia would not be a considerable supplier of war material to Britain or her allies, but her co-operation would be invaluable in denying Russian sources of raw material to Germany.

A change for the worse on May 4th preceded their next meeting. Maxim Litvinov, the protagonist of a Western alliance was replaced as Soviet Foreign Commissar by Vyacheslav Molotov. When the Committee on Foreign Policy met on Friday, May 5th, the Prime Minister had thickened its composition by asking in Mr W. S. Morrison again and Sir John Simon. Mr Butler, Sir Horace Wilson and Sir Alexander Cadogan were also present. Sir Robert Vansittart was still the uninvited Chief Diplomatic Adviser.

The draft reply to the Russian proposals of April 18th was still undelivered and Lord Halifax had no certain feeling that the Russian Government would be converted to the British view that a unilateral Russian declaration of intent was desirable. The Committee speculated on the dismissal of Litvinov, but nobody ventured an explanation.

It was known that Russia had been pressing for conditions that would afford her assistance if she went to war on behalf of the Baltic states. Lord Halifax said that the French "agreed with us that it would be excessive at present to extend our guarantee to the Baltic states".[1] It was clear that Russia, however, wished such a guarantee to apply less to the Baltic states than to herself, and this contingency was covered by a new formula submitted by the French.

> If France and Great Britain find themselves in a state of war with Germany as a result of the action which they had taken with a view to preventing all changes by force in the *status quo*, in Central or Eastern Europe, the U.S.S.R. would immediately lend them all aid and assistance. If the U.S.S.R. found itself in a state of war with Germany as a result of the action which it had taken, with a view to preventing all changes by force of the existing *status quo* in Central or Eastern Europe, France and Great Britain would immediately lend it aid and assistance. The three Governments would concert without delay on the nature, in both cases contemplated, of this assistance and will take all steps to ensure its full efficacy.

The Committee addressed itself to a series of Russian demands contained in Sir William Seeds report of April 18th and sought to find replies to them. It was for instance agreed that "it was objectionable and dangerous to refer specifically to Germany by name", as the fourth Russian proposal suggested, whereas the British guarantee to Poland "had been in quite general terms without mentioning any aggressor". They discussed the Russian fears lest a quick victory by Germany over Poland might expose Russia alone to military vengeance, and though Sir Samuel Hoare and Mr Oliver Stanley argued for some reassurance to Russia against a separate peace, Sir Thomas Inskip decisively opposed such an extended commitment. He had with Mr Butler presided at a meeting with the Commonwealth High Commissioners on April 18th and had asked the Dominions Governments for their views. On April 22nd he had received from the South African Government an *aide-mémoire* which strengthened his hand. General Hertzog's Government opposed any irrevocable commitment to Russia and described an Anglo-Soviet pact as the ingredient that would probably decide Hitler in favour of war. These views had been circulated to the previous meeting of the Committee and Sir Thomas now objected to the Soviet sixth

[1] Cab. 27. 624, p. 329

proposal that "Britain, France and the Soviet[1] should under-take, following an outbreak of hostilities, not to enter into separate negotiations for peace". Sir Thomas said that he was considering a position in war in which a deadlock had been reached. He mentioned the Lansdowne letter on a peace initiative in the Great War. Lord Chatfield commented that he "could not conceive that we should wish to make a separate peace with Germany unless, indeed, we were faced with certain defeat. In any other circumstances it would be imperative to continue the war until victory was attained." Mr Chamberlain "suggested that we might give an assurance that if in conse-quence of a Declaration made by the Soviet, the three Powers engaged in war with an aggressor, none of them would make peace or negotiate with the aggressor without prior consultation with the other Powers". The Prime Minister however added a rider to this unexpected opinion: "It would be impossible to foresee every contingency that might arise. For example, we might wish to make a separate peace by reason of some inter-vention on the part of President Roosevelt."[2]

Mr Oliver Stanley and Sir Samuel Hoare adhered to the view that the Russian demand for an assurance against separate peace intiatives should be met. Sir Samuel "attached great importance to securing this unilateral Declaration from the Soviet". Mr W. S. Morrison retorted that a clause against a separate peace would "involve a Three Power agreement quite inconsistent with our policy". He was in favour of postponing any such decision. The Prime Minister "warned the Committee that it might be highly embarrassing to enter into any definite commitment in regard to this matter at the present time when we do not know whether the dismissal of M. Litvinov really means that the foreign policy of the Soviet Government was going to be changed or not". Lord Halifax "thought that there was great force in the observations of the Chancellor of the Duchy of Lancaster that by making a 'no separate peace' agreement we should be approaching much nearer to an alliance with the Soviet than we had hitherto contemplated". . . . The Foreign Secretary feared that if we were to accept this 'no separate peace' proposal it would be generally assumed that we had in fact entered into such an alliance. The Prime Minister

[1] Referred to in these words   [2] Cab. 27. 624, p. 333

endorsed this view, and Sir Thomas quoted South Africa and
Canada as deprecating an alliance with Russia and New
Zealand as recently having decided to adopt the same attitude.
Lord Chatfield added that closer concert with the Soviet might
alienate Spain and Portugal. Mr Oliver Stanley was not to be
convinced that the Russian demand was unreasonable and Mr
Malcolm MacDonald spoke in support of him, since "I am
satisfied that there is a grave danger of our negotiations with the
Soviet Government breaking down. . . . The Chiefs of Staff have
warned us on the very real danger of Russia remaining neutral
in a war."

Lord Halifax returned to his assertion that "if to the somewhat looser and indefinite unilateral declaration, we joined a
firm and definite 'no separate peace' tripartite agreement, we
should be changing the whole basis of our policy and risking the
alienation of our friends".

The Committee sought to surmise the policy that Mr Molotov
might pursue, whether of reversing the Litvinoff proposals or
even, as Lord Halifax suggested, "possibly standing for closer
relations with the Western powers".

The infusion of this uncertainty seemed to conclude the
argument and it was agreed to revise and submit to the Prime
Minister forthwith a reply to the Russian proposals. This would
be preceded by an instruction to Sir William Seeds, in view of
the change made in the Commissariat for Foreign Affairs, to
inquire of M. Molotov whether the proposals of M. Litvinov
still stood unaltered. If his reply was in the affirmative, the
British responses would be given to M. Molotov. If the Litvinov
proposals were withdrawn or modified, the British answers
would be withheld pending further instructions.

Instructions to Sir William were sent by cypher telegram on
May 6th 1939, at 7.30 p.m. and were followed an hour later by
a fuller and more formally worded British note. In his own
instructions on the vexed question of Soviet point 6 (no separate
peace) Sir William was told:

His Majesty's Government would hope that it might be possible
for you to persuade the Soviet Government not to press this point,
which is one of obvious difficulty. Should it however appear that
the point was one likely to exert decisive influence on Soviet

decision as to unilateral declaration proposed, His Majesty's Government would wish that, while leaving them complete freedom for further examination of issues raised, you should do your best so to handle matter as to prevent negotiation breaking down finally on this or indeed on any other ground.

The instructions went on that if Russia would first make a unilateral declaration, "His Majesty's Government would be very willing to discuss with the Soviet Government any further questions which might arise therefrom,"[1] but Russia would not be drawn on these terms.

The Committee on Foreign Policy came back to the subject of Russia. It had to consider a new *aide-mémoire* by the Chiefs of Staff, in which they had broken forth from the strict limits imposed on their Report on the Military Value of Russia as an Ally. Now they delivered themselves of a rounded opinion on both the strategic and the general aspects of the negotiations with Soviet Russia. The Prime Minister had thoughtfully added Mr Leslie Burgin, Minister Without Portfolio, to the Committee, which by now contained half the Cabinet, but none of the three Services Ministers.

Lord Halifax explained the exchange of telegrams with Moscow and the most recent British proposals, in line with the refusal to extend the guarantee to the Baltic states. He confirmed in reply to a question from Sir John Simon that "if Germany attacked Lithuania and Latvia and Russia came to their assistance, we should not be obliged to come to Russia's help".[2]

Lord Chatfield said that he had asked the Chiefs of Staff to consider the position afresh, and at a meeting with them that morning, they had somewhat modified their views. They saw the danger of Russia, after failing to reach agreement with us, standing aside in a future European war and hoping thereby to secure advantage from the exhaustion of the Western nations. The Chiefs of Staff *aide-mémoire* was emphatic.

The strategical and political aspects are closely related in a problem of this kind. . . . A full-blown guarantee of mutual assistance between Great Britain and France and the Soviet Union offers certain advantages. It would present a solid front of

[1] F.O. Telegrams 98 and 99. 6.5.39. Cab. 27.624, p. 351
[2] Cab. 27. 625, p. 26

formidable proportions against aggression. . . . The whole hearted accession of Russia to the anti-aggression cause might influence certain waverers towards our side. . . . If we fail to achieve any agreement with the Soviet, it might be regarded as a diplomatic defeat which would have serious military repercussions, in that it would have the immediate effect of encouraging Germany to further acts of aggression and of ultimately throwing the U.S.S.R. into her arms. . . . Furthermore, if Russia remained neutral, it would leave her in a dominating position at the end of hostilities.

The Chiefs of Staff thought that an occupation of the Baltic states by Germany would "turn the Baltic into a German lake" and "complete the encirclement of Poland," but would "not justify us in going to war unless it was certain that the whole of the Eastern front of Europe, particularly Poland and Russia, would also actively intervene . . . making it a two-front war for Germany".

The Chiefs of Staff reviewed the difficulties that would confront Germany in attacking Russia other than through Poland and thought that "we should gain more than we should lose" by giving Russia a guarantee of assistance in the event of a direct attack or an attack through the Baltic states. The Chiefs of Staff then addressed themselves to an extraordinary question that had been put to them "at very short notice on May 10th", as to the balance of value in war as between Spain as an enemy and Russia as an ally. They concluded that "the possibility of antagonising Franco-Spain should not from the military point of view be allowed to stand in the way of the conclusion of a pact with Russia".

The Prime Minister proceeded to argue against the Chiefs of Staff case. If military and strategic considerations pointed one way, he said, and political considerations pointed in another direction, care must also be taken not to overlook the importance of the latter. He wondered whether the Chiefs of Staff based their present appreciation on the supposition that an arrangement with Russia was not possible unless we were prepared to enter into a full alliance with her.

Lord Chatfield objected that "the Chiefs of Staff were very anxious that Russia should not in any circumstances become allied with Germany. Such an eventuality would create a most dangerous situation for us".

"What effective help Russia could in fact give us?" inquired the Prime Minister.

Lord Chatfield replied that Russia would contain substantial enemy forces, but the tepid flavour of the previous Chiefs of Staff memorandum of April 24th remained in the memory of those Ministers with whose views the new *aide-mémoire* conflicted. Even Lord Chatfield though describing "the possibility of war with Russia" . . . as "a great deterrent" to Germany, added that "Russia was not a great military power". The Prime Minister foresaw that an alliance with Russia would give rise to "serious difficulties with certain of the Dominions". To Lord Chatfield's objection that Poland was in a weak strategical position, the Prime Minister rejoined that previous advice had been that Poland could resist German attacks successfully "for some weeks at least". He was alarmed, he said, at the views of the Chiefs of Staff in favour of greatly increasing our liabilities. Lord Chatfield repeated the Services' view that to avoid the very real danger of Russia remaining neutral, "it would be better to go somewhat further than was now proposed. Issues of great strategical importance were involved. (His colleagues would realise how distasteful it was to Lord Chatfield personally to contemplate any alliance with the Soviet.) . . . It was not possible to say that that great country standing behind Poland would have no military or economic value. . . . Weaknesses of Russia must not be lost sight of, but if for fear of making an alliance with Russia we drove that country into the German camp, we should have made a mistake of vital and far-reaching importance." Sir Samuel Hoare followed his previous arguments by repeating that "the Chiefs of Staff had laid great stress on the deterrent effect . . . of Russia entering a European war. There was great force in this consideration. We should be wise to reinsure by doing everything in our power to bring in Russia on our side, in order to avoid a Russo-German agreement."

Leslie Burgin, who had been brought in to the Committee for the first time, "doubted whether we had reached the point of a breakdown of negotiations with Russia". Lord Halifax "felt the greatest reluctance to being bluffed off a good and sound policy by Russian insistence".

The outcome was that Sir Robert Vansittart, at no point

present at this meeting, was to be instructed to arrange another personal meeting with M. Maisky and propose to him a bargain whereby Russia would forgo a Western guarantee for the Baltic states in exchange for military staff conversations and, as Mr Chamberlain put it, "an agreement on the lines now proposed without prejudice to the possibility that a closer form of agreement might prove possible at a later date".

This proposal would be submitted in written form and legal phrasing, which as Lord Halifax explained to the Committee would be likely to impress the Soviet Government. It began that "whereas the United Kingdom and France have made declarations undertaking obligations to Poland and Roumania and whereas the Government of the U.S.S.R. have on (date of parallel declaration about Poland and Roumania) declared that . . ." It then proceeded that if Britain and France were already involved in their obligations,

(1) "it results that the three Governments will in these circumstances be engaged in the common task of resisting the act of aggression . . . the three Governments will give each other all the mutual support and assistance in their power."

(2) They will concert methods of mutual support and assistance.

(3) The three Governments are willing to consider similar declarations in regard to other European countries, to which the provisions of (1) and (2) would equally apply.

The two diplomats met on May 17th, but on May 19th Maisky had to inform Lord Halifax that the proposals made through Sir Robert Vansittart "were not acceptable to his Government and that the only basis on which the Soviet Government were prepared to proceed was that of a Triple Pact between Great Britain, France and Russia".[1]

The Committee therefore agreed on May 19th that Poland and Roumania might be asked to reconsider their own objections to Russia. It should be put to them that if the Triple Pact, to which they had previously objected, were not concluded, Russia might well gravitate towards Germany. Would not this in their view also tend to precipitate a European war?

At this point Lord Halifax then introduced a subtle argu-

[1] Cab. 27. 625, p. 59

ment by the German Ambassador, who had engaged him on May 18th in a long conversation. Herr von Dirksen referred to Herr Hitler as a "reasonable and sensible man, and said that no reasonable and sensible man would think of making war against the forces which Great Britain had (unjustifiably) mobilised against Germany. These included the whole of the British Empire, France, Poland, Roumania, Greece and Turkey, with the United States standing behind." Whatever decision the Cabinet might reach would not prevent Germany from accusing us of being the inventor of the encirclement policy. At the same time he, Lord Halifax, had the strongest distaste for a policy of acquiescing in Soviet bluff and blackmail.

The Prime Minister took this up readily. An alliance with Russia would constitute an entirely new factor, he said. Many influential people in Germany were trying to persuade Herr Hitler that the time for him to strike was when the Three Power Pact was concluded. "The conclusion of such a Pact would unite Germany as nothing else could do."[1] This argument did not convince Sir Samuel Hoare that the German Government would be deterred by anything else but fear, but Mr Morrison then asserted: "The whole Empire would stand in with us if we entered into war with Germany because of German aggression against Poland or Roumania. . . . He doubted whether this would be the case if we got involved in a war of aggression by Germany against Russia, in which the other Eastern European countries were not involved."

The geographical impossibility of this, as pointed out by the Chiefs of Staff, seemed to have escaped Mr Morrison, but the Committee decided to postpone a reply to the message from Maisky and refer the matter to the full Cabinet on May 24th. They would also see what France, Poland and Roumania might say to a Triple Pact with Russia.

On June 5th the Committee was perplexed still further. They had conceded that Western guarantees might be extended to the Baltic states, but Russia was refusing any obligation to act in the case of aggression against Holland or Switzerland. (Neither of these countries belonged to any kind of defensive alliance,

[1] Sir Nevile Henderson had by this time returned to his Berlin post and was continuing to write letters direct to the Foreign Secretary and the Prime Minister in criticism of the negotiations with Russia.

which might give reciprocal assistance to Russia.) Thereafter Russia raised another objection that soon became serious. Russian proposals spoke of the possibility of "aggression from within", internal action in the Baltic states which might be so serious as to warrant Russian intervention. This at once suggested to the British that Russia herself contemplated a pre-emptive aggression; but by June 1939 disenchantment had gone far on both sides to frustrate any possibility of final agreement. Quite apart from their Russian deadlock, the British were in unimaginable difficulties[1] of draftmanship; for their guarantees had been first drafted to avoid giving offence of naming Germany as the potential aggressor. Consequently the obligations they were assuming could be interpreted as guaranteeing the states of eastern Europe in all directions against both Germany and Russia and even each other, an impossible proposition.

Sir John Simon made a remark in the Committee which went far to explain its dilatory methods: "we are not preparing for war, we are constructing a peace front." That much was fully understood by Joszef Stalin. The Soviet Government had already received a German "trade delegation" in Moscow secretly. Rumours of this had reached the West, but although the British Chiefs of Staff were thoroughly alarmed, the Chamberlain Cabinet continued to seek new legalistic terms for their own proposals and to find the arguments of "the Soviet" inadmissible.

[1] Lord Halifax explained these complications to the Committee in these terms. "The existing guarantees to Poland and Roumania, and our prospective guarantee to Russia all apply not merely to aggression by Germany, but to aggression by *any European state.*" In effect this means that we guarantee Russia *inter alia* against all her neighbours including Poland, and that we guarantee Poland and Roumania against Russia. Since the prevention of aggression by Germany is the sole object of our entering into agreements with these countries, it is superfluous and might be embarrassing that our guarantees should be extended so as to cover aggression by these countries against each other . . . By limiting our guarantee to aggression by Germany we are giving Germany further proof in support of the argument that our policy is being directed solely against Germany and aimed at encirclement. Nevertheless this effort at limitation should be made in all our undertakings, since it has already been achieved in the case of Poland, "and the Poles will be greatly offended if we refused to guarantee them against Russia, while guaranteeing Russia against Poland". Cab. 27. 625, p. 92

CHAPTER XVIII

Acceleration and Delay

NOT EVERYTHING THAT the Chamberlain Government essayed was to be so blighted as its diplomacy. An instance of success in action was the Committee on Defence Programmes and their Acceleration, formed in the week after the German march into Prague. A small volume,[1] compiled on its activities, begins on March 20th 1939, after the Cabinet meeting of March 18th brought it into being. Admiral Lord Chatfield, Minister for Co-ordination of Defence, and the three Services Ministers, the President of the Board of Trade, and the Minister of Labour were among its regular members. The Prime Minister, whose gifts for practical organisation would have been well bestowed upon this sort of work, did not participate, leaving the Chancellor of the Exchequer to watch over finance and Treasury approval. Among its several representatives from the Armed Forces was Sir Harold Brown, Director-General of Munitions Production in the War Office, whose desperate appeal for decisions early in 1937 is quoted in the second chapter of this book. The Prime Minister had, late in 1938, raised the practical efficiency of his Cabinet by bringing in Sir John Anderson, a retired member of the Indian Civil Service, as Lord Privy Seal in charge of Civil Air Defence. He now freed Mr Leslie Burgin from Departmental duties by replacing him as Minister of Transport with Captain Euan Wallace and designated Burgin as Minister Without Portfolio, becoming Minister of Supply on July 26th 1939. The meetings of the Acceleration Committee were not more than half a dozen in all, held at 6 Richmond Terrace, in the room of General Sir Hastings Ismay, Secretary to the Committee of Imperial Defence, who in war became Chief of Staff to the Defence Minister.

The Committee was required to speed up defence preparations within the second quarter of 1939. Lord Chatfield suggested at their first meeting on March 20th that their main duty was to accelerate short term preparations, though

[1] Cab. 27. 657

both Sir Kingsley Wood and Mr Hore-Belisha urged that some longer term projects could also be improved, if authority were given immediately. Lord Chatfield wanted industry put on a war basis, not at the expense of the export trade but by curtailing home consumption, but this proposal was not adopted. Proposals for acceleration of equipment for the Armed Services and Civil Defence preparations were called for within forty-eight hours, and at a notable meeting on March 23rd, Lord Chatfield asked for an assumed date as zero day, to which they would work. He proposed August 1st 1939, and laid down the principle that they make "every effort to do now what it would be possible to do in war, unless such action was politically impossible".

Mr Hore-Belisha reported that a delay of 50–60 months existed in ordering machine tools for equipping the Army's projected nineteen divisions. The Committee agreed to ask the Prime Minister to make a private appeal to industry to give to all authorised orders for the rearmament programme priority over normal trade orders.

Outside the terms of reference of this Committee lay conscription, the biggest single step towards acceleration of defence, but which Lord Chatfield would still have termed "politically impossible". Mr Chamberlain, though he had told the Cabinet, concerning Mr Baldwin's pledge of air parity with Germany, that "no pledge lasts for ever", and that he was prepared to defend a departure from it, was not, however, willing to depart from a second pledge given by Baldwin, that conscription would not be introduced in the present Parliament. Yet both conscription and legislation for a Ministry of Supply came about within the next two months.

Neither came about through any initiative of Neville Chamberlain and conscription came against his will. Discussion was in characteristic manner referred first to a few political advisers rather than the full Cabinet. Mr Hore-Belisha spoke impatiently at Bermondsey on March 31st of the "inestimable benefits that conscription could bring". After the seizure of Albania by Italy on April 7th, he had occasion to meet Sir Horace Wilson and spoke of his relief that the Prime Minister was reconsidering a Ministry of Supply. Sir Horace in turn

¹ Cab. 27. 627

expressed his own amazement that nobody in the War Office supported a proposal of the Prime Minister that the Territorials after their ordinary day's work should man guns and search-lights at night that summer for a matter of three to six months.[1] This impracticable scheme remained in Chamberlain's mind as a substitute for conscription. On April 11th, Lord Gort, the C.I.G.S., advised that the Army would have to be partially mobilised, as without reservists there was no way of keeping anti-aircraft defences in a state of continuous readiness. Hore-Belisha, who had been invited to dine with Winston Churchill at Chartwell on April 11th, and was warned by him of the consequences of inaction to his own career, then "took his political life in his hands".[2] He sent the Prime Minister at Chequers on Saturday, April 15th, the proposals for mobilisa-tion submitted by the War Office, with the request that he might be allowed to circulate them to the Cabinet on Monday. He attached a note of his own concluding that "it behoves us to take steps that will remove the deficiency (of personnel) by a compulsory scheme". On Monday 17th, the Secretary of State for War "had a telephone message . . . to say that the P.M. was considering the War Office papers, but that he did not wish me to circulate them to the Cabinet. In the meantime he wished Chatfield and the Treasury to consider them."[3] Hore-Belisha complied, but he had sent a set of the War Office papers to Lord Halifax, and called on him at the Foreign Office that afternoon.

Lord Halifax "said he had good reason to believe that con-scription was the only course that would have any effect on Germany. . . . He would speak to the P.M. about the War Office papers and he would not mention that I had shown them to him."[4] Hore-Belisha, past caring, asked that the truth should be made known. On April 18th, he saw Mr Chamberlain. "It was not a pleasant interview."

"I understand you wished to see me," began Hore-Belisha.

"You wished to see *me*," replied Chamberlain. Hore-Belisha then broached the subject of the War Office demands. "The Prime Minister said I was adding to his difficulties and that I had made up my mind; that I had a bee in my bonnet about

<hr/>

[1] Private Papers of Hore-Belisha   [2] Churchill, *The Gathering Storm*
[3] Private Papers of Hore-Belisha   [4] *Ibid.*

conscription; that the War Office wanted it and that I had therefore a biased view." Mr Chamberlain feared trouble from the Trades Unions and the Labour Opposition—he still seemed to think that the Territorials could be called up nightly to man A.A. defences. He sent away the Secretary of State for War to think again; but the Army Council meeting that after-noon agreed unanimously that there was no alternative to a partial mobilisation, if conscription was not adopted. Next day, Mr Chamberlain sent for Hore-Belisha again—his manner had completely changed and he offered to let him raise the subject of the War Office papers verbally in Cabinet but without circulating the papers.[1] Such was the diary note made by Hore-Belisha, but all happened otherwise. A Secret Memoran-dum was circulated by direction of the Prime Minister, the Cabinet Minutes tell us, on April 22nd, containing his own proposals for Compulsory Military Training, in a Note that bore the imprint of the Chamberlain mind: "as an earnest of our intention to resist aggression and also to provide the solution for certain urgent problems of defence preparedness during prolonged periods of tension . . . powers would be taken in a Military Training Bill to call up all the men born in a particular year, each year between 200,000 and 250,000."[2] Mr Hore-Belisha is not recorded as raising the subject in Cabinet. In fact Chamberlain raised it himself.

> The Prime Minister said that personally he had long been in favour in principle of a scheme of compulsory military training, but until recently had regarded the introduction of such a scheme as impracticable by reason of the Opposition it would arouse in Trade Union circles. He referred to the pledge which had been given by Lord Baldwin on April 1st 1936, that he would not introduce a measure of conscription so long as peace prevailed. He himself had renewed that undertaking; but he thought that, while we were not actually at war, it was a mockery to call the present conditions "peace", and these undertakings did not therefore disturb him.[3]

Sir Samuel Hoare thought all his colleagues in favour of compulsory military training ("conscription" being the term that many of them had previously resisted, this word is nowhere

[1] C.P. 91 (39)   [2] Cab. 23. 99, pp. 6–8   [3] Cab. 23. 99, p. 8

used in the minutes). He did foresee some parliamentary delay to the accompanying Emergency Power Bill, and Lord Halifax asked whether some Territorials and Reservists could not be called up by an immediate declaration of a state of emergency. Advice had been given, said the Prime Minister, that this might have disastrous effects on the City, not perhaps on British but on foreign holders of sterling securities.

There were innumerable lesser problems in the acceleration of rearmament, such as that involved in War Office continuation orders for munitions production. These long-term orders would be in excess of the Treasury authority given for equipping the Field Force of ten Divisions, but if not placed immediately would result in some ordnance firms going back from double to single work shifts at a time when the Army was desperately short of ammunition. Under existing arrangements the Second Contingent of the Field Force would not be completely equipped with war reserves till July 1940, but if the continuation orders were placed, an earlier date could be attained and they would provide some material as well for nine other Divisions envisaged. The War Office was asked to negotiate for authority direct with the Treasury. In the course of other Acceleration Committee discussion, such gaps were revealed as a total lack of light A.A. artillery personnel for the First Field Force contingent of five Divisions, making it necessary to borrow from the Indian Army. Lord Gort explained that the three Services each ran separate Intelligence Services in the Middle East, which must be unified. Gibraltar had only half its complement of A.A. Gunners. War reserves of material had to be considered for Hong Kong, Aden, Malta, Gibraltar, Trincomalee, Penang and Singapore. Defence of Egypt and Port Sudan had to be organised and the overland routes from Egypt to Basra completed and protected. In raising the Territorial Army to war establishment, authority had to be sought for over-recruitment by 15 per cent to provide for wastage, and a similar permission to over-recruit for Air Defence of Great Britain units was necessary. The War Office proposals, if they were to ensure that nineteen Divisions of a Field Force could go abroad twelve months after the outbreak of war, required a whole series of enlarged Treasury permissions.

On munitions production, on continuation orders, on

earmarking of metals, redisposition of British units overseas, on storing war reserves at ports abroad, Mediterranean and Middle East defence measures, and increased personnel demands, Cabinet and Treasury approval was obtained by April 23rd. There was also an increase from 15,000 to 25,000 approved in the numbers of the National Defence Companies, the embryo Home Guard.

Proposals on March 22nd for canned meat, fish and milk reserves, wheat and flour reserves, whale oil and cotton seed, farm foodstuffs and oilseed were all approved by April 24th. The Air Ministry acceleration proposals were broadly agreed by May 10th, though a plan for an order for 1,200 more air frames was cut back to 1,000, while the provision of air war reserves on a 90 days coverage basis was to be submitted in detail with the Treasury. Reserves of aviation spirit and provision of additional tankerage and storage had been agreed by May 31st.

On June 20th 1939, the Chairman of this remarkable Committee, Lord Chatfield, put forward the view that since decisions had been taken on all short term projects and had been taken or were pending in all long term projects put forward, the Committee on Defence Programmes and their Acceleration "might now be wound up". On July 12th, General Ismay, as Secretary, informed members that all had assented to this proposal.[1] It remains true that thereafter problems remained; the Ministry of Supply was still being formed and the Army terribly short of tanks and guns; designs were not completed and factories unequipped with tools to fulfil orders. A start had, however, been made.

Once the immediate risks appeared to have been averted by the Acceleration Committee, Sir John Simon took steps to protect his somewhat shaken fiscal authority. The Cabinet of May 23rd had before it a Memorandum of the Chancellor of the Exchequer,[2] entitled "Control of Expenditure", which drew attention to "the seriousness of the situation" and asked "for closer control of ordering and spending". "The Treasury was receiving a continuous flow of demands from all quarters involving heavy expenditure . . . we were reducing our resources at a rapid rate . . . the limit to the rate at which we could raise

[1] Cab. 27. 65. 7   [2] C.P. 118 (39)

money had already been reached. . . ." Sir John Simon said "he was sure his colleagues would agree that the Treasury had not in any way opposed the rearmament programme. . . . There was grave danger, however, that in six or twelve months we might find ourselves in a very serious (financial) situation." The replies of the three Services Ministers were courteous but emphatic that adequate Treasury controls already existed. The Prime Minister then went to Sir John's rescue. Mr Chamberlain "felt that the Cabinet should agree to the proposal of the Chancellor (for a Committee of Control). . . . It was impossible for the Government to continue the present rate of expenditure indefinitely." The Prime Minister had his list of members ready, and the composition of the Committee set up reflected close support for his personal policy of fiscal caution. Lord Chatfield, Minister for Co-ordination of Defence, was not a member, nor were any of the three Services Ministers. Mr Chamberlain selected the Lord President of the Council, Viscount Runciman, who had returned to the Cabinet in this guise; Lord Chancellor Maugham, who had just objected to a Chiefs of Staff proposal for a summary issue of Defence Regulations in an emergency; Sir Samuel Hoare; Mr W. S. Morrison (the ubiquitous Chancellor of the Duchy of Lancaster); Sir Thomas Inskip (Dominion Affairs); and Mr Oliver Stanley, President of the Board of Trade.[1]

It may be that the departure of Sir Kingsley Wood from the Cabinet room, noted at this moment, was an expression of disapproval at this new drag on the wheel of rearmament.

The Cabinet had been let into the Russian negotiations on May 17th, when Lord Chatfield explained that the Chiefs of Staff had prepared three Reports; the first dealing with the military value of Russia as an ally, making clear that this value was not so great as commonly supposed; the second dealing with the balance of strategic value of Russia as an ally and Spain as an enemy; the third Report had been prepared in great haste on the previous day (May 16th). The Chiefs of Staff had been shown two telegrams to the British Ambassador in Moscow, proposing a middle course between a system of mutual guarantees by Britain and Russia and a complete military alliance. The Chiefs of Staff opinion on the middle

[1] Cab. 23. 99, p. 244

course proposed was that "on the whole it would be advantageous that we should go somewhat further ... a military alliance involving very little extra liability and giving a much better assurance of help from Russia". "The Chiefs of Staff were, of course, only concerned with the military aspect of this problem," repeated Lord Chatfield. "If they had been present at the meeting of the Foreign Policy Committee and had heard the arguments there adduced, they might perhaps to some extent have changed their views."[1]

It may be remarked that it was open to the Prime Minister to have invited the Chiefs of Staff to attend the Policy Committee, but not open to them to propose their own attendance. There were a series of questions in Cabinet on this disturbing divergence of views and "the Prime Minister agreed to the circulation of the papers in question, saying that it was certainly his intention, if a choice had to be made, to call a meeting of the Cabinet with full opportunity for discussion".

The Cabinet on May 17th had before it the Military Training Bill and the Reserve and Auxiliary Forces Bill, in which form conscription was being rushed through Parliament. The Cabinet also authorised a procedure for revising the Government War Book and printing and storing Defence Regulations for issue in an emergency by Order-in-Council, should Parliament not be sitting at the time,[2] though not without some previous grumbling by the Lord Chancellor, Lord Maugham, about "illegal proceedings".

The Cabinet met on May 24th to study the Chiefs of Staff papers on a Russian alliance and a Memorandum by the Secretary of State for Foreign Affairs, who had just returned from discussions in Geneva with M. Maisky. The Russian arguments in Geneva had still been firmly for absolute reciprocity of engagements. "We were now faced with a clear choice of alternatives," said Lord Halifax. He then declared his own view to be in favour of "a direct mutual guarantee agreement 'with the Soviet Government. . . .' He thought that Herr Hitler was more likely to be provoked into starting a war if we failed to oppose him with a solid bloc of states pledged to resist aggression."[3]

[1] Cab. 28 (39). Cab. 23, p. 99   [2] Cab. 23. 99, pp. 205, 208, 209
[3] Cab. 23. 99, p. 275

Mr Chamberlain reluctantly conceded his agreement to this view, but said that it was important to present the agreement "rather on the lines of a regional pact on the Locarno model". This was no mere *façade*, he said. Arrangements under the Covenant of the League, would meet less opposition in the country. He mentioned a letter just published in *The Times* from Sir Henry Page Croft, M.P., a powerful Conservative, "expressing his dislike of a naked military alliance with Russia, which might put a millstone round our necks for years and result in our sons being called up to fight for Russian interests".

Sir Thomas Inskip reported the reluctant agreement of the Dominions Governments to extending the negotiations with Russia, if they were in danger of breaking down altogether. Lord Chatfield then put to the Cabinet the serious position discovered at the Anglo-French Staff conversations of May 3rd, his remarks being classified as Most Secret and given no circulation in the minutes.

> The French intention in the event of a war between Germany and Poland was to stand on the defensive on the Maginot Line. . . . The British Chiefs of Staff were considerably disturbed at the prospect of complete inaction on the part of the French and the consequent failure to exploit the two-front war. . . . If the French were going to do nothing to draw off the weight of a German attack on Poland, the assistance of Russia would be of great value to the latter.

The Cabinet agreed to authorise the Foreign Secretary to continue negotiations with Russia, basing British obligations on Article XVI of the Covenant of the League of Nations, and agreed to a statement in the House of Commons to this effect.

At this point Sir Thomas Inskip made a suggestion in his capacity as Secretary of State for the Dominions. He had on the previous day discussed the Anglo-Russian negotiations with the Dominions High Commissioners. . . . "The suggestion . . . which had emerged . . . and had a good deal in common with the suggestion made recently by the Foreign Secretary to the German Ambassador. . . was that . . . when we had strengthened

H

our position by making an agreement with the Russian Government we should take the initiative in a renewal of the search
for appeasement. . . . We should be in a position to make such
an approach from strength. . . . There was more likelihood that
Germany would be willing to listen. . . . We might indicate
that we had no intention to encircle Germany economically
and were ready at any time to discuss any matters in dispute."[1]
The Prime Minister thought this "premature", though "he did
not reject the suggestion. . . . "It was necessary not merely to
be strong but that others should realise the fact" . . . Lord
Halifax then repeated the substance of an unwritten comment
that he had made to Herr von Dirksen at their most recent
interview—Britain might appear to be putting out a notice
"Keep off the Grass", but "he had added that there was, however, also a positive side to our policy".

On June 7th further obstacles to agreement with Russia
were described by Lord Halifax. The Soviet Government wished
countries to be named in the documents of guarantee, though
some countries did not wish so to be named, while others which
Britain wished to be named, at least in secret protocol, such
as Switzerland and Holland, were omitted from the Russian
draft. It was noted that Sir William Seeds would return from
Moscow to London for further instructions, but at the next
Cabinet on June 14th, it was explained that Sir William was
suffering from influenza and that it had been decided instead to
send to Moscow Mr William Strang, Head of the Central
Department of the Foreign Office. A very comprehensive
memorandum for Sir William Seeds had been prepared, and
Mr Strang had "authority to submit various suggestions".
Lord Halifax quoted an extract from the instructions to the
British Ambassador in Moscow—"The draft treaty should be as
short and simple in its terms as possible. It is better that agreement should be quickly reached than that time should be spent
in trying to cover every contingency." Loopholes were "prefer-
able to a long delay" and "less serious than detailed provisions
which, if the treaty ever came to be executed . . . might be found
to limit His Majesty's Government more effectively than the
Soviet Government".[2] He had to tell the Cabinet nevertheless,
on June 21st, that "M. Molotov's attitude does not seem to

[1] Cab. 23. 99, p. 286   [2] Cab. 23. 99, p. 338

be very helpful". The Soviet Foreign Minister was now saying
that if difficulties over the precise form of guarantee of the
Baltic States were becoming insurmountable, "the best plan
might be that Great Britain, France and the Soviet Union
should enter into obligations limited to mutual assistance in the
event of direct attack by an aggressor on the territory of one or
other of the three Contracting Parties".[1] M. Maisky was still
attaching great importance to the Russian conditions for "no
separate peace". Lord Halifax wondered whether M. Molotov
was not seeking an excuse to break off the negotiations. The
Agreement of Britain with Poland had been a long time in the
process of drafting but was now practically complete. Talks
were proceeding on "non-commercial credits" with a Polish
delegation, and as "on the political side we are living in what is
virtually a state of concealed war . . . engaged in an attempt to
form a coalition of actual or potential allies. . . . I think the
time has come when the financial help afforded to Poland and
Turkey must be regarded from the military rather than the
commercial point of view." He thought that Poland would
require a great deal of assistance. "The whole future of Europe
might depend on Poland being sufficiently strengthened to
resist attack by Germany."[2]

To this view Sir John Simon opposed his own. "The expression
that 'the sacrifice must be made' was fundamentally a false
view. . . . The real question was how much it was within our
power to do, even at the cost of weakening our own position. . . .
The Foreign Office had recently agreed to a limit of £10m. on
new non-commercial foreign credits. There would now seem
to be no limit to the demands which might be made upon us,
since the Foreign Secretary had spoken of aid for Poland,
Roumania, Turkey, Greece, Portugal, Egypt, Iraq, Yugoslavia,
Bulgaria, Afghanistan and Saudi Arabia." This was later found
to amount to £51m., which Sir John found "rather disturbing".[3]
The Cabinet agreed to increase the limit beyond £10m., but
directed that political loans and credits should be submitted
in the form of a statement by the Foreign Secretary to the
Chancellor of the Exchequer.

Lord Halifax by June 28th thought that Britain might have

[1] Cab. 23. 100, p. 4   [2] Cab. 23. 100, p. 21
[3] Cab. 23. 100, June 28th 1939

to yield to the Russian demand for naming the states to be guaranteed in the treaty instruments. He returned to the subject on July 5th, repeating the grave doubts of the Foreign Policy Committee of the Cabinet about Molotov's definition of "indirect aggression". Molotov saw a right to immediate action if "an internal *coup d'état*" took place, "or a reversal of policy in the interests of the aggressor". It is easier now with hindsight to visualise the need for such a provision, in view of the very precarious condition of the Baltic States, with which Stalin and Molotov must have been closely concerned; but at the time, this proposal outraged the cautious and legalistic thinking of Chamberlain and was the occasion for further delay. Mr Walter Elliot, however, maintained in Cabinet on July 5th that "if the new technique of indirect aggression should be applied to the Baltic States, Molotov's point is a crucial one in any arrangements to meet aggression". . . . "What", he asked, "is the gap in British and Soviet views on this subject?" The difference was, so Lord Halifax explained, that the Anglo-French draft prescribed "consultation", whereas in the Russian draft, if Russia acted against such a policy reversal in Finland for instance, "We might well find ourselves involved in war."[1]

On July 12th, Lord Halifax reported further that the Foreign Policy Committee was adhering to its own formula since M. Molotov had submitted a definition of indirect aggression "which appeared to the Committee to give the Soviet Government a wide right of intervention in the internal affairs of other countries and on this ground to be open to grave objection".[2] The comment of Mr Chamberlain was that "on the whole I am disposed to think that the Soviet Government intends to make an Agreement with us, but is probably in no hurry to do so". When the Cabinet, on July 26th, reviewed the prolonged wrangle over the definition of indirect aggression, the Prime Minister concluded "that he could not bring himself to believe that a real alliance between Russia and Germany was possible".[3]

The German nerve war against Poland over Danzig was at its height, and Lord Halifax on July 5th referred to current

[1] Cab. 23. 100. 78   [2] Cab. 23. 100. 146
[3] Cab. 23. 100, p. 187

rumours of an imminent German *coup* against Danzig. The Cabinet agreed to a proposal to send out General Ironside, Inspector General of Overseas Forces, to find out what kind of resistance the Poles would offer if the Germans seized Danzig. Ironside presented himself at 10 Downing Street at noon on July 10th, and found Chamberlain and Halifax awaiting him. "I must say that Chamberlain looks very young for his years, plenty of hair with very little grey at the temples. He talked quietly and easily and without hurry."[1] Ironside was "glad to see that he had no belief in Hitler's promises", but noted also that when faced with the idea that Hitler might confront them with a *fait accompli* over Danzig, the two Ministers said "that we must settle Danzig so that Hitler could not say that he had had a success through threatening force" . . . "Chamberlain said that it seemed impossible to come to an understanding with Russia. Did I think it was right?" To Ironside's remark that an agreement with Russia "was the only thing we could do", Chamberlain exclaimed—"the only thing we cannot do". On July 26th, Ironside told Hore-Belisha that he had discovered the Chamberlain policy to be "not hurrying on getting in Russia".

On July 5th, Cabinet time was given to the activities of the Irish Republican Army in Britain after what had become known as the Piccadilly bomb outrage. The Cabinet approved an outline Bill proposed by the Home Secretary to empower him to deport Irish suspects.

Later that day, Sir John Simon presented a Memorandum on the Financial Situation,[2] in which he described as "The War Chest" those assets "which represented our staying power in war". These were:

(1) The British export trade;
(2) Stocks of gold;
(3) Foreign securities owned by British subjects which the Government could acquire;
(4) Loans abroad.

The Chancellor considered the British favourable balance of trade far less strong than in 1914, while the gold stocks of

---

[1] The Ironside Diaries, p. 77   [2] C.P. 149 (39)

the sterling bloc were falling at the rate of £80m. a year. There were disadvantages in allowing the level of the pound to drop. As to foreign borrowings, Britain had in the Great War borrowed £250m. from private investors abroad, which had been repaid, but the loans borrowed from the United States Government had not been repaid and under the Johnson Act the position in 1939 was that Britain could no longer borrow from the United States. The broad upshot, concluded Sir John, was that the Cabinet should know that the War Chest was being steadily depleted. It was impossible to say when war might break out, but if it should break out some years hence, those responsible for policy should know that British financial strength would be much weaker than in the summer of 1939. A related paper on the German Financial Effort for Rearmament[1] showed a much higher rate of taxation on the German working population and a far lower expenditure on their social services.

Sir Richard Hopkins of the Treasury, whose review in detail was rather less pessimistic than that of Sir John Simon, gave the Cabinet an account of the world position of sterling. A maximum effort now would be well applied, Sir Richard said, if the prospect of a reasonably short war was assumed. Even if this assumption should prove wrong, the attitude of the United States in a more prolonged war would be sufficiently favourable to enable Britain to use it. Mr Oliver Stanley drew the conclusion from these arguments that "a point would ultimately come when we should be unable to carry out a long war". The President of the Board of Trade, who had a month previously offered to resign in favour of Mr Churchill entering the Cabinet, went on to produce what must have been for Sir John Simon a most unpalatable argument. "There would therefore come a moment which, on a balance of our financial strength and our strength in armaments, was the best time for war to break out." "It might be desirable to consider whether at such a period Great Britain should apply strong pressure to Germany to relax the international tension."[2]

The Cabinet took note of Sir John Simon's warnings, "in particular of the measures necessary to make money available for the Defence Programmes". His first conclusion—and this

[1] C.P. 148 (39)   [2] Cab. 23. 100, p. 131

rang a knell of the hopes of the Polish Government—was that
"the primary need is to conserve our resources in gold and
foreign exchange, which represent staying power in war".
Sir John appraised the Cabinet on July 12th of the Polish
requests for export credits and a cash loan, to which he thought
Britain should agree provided that France acted with her in the
matter. Sir John thought it might be suggested to Poland that
it would also be salutary to devalue the Polish zloty, a course of
diplomacy upon which Lord Halifax expressed some misgiving.
It appeared from a further statement in the Cabinet on July
26th that export credits amounting to £8m. would be available,
but Sir John Simon was not disposed "to give Poland gold,
which Poland would store in vaults in Warsaw and make the
basis for further expansion of her paper currency".

The Cabinet on July 26th heard from Lord Halifax the
impressions of General Ironside concerning the danger and
risks attendant upon a German *coup* in Danzig. The General
thought that Poland would not resort to military action unless
there was a definite military invasion of Poland by the German
Army. Marshal Smygly-Rydz, the Commander-in-Chief,
appeared to take the view that German ambitions were
incompatible with the existence of a Polish state and that war
was inevitable, though he did not expect it in August. Lord
Halifax seems not to have related that General Ironside had
wired the Government on July 18th "that we ought not to
make so many conditions to our financial aid, that time is
short".[1]

The Foreign Secretary informed the Cabinet of a conversation that he had just held with Dr Burckhardt, League of
Nations Commissioner for Danzig. The Gauleiter of Danzig,
Herr Forster, had returned there from Berchtesgaden, saying
that Hitler thought "the question (of Danzig) could wait, if
necessary, till next year. Nothing would be done on the German
side to provoke a conflict." Was this a blind to cover up the real
motives of Germany, asked Lord Halifax, or was she impressed
with the firm attitude of the Peace Front? Plainly, Lord Halifax
was uncertain himself that a *détente* was on the way, but he
told the Cabinet that "we have informed the Polish Government that we have information that the Germans are working

[1] The Ironside Diaries, p. 81

for a *detente* and that it is of the utmost importance that the Poles should direct their endeavours to the same end".[1]

This was evidently "the more positive side" to the British "Keep off the Grass" policy, to which Lord Halifax had earlier drawn the attention of the German Ambassador. Their pressure on Poland to negotiate on Danzig brought a knock on the Cabinet door from Mr Winston Churchill. The great backbencher had something to say at this stage, which Lord Halifax thought important enough to repeat in the first Cabinet of August 1939.[2] Lord Halifax first delivered himself of a somewhat equivocal statement on Danzig. "He had been at pains to correct a statement that we were committed to fight for Danzig. The true position was that Danzig of itself . . . was not . . . a *casus belli*. If, however, a threat to Polish independence arose from Danzig, then this country would clearly become involved." . . . "Mr Winston Churchill had said that he had no wish to be more Polish than the Poles, but he was anxious that the Government should not put pressure on the Polish Government to take action which, in their view, would be destructive of their State."

There were voices raised for keeping Parliament in session during August. Lord Lloyd, an active Conservative peer, had argued in an end of session speech that it would have required repeal of the American Neutrality Act as well as the signing of an Anglo-Russian Agreement to avert the threat of war, but that neither of these steps had been achieved. Such voices were raised in vain and Parliament scattered at the end of July to holidays at home and abroad. Sir Alexander Cadogan did manage to deflect the Duke of Kent from visiting a sister-in-law in Munich, but the Cabinet rose in a mood that was not alarmist, with the report of a *détente* fresh in mind. The truth is now realised of reports that as early as April 3rd 1939, Hitler had directed that the Wehrmacht be ready in every particular for war by August 25th. Even at the time it had not really been possible to conceal the extent of German preparations. Lord Halifax went up to Yorkshire and Mr Chamberlain went fishing in Scotland, leaving Sir Horace Wilson to explain to the Poles why there could be no loan, because Britain must

[1] Most Secret Annex to Item 2 of Cab. 39 (39), July 26th 1939
[2] Cab. 40 (39), August 2nd 1939

preserve her economic strength in case of a long war. In the Cabinet Room the shutters went up after the meeting of August 2nd, and no further meeting took place until August 22nd when the Cabinet was hurriedly reassembled in the wake of a dire event.

CHAPTER XIX

"If Time Is Given"

JUST BEFORE DINNER on August 18th, Sir Robert Vansittart
telephoned to Lord Halifax in Yorkshire and was "very insistent
that I ought to return to London the following morning".[1]
Sir Robert, through a German diplomat in the Hague, had
received information that an attack by Germany on Poland
within two weeks was a practical certainty. He was guarded
on the telephone and Lord Halifax, with his eye on Cricket
Week and a little farming at Garrowby, was reluctant to be
drawn. He played for time, suggesting that Vansittart should
consult with Sir Alexander Cadogan and if both agreed, "I
would come up by the early train."

Cadogan advised him to come, "although it was impossible
to feel certain about (Van's) information", and at noon on
Saturday, August 19th, Halifax met both men "at the Office".
"I rather think we got Horace Wilson into this talk which
concerned the information Van had received as to the date of
the prospective German attack on Poland." They agreed not to
fetch the Prime Minister back from Scotland, as he was due
back on the 21st, but that a telegram should be sent to Rome
urging that Mussolini should use his influence with Hitler.
They would also prepare a draft letter to Hitler on lines
suggested to the Prime Minister earlier that summer by Sir
Nevile Henderson.

An R.A.F. machine then flew Lord Halifax from Heston to
Driffield and he managed some farming and cricket that
weekend before going to 10 Downing Street on Monday
morning to see Chamberlain. Halifax noted in his confidential
Record of Events that " 'C' tells us[2] that he has received an
approach, suggesting that Goering should come to London if
he can be assured that he will be able to see the Prime Minister.

---

[1] F.O. 800. 317. "A Record of Events Before the War." Précis by Lord
Halifax, 1939

[2] 'C' was the pseudonym of the Head of the Foreign Intelligence Service,
Major-General Sir Stuart Menzies.

It was decided to send an affirmative offer to this curious suggestion and arrangements were accordingly set in hand for Goering to come over secretly on Wednesday, the 23rd." Among the preparations for such a conspirational meeting they decided to land the Field-Marshal "at some deserted aerodrome" and motor him to Chequers, where the telephone would be disconnected and "the regular household given *congé*". Lord Halifax anticipated "a dramatic interlude" but there was no news from Berlin next day as to Goering before the Cabinet met at 3 p.m. to approve the Chamberlain letter to Hitler. Another dramatic interlude, however, had erupted in the night of August 21st–22nd. Soviet Tass Agency announced that Herr von Ribbentrop was flying to Moscow to sign a Non-Aggression Pact with the Soviet Union.

The Prime Minister on July 26th had told Cabinet Ministers that "it was very difficult to give any definite guidance as to the date when normal weekly meetings of the Cabinet would be resumed after the Recess". He had therefore proposed to proceed as in the previous summer by holding an occasional meeting of Ministers, and only to call the full Cabinet if some event arose "of the first importance". He had been kept informed in Scotland through Lord Halifax at Garrowby of the contacts with Field-Marshal Goering, which were being mysteriously arranged by a Swedish business man, Birger Dahlerus, whose apparent aim was to by-pass both Ribbentrop and the British Foreign Office. Mr Chamberlain summoned all Ministers on August 22nd, and told them that they met "in circumstances which could only be described as grave". He asked Lord Halifax to speak on the international situation. "Rather over a week ago," related Lord Halifax in his best dry manner, "the Anglo-French military delegation had been in 'very amicable' conversations with the Russians in Moscow when the Soviet Government asked whether permission could be obtained from Poland and Roumania to operate through those countries in case of war." It would otherwise, in the view of the Soviet Government, be useless to continue the conversations. The Polish Government had told the British Ambassador in Warsaw their opinion that the Russian purpose was to find an excuse for occupying Polish territory permanently. Colonel Beck had, however, added that the Polish attitude, rejecting the Russian demand, might be modified if war broke out.

The British Military Mission in Moscow had inquired of the Foreign Secretary whether he agreed with the French view of a Russian right of passage "as soon as Poland is at war with Germany", but Lord Halifax had not thought it right to send any answer to this question "until we knew more about the real meaning of the German negotiations with the Soviet Government".[1] "Were the press reports true?" asked Sir John Simon. "Had the Soviet Union signed a non-aggression pact with Germany and could the Anglo-French military mission remain any longer in Moscow?" Lord Halifax replied that on the Russian side it was indicated that no definite arrangement had been made. As to the situation of tension between Germany and Poland over Danzig, Mr Chamberlain said that a letter from himself to Herr Hitler might help. The Cabinet agreed that Parliament should be summoned to meet on August 24th, and asked to pass the Emergency Powers Bill through all stages the same day.

They agreed also that a statement should be prepared making it plain that the conclusion of a non-aggression pact between the Soviet Government and Germany would make no difference to the British obligation to Poland, and that the personal letter that lay in draft before them on the Cabinet table should be sent by Mr Chamberlain to Herr Hitler. Sir John Simon told the Cabinet as a matter of extreme secrecy that the loss of British gold reserves had been very heavy in the last few days, amounting to £30m. in one day. He thought it would be necessary to take action, since the amount of gold remaining in the Exchange Equalisation Account must now be regarded as the minimum required for the War Chest. It might be necessary to introduce currency exchange control. The Chancellor obtained authority to alter, if necessary, the existing Bank of England system, whereby the pound was maintained at 4.68 dollars.[2]

The Chamberlain letter explained to Hitler certain British defence measures, and continued that

> apparently the announcement of a German–Soviet Agreement is
> taken in some quarters in Berlin to indicate that intervention by

[1] Cab. 23. 100, p. 310   [2] Cab. 41 (39) Most Secret Annex

Great Britain on behalf of Poland is no longer a contingency that need be reckoned with. No greater mistake could be made. Whatever may prove the nature of the German–Soviet Agreement, it cannot alter Great Britain's obligation to Poland, which His Majesty's Government have stated in public repeatedly and plainly and which they are determined to fulfil.

It has been alleged that if His Majesty's Government had made their position more clear in 1914, the great catastrophe would have been avoided. Whether or not there is any force in that allegation, His Majesty's Government are resolved that on this occasion there shall be no such tragic misunderstanding. If the need should arise they are resolved and prepared to employ without delay all the forces at their command, and it is impossible to foresee the end of hostilities once engaged. It would be a dangerous delusion to think that, if a war once starts, it will come to an early end, even if a success on any one of several fronts . . . should have been secured.

I trust that Your Excellency will weigh with the utmost deliberation the considerations that I have put before you.

This letter met with the prompt retort that Great Britain, with her "unconditional assurance to Poland", was emboldening that country to resist reasonable German demands and to terrorise the many German inhabitants of Poland. The Soviet–German Pact was signed late on the night of August 23rd, and when the British Cabinet and Parliament met on August 24th, the text of the Pact had been published in all newspapers.

Mr Chamberlain told the Cabinet on the 24th that he had not asked them to meet in order to take decisions, but in order that they might be informed of developments. As to his exchange of letters with Herr Hitler, Sir Nevile Henderson had (mistakenly) told the German Foreign Office that these would not be published, but he, the Prime Minister, felt it necessary at least to give the House of Commons the gist of the letters, since it was believed his own letter "contained threats only and no constructive proposals".[1]

The Cabinet was informed that Sir Percy Loraine had reported from Rome that he was strongly of the opinion that Italy would not participate in a war started by Germany over Poland, and that Signor Mussolini envisaged some peace

[1] Cab. 23. 100, p. 353

conference on the basis that Poland's vital rights in the Free Port of Danzig would be ensured. This day matters were made worse by a proclamation in Danzig making Herr Forster, the Nazi Gauleiter, Head of State.

Lord Halifax noted the results of the Cabinet of the 24th as "a telegram to Mussolini explaining that we cannot press Poland to agree to the incorporation of Danzig in the Reich, but that if Hitler will agree:

(a) that Polish rights must be safeguarded, and
(b) that a settlement must be internationally guaranteed, that would give us a basis on which we might approach the Poles. . . ."

"I had luncheon alone with the King, who had come down from Scotland and was very calm and steady." According to Lord Halifax the reception of the Chamberlain statement in the House of Commons that afternoon, showed that "everybody felt that, if Hitler insists on invading Poland, there is nothing to do but to try and smash him". "The Goering idea has, temporarily at least, faded out, a message being conveyed that Hitler does not think it would be immediately useful."[1]

As to the signing of the Russo–German Pact, Lord Halifax read out in Cabinet a telegram from the British Military Mission that they proposed to leave Moscow that night, and the Cabinet agreed that no useful purpose would be served in staying there. Coast Defence and Anti-Aircraft Units, reported Mr Hore-Belisha, were being called up. The Prime Minister proposed to adjourn Parliament for a week and to keep his Ministers available at short notice.

On August 25th, the long delayed Ratification of the Anglo-Polish Treaty of Mutual Assistance took place. Reasons had been found on the British side for not signing it earlier because Colonel Beck had refused to specify the aggressor by name. As Lord Halifax had already told the Cabinet, Britain did not want to enter commitments operable in all directions. He received that afternoon a short telephone message from Sir Nevile Henderson, who had seen Hitler at 1.30 p.m. "Henderson rang up to say that Hitler had made a communication to

[1] F.O. 800. 317

him and had suggested that the Ambassador should fly back to London. This we tell him to do." A telegram later summarised Hitler's proposals. "These are to the effect that the Polish question must be settled first; after that is done, he will make an offer to England."[1]

Sir Nevile Henderson arrived in London in time to be invited to attend the next Cabinet on August 26th. It was all a painful repetition of the bad melodrama of the previous summer, the Prime Minister saying that he thought the whole Cabinet should share the opportunity of discussing the situation with the Ambassador. No representative of the Foreign Office was invited, nor was Sir Robert Vansittart, the Chief Diplomatic Adviser to the Prime Minister. Sir Nevile was the bearer of a letter containing Hitler's reply to Mr Chamberlain, the purpose of which Lord Halifax discerned to be "to divide Britain from France and Poland. . . . Did Hitler want a settlement with Poland on his own terms more than he wanted to avoid war with Great Britain?" Lord Halifax "felt no confidence as to the answer to this question".[2] "Fairly precise information from sources alleged to be reliable had reached us to the effect that Germany intended to march into Poland that night or next morning."[3] He himself thought, however, that for the German Government to arrange for our Ambassador in Berlin to fly to this country with a special message in a German aeroplane was not consistent with such an intention. . . . Even if the matter was viewed in the most sinister light as another attempt to get a peace offer on record, there was no point in making such an offer and affording no time for a reply. Lord Halifax then told the Cabinet that a "neutral person in touch with Field-Marshal Goering",[4] had described to him the signing of the Anglo-Polish Treaty as "a dreadful action", but "other information is that the effect in Berlin has been considerable".

Lord Halifax did not propose to rest on the previous message to Hitler, but was giving "a good deal of thought" to a further letter to Hitler, expressing anxiety for a peaceful settlement but

[1] Hitler also "pledged himself personally to the continued existence of the British Empire".
[2] Cab. 923. 100, p. 371
[3] August 25th was the date named in the Vansittart intelligence.
[4] Birger Dahlerus.

THE CHAMBERLAIN CABINET

Sir Nevile was then questioned by Ministers, who asked whether
Hitler still entertained any doubts on the point that if Germany
invaded Poland, Great Britain would make war on Germany.
The Ambassador replied "that no reasonable person could
have any doubt on the subject". "He thought, however, that
we must not rule out altogether the possibility that Herr Hitler
might still hope that he could detach us from the Poles and get
us to dishonour our obligation ... The (Hitler) letter might have
been partly written to provide useful propaganda material."
Sir Nevile was determined to cover all the possibilities. "Another
was that Hitler had never intended to go beyond the limits of
bluff and now sought a solution without war." Once more, as
in the previous summer, Henderson would not have it that
Hitler had made up his mind. The Ambassador thought that
"the least which Herr Hitler would accept without going to
war was to incorporate Danzig in East Prussia and include the
whole of the Polish corridor in Germany". The Prime Minister
summed up that "the basic idea" of Hitler's letter was that "if
Britain would leave Herr Hitler alone in his sphere (Eastern
Europe), he would leave us alone". In reply to another
question, Sir Nevile said that he still thought it would be
possible for Hitler and Colonel Beck to negotiate amicably,
an idea that Mr Dahlerus was propagating too. Sir Nevile
considered that "the real value of our guarantee is to enable
Poland to come to a negotiated settlement with Germany" ...
"Herr Hitler is quite well disposed towards Colonel Beck."
The Cabinet thus drifted away from the firm attitude in the
first Chamberlain letter and towards the idea of negotiations
on the basis of an exchange of German and Polish minority
populations. Ministers devilled away at a draft reply from Mr
Chamberlain to Herr Hitler. "This went on until 8.30 and
was, as always, most wearisome," noted Lord Halifax.[1]
Mr Chamberlain said that "he would be very glad to know the
impression that the draft made on his colleagues, who, unlike
himself, came to it fresh".[2] He had already worked over it
with Lord Halifax, Sir Horace Wilson and Mr R. A. Butler.
Several Ministers thought the draft "somewhat too deferential",
"appearing to treat Herr Hitler's suggestions with somewhat

[1] F.O. 800. 317   [2] Cab. 23. 100, p. 382

too much respect". It was noted that the High Commissioners of Canada, South Africa, Australia and New Zealand, reported their Governments as favouring a discussion with Germany, but a suggestion from Mr Mackenzie King that King George VI should be invited to send a letter to Herr Hitler "met with no favour". The Cabinet agreed that the Chamberlain letter should once more go to a small group for drafting, consisting of the Prime Minister, Lord Halifax and Sir John Simon. They passed on to a review of defence dispositions. Lord Halifax took the draft over to the Foreign Office after dinner to try to improve its appearance and was sitting next morning in No. 10 for "more work on this wretched draft".

Birger Dahlerus was back in London to tell Lord Halifax that "Goering was very pleased with some platitudinous message expressing the general desire for peace that I had sent him on Friday". Lord Halifax took Dahlerus over to No. 10 to see the Prime Minister just before the Cabinet met that afternoon. "He did not really add much to what we know, but insisted that Goering was working very hard for peace and that things were by no means hopeless."[1] Dahlerus left that day again for Berlin.

The Cabinet meeting was at 3 p.m., with Sir Nevile Henderson again inflicting his advice on them. The Ministers were given a telegram from Rome with a suggestion by Count Ciano "that we should work for time". With Ciano adding to the continuous hopes just received from Dahlerus and Henderson, Mr Chamberlain was strongly in favour of the Italian Foreign Minister's advice. "If time is given, it is harder for any Government to take action resulting in war breaking out," he said.

Lord Halifax let his colleagues into the secret of the Dahlerus link with Goering (now that the visit had "temporarily faded out"), relating that "Mr D." had arrived in Croydon in the impression that he was carrying "definite peace proposals in regard to Danzig and the Corridor" from Hitler and Goering.[2]

Lord Halifax explained that he and the Prime Minister during their interview with him had made it clear to Mr D. that it was not practicable to start discussions with Germany on a

[1] F.O. 800. 317   [2] Cab. 44 (39) Most Secret Annex

number of diverse topics . . . while all the time there was the
possibility that Germany might any day invade Poland, but it
had been arranged that some rough notes, approved by the
Prime Minister and the Foreign Secretary, should be taken
back to Germany by Mr D. that night, though Mr Chamberlain had said that he could see no chance of a settlement on the
basis of Poland ceding the Polish Corridor and the status of
Danzig. The role of Goering was then mentioned and Sir
Nevile Henderson "agreed that when the negotiations were near
the point of agreement, Field-Marshal Goering would like to
come to London to deal with the concluding stages".[1] The
Prime Minister appeared to be himself in control of these
unofficial channels and Lord Halifax observed in Cabinet that
"he was rather afraid that the issue might be somewhat confused . . . by these rather informal and secret communications".[2] In his diary he noted that "the Cabinet sat a long time
on the revised draft, which was again remitted for revision to
Simon, Horace Wilson and Alec".[3]

The Prime Minister on Monday, August 28th, told the
Cabinet that it was desirable to have Parliament meet on the
Tuesday. Sir Nevile was still in the Cabinet Room, waiting for
the Prime Minister's letter to Hitler. The Cabinet was told that
Hitler had also been in communication with M. Daladier,
and that Poland had taken some mobilisation measures. Once
more they turned to the draft Chamberlain message, paragraph
by paragraph.

Mr Hore-Belisha repeated with emphasis a military objection
to the proposal that it contained in paragraph 4, for an international guarantee. Did the Poles want it? Lord Halifax
explained that "some time ago" he had proposed this to the
Polish Ambassador, Count Edward Racynski, who "nodded his
agreement". Hore-Belisha objected that if an international
guarantee superseded the Anglo-Polish Treaty, Britain would
no longer have the possibility of reciprocal military aid and two
fronts in the event of war. The Prime Minister replied that the
guarantee that he had in mind was "not incompatible" with
reciprocal treaty arrangements with Poland".[4] The Cabinet
agreed to leave the final draft with the Prime Minister and

[1] Cab. 23. 100, p. 402   [2] *Ibid.*
[3] F.O. 800. 317   [4] Cab. 23. 100, p. 411

Lord Halifax, "to bring into line with any further developments that might take place before Sir Nevile Nenderson left in the course of the afternoon". Henderson saw Hitler on the evening of the 28th and presented the British proposals. There was a chirp from Dahlerus early next morning that "things were satisfactory and that he hoped that nothing foolish would be done by either side to upset them".[1] Of this message Lord Halifax, walking with his wife, apprised Mr and Mrs Chamberlain that morning on a stroll in St James's Park. But by 10 p.m. a summary of Hitler's reply looked "pretty bad" and they we redrafting "rather a sharp" answer in 10 Downing Street till 2.30 a.m. on the 30th.

Hitler had disregarded appeals from President Roosevelt, M. Daladier, Queen Wilhelmina, King Leopold and the Pope, and had demanded that a Polish negotiator with full powers should proceed to Berlin.

On studying the full text after sleep and breakfast, Lord Halifax revised his worst impressions of the previous night, forming the new opinion that Hitler "might be playing for time or for a break[2] in the negotiations". Mr D. alighted in Croydon again, and was taken to Downing Street. There he told Chamberlain of the "remarkable effect" the British proposals had made and that but for them war might have broken out on the 29th. He said also that Goering appeared hopeful that Hitler might offer a plebiscite. His report was given some credence at 10 Downing Street and set the Cabinet ruminating yet another personal message from the Prime Minister to the Reich Chancellor. The German radio had meanwhile been blaring about attacks on persons of German race in Poland, and there was an atmosphere of extreme tension. When the Cabinet fell to discussing the German demand for a Polish negotiator, it was Chamberlain who described this demand as "the most unsatisfactory thing in Hitler's reply . . . This definitely represents part of the old technique. It is essential that we should make it quite clear that we are not going to yield on this point."[3]

Of this day and Mr D.'s efforts at mediation, Lord Halifax

[1] F.O. 800. 317
[2] In the optimistic context of his Diary Notes this should probably be read as "pause".
[3] Cab. 23. 100, p. 425

wrote that "Goering appeared to insist that a Pole should come from Poland at once to get the terms. I told Dahlerus this was clearly unreasonable."[1] Nevertheless, it seemed to them at 10 Downing Street that Hitler might offer a plebiscite on certain conditions and "we told Dahlerus to rub into Goering that the essential thing was that any proposals Hitler may make should not be couched in the form of a *Diktat* to the Poles". In the Cabinet the Prime Minister discussed means of arranging a meeting between Germans and Poles on neutral ground.

By this time, Hitler had either won the extra time that he required for his general mobilisation or had convinced himself that there was no prospect of altering the British attitude by further parley. On August 31st, he ordered the attack on Poland to be made next day. On that same Thursday, Lord Halifax noted Henderson's report of a midnight interview with Ribbentrop, at which the German Foreign Minister gabbled out sixteen German conditions to Poland—"not very encouraging," the Foreign Secretary commented.

Count Ciano telephoned from Rome at 11 a.m., suggesting that "if we could get the Poles to give up Danzig, Mussolini would use his influence with Hitler to make him agree to a conference". The Count rang again at 12.50, while Lord Halifax was at No. 10 Downing Street, and "said that Mussolini wanted to propose a conference for 5th September to revise the Treaty of Versailles". That evening the German radio broadcast that the sixteen point offer to the Poles to negotiate must be considered to have expired. "Alec called for me at Eton Square about 9 a.m., wrote Halifax. "He told me that he had heard at 7 that Danzig had declared its incorporation in the Reich and a little later that the Germans had crossed the Polish frontier."

[1] F.O. 800. 317

CHAPTER XX

The Ultimatum

ON SEPTEMBER 1ST at 11.30 a.m. Mr Chamberlain told the Cabinet that they met "under the gravest possible conditions. The events against which we have fought so long and so earnestly have come upon us. But our consciences are clear and there should be no possible question where our duty lies". The German invasion of Poland had begun. Lord Halifax saw "the principal obstacle to progress (in negotiations) in the difficulty of contact between Germans and Poles". A British telegram to Warsaw on the previous night had urged that the Polish Ambassador in Berlin, M. Joszef Lipski, should call on the German Government. "All this is rather ancient history," continued Lord Halifax. "Since then reports have been received of the invasion of Poland. There are also reports of the bombing of a number of Polish towns." The Polish Ambassador in London had that morning put the view to the Foreign Secretary that this called for implementation of the British guarantee. Lord Halifax had replied to Count Raczynski that "if the facts were as stated, he did not suppose that we should differ". In his Record of Events, Lord Halifax gives a slightly fuller version of his words than appears in the Cabinet Minutes. "I told him that, if the facts were as stated, I had no doubt that we should have no difficulty in deciding that our guarantee must at once come into force."[1]

Mr Joseph Kennedy, the American Ambassador, had telephoned to express "great satisfaction with the British attitude". Sir Percy Loraine reported Count Ciano as saying that "there was at present no very definite information as to hostile action", and Sir Nevile Henderson telegraphed that Hitler was about to deliver a speech in the Reichstag, and after that, "there might be some further peace effort on the part of Hitler".[2]

Lord Chatfield told the Cabinet that after discussion with the Lord Privy Seal and the Chiefs of Staff, the evacuation of the

[1] F.O. 800. 317, September 1st 1939   [2] Cab. 23. 100, p. 446

British civil population from large urban areas had just started: "from that point of view it is obviously desirable that there should be a further delay before we send a communication in the form of an ultimatum". Broadly, the Chiefs of Staff view had been that once an ultimatum had been delivered, the enemy might take immediate action. The Foreign Office view, as put to Sir John Anderson, had been that the period of an ultimatum should not be longer than six hours. In 1914 the period had been four hours. On the important question of when to deliver it, "the general view of the Chiefs of Staff was that if we reached the conclusion that circumstances had arisen in which we were bound to implement our guarantee, the right course would be to dispatch a communication in the nature of an ultimatum to Germany without delay".

Once more that morning the activities of Mr Dahlerus were described in Cabinet discussion. He had telephoned from Berlin Sir Alexander Cadogan that "the Poles had blown up a bridge . . . and this had started the fighting. . . . Herr Hitler did not want to start a world war and wanted direct negotiations with Great Britain." The Cabinet agreed that the reply to Mr D "should be stiff".

As to the immediate prospects, there had been a Chiefs of Staff paper of July 28th which concluded that "if Germany holds in the West and attacks in the East, there is little that we can do at sea or on land to relieve the pressure on Poland, and therefore the problem resolves itself into what we can do in the air". In the air, however, the Cabinet itself had decided views as to what could or could not be done, and they were haunted by the vulnerable condition of London.

On August 22nd "most stringent instructions"[1] had been issued to British military commanders that "only purely military objectives in the narrowest sense of the word were to be bombarded". The permissible targets specified were naval forces at sea, army units, air units, troop transports, military stores, but not military factories, field dumps and troops on the move, though not small detachments in towns, if there were an unjustifiable risk to the civil population. Ships alongside in port were to be spared in the same circumstances. This caution

[1] These are contained in C.O.S. Paper 961 (39), "Bombardment Policy at the Outset of War".

was necessary to the strategy of a nation whose air defences were still far from sufficient.

If Germany attacked "purely military objectives", the Chiefs of Staff in a paper of August 31st had recommended reprisals limited to air attacks on Wilhelmshaven naval base and on German warships at sea, while leaflets should be dropped on Germany at night. It was clear that such a cautious strategy would extend itself to the sort of ultimatum to be delivered to Germany, but the time factor did constitute a matter of international propriety. The Anglo-Polish Treaty pledged Britain "at once to lend the Polish Government all the support in their power".

The Cabinet had thus on September 1st to consider the remarks of Sir John Anderson that some delay would be advantageous to evacuation of the civil population, but presumably only if there were to be immediate *Luftwaffe* attacks in the West. Mr Hore-Belisha, Sir Kingsley Wood and Lord Stanhope put no such request for delay on behalf of the three Services. There was some discussion of a time limit when Lord Halifax read out a draft of the British ultimatum. Mr Chamberlain pointed out that "on receipt of this telegram, the Germans might start an attack on our merchant shipping".[1] The shipping magnate, Viscount Runciman, who had been dropped from the Cabinet in May 1937 and had played the somewhat ludicrous role of mediator over Czechoslovakia, had surprisingly returned to the Cabinet after the Munich Agreement, occupying the high office of Lord President of the Council. Neither he nor the President of the Board of Trade had anything to say to this comment about shipping, but it was decided to leave to the Prime Minister and Lord Halifax the form of an ultimatum. It was still unclear when the Cabinet rose whether, if Henderson received an unsatisfactory reply, the Ambassador was to ask for his passport of departure. On this important point "the Prime Minister and the Foreign Secretary had been authorised to take such action as they thought fit".[2] The Prime Minister proposed and the Cabinet agreed that the communication as amended should be sent off as soon as an agreement had been reached with the French" (whose views were that it should not be in the form of an ultimatum).

[1] Cab. 23. 100, p. 449   [2] Cab. 23. 100

The instructions sent to Sir Nevile Henderson contained the text of a Note accusing Germany of an attack on Poland, but concluding in imprecise terms that "I am accordingly to inform Your Excellency that unless the German Government has suspended all aggressive action against Poland and are prepared promptly to withdraw their forces from Polish territory, His Majesty's Government in the United Kingdom will without hesitation fulfil their obligations to Poland."[1]

To the German eye, practised in detecting the inner meaning of British notes, the perfect tense would be no substitute for a time limit. Moreover, no close reading was necessary to Herr von Ribbentrop; for Lord Halifax in noting that "Henderson called on Ribbentrop in the evening to present him with a warning", adds "we authorised Henderson to say (it) was a warning and not an ultimatum. . . . He did not in fact say this to the German Government, but I said it to Ciano on the following day."[2] Ciano did not miss the opportunity to get the Italian Ambassador in Berlin to confirm with Henderson that the Note delivered to Ribbentrop "did not have the character of an ultimatum". The Italian then announced that fact.

Lord Halifax noted on September 2nd that there was "no answer from Berlin. . . . We drafted a statement for Parliament. . . . The great difficulty was the French, who did not want to present any ultimatum till noon tomorrow (September 3rd) with a 48-hour time limit."[3]

Mr Chamberlain had concluded at the Cabinet of September 1st, after a review of defence and fiscal arrangements for war, with the observation that "he felt sure that it was in the minds of his colleagues that if war came, it would be necessary to make some changes in Cabinet arrangements. . . . He had no doubt that the right course was to set up a War Cabinet at once on the model of that established in the last war, and this was the course that he intended to follow. . . . It might be

[1] F.O. 311, September 1st 1939   [2] F.O. 800. 317 Record of Events
[3] *Ibid.*, Col. General Halder, Chief of German Army General Staff, wrote in his Notebook on this date what may have been an additional consideration: "English want to have their entire merchant fleet in safe ports by September 3." Documents on German Foreign Policy, Series D, Vol. VIII, p. 571.

necessary to make certain other alterations in the Cabinet. Might he assume that his colleagues were prepared to place their resignations collectively in his hands?" His colleagues, the minutes state, "willingly agreed". Such had been the procedure upon the retirement of Mr Baldwin and the formation of the Chamberlain Cabinet, but although he had seen Mr Churchill that morning about entering the Government, there was this time no smooth transition.

It was the same Cabinet that met again on September 2nd in the afternoon, and it was, Lord Halifax noted, "in an extremely difficult mood".[1] Ministers were puzzled that the communication sent on the previous day by Chamberlain and Halifax had met with no response from Berlin. Lord Halifax explained that the Note had not been sent in ultimative form, so that further consultation between London and Paris could take place after a German reply had been received. Messages from Italy about mediation had also made it necessary, he said, to postpone statements in Parliament on the British attitude.

Of this day's events he noted that "Ciano rang me up again at the Office to tell me that Mussolini wished to propose a Five Power Conference, Germany, France, Russia, Italy and ourselves. . . . I never remember spending such a miserable afternoon and evening . . . telephoning to Bonnet and Ciano that we could not accept the conference idea unless German troops were withdrawn. Ciano said it was quite useless to press that." "The Cabinet met at 4.30 or 5,[2] and were pretty unanimous in their feeling that in the statement, for which both Houses of Parliament were, while the Cabinet was sitting, anxiously waiting, some pretty short time limit should be announced."

"We should be prepared to allow the Germans till 12 noon tomorrow (September 3rd) for consideration," Lord Halifax proposed to the Cabinet. He also spoke of a conference to settle the dispute, "if this course was desired by the two countries" (Poland and Germany). Mr Chamberlain said that he had described the British Note of September 1st to Germany as "a last warning". Sir Samuel Hoare complained that he thought "this communication had been generally regarded as

[1] F.O. 800. 317   [2] The Cabinet Minutes record 4.15 p.m.

in the nature of an ultimatum. There would be tremendous risks in accepting any delay." The Foreign Secretary mentioned French wishes for 48 hours respite. The Services Ministers then spoke in turn. Lord Stanhope began that the Naval Staff did not attach much importance to "catching the liner *Bremen* at sea", but were opposed to any appreciable delay and wished to carry out an early reconnaissance of the German naval forces. Mr Hore-Belisha stated a strong objection to delay and suggested that the Italians might be acting in collusion with the Germans. Midnight on September 2nd to 3rd was proposed by several Ministers as the latest time to be allowed to Hitler for consideration.

At this heated point Mr Chamberlain read out a message to him from the Polish Government:

> Request immediate fulfilment of British obligations. . . . Battle today over the whole of the front has increased and has acquired very serious character. Our troops are opposing strong resistance. The whole of German Air Force is engaged against Poland. Villages and factories bombarded. The engagement of German aircraft by allied forces of greatest urgency.

There was by then a consensus of the Cabinet for an ultimatum by midnight, but the Prime Minister in his summing up appeared still to envisage that there might be a way out. For he said that it was agreed that "there could be no negotiation without German troop withdrawals first". He concluded that the Cabinet agreed "that it was undesirable to allow Germany any longer than until midnight to make up her mind. . . . A communication in this sense clearly constituted an ultimatum. . . . At the same time, it was evident that the precise terms of the communication to Germany and the statement in Parliament that afternoon would have to be made in consultation with the French."

The tenacious old man was this time overstretching the patience of the waiting public and of Parliament. Winston Churchill in two letters to him of September 2nd reminded him that "the Poles have now been under heavy attack for thirty hours . . . I trust you will be able to announce our Joint Declaration of War at latest when Parliament meets this afternoon." In the second letter he wrote "I really do not know what has happened during the course of this agitated day; though it seems to me that entirely different ideas have ruled from those which you expressed to me when you said (on September 1st) 'the die was cast'." Even when writing his War Memoirs Sir Winston Churchill remained under the misapprehension that the Note of September 1st had been "a British ultimatum" and spoke of two British ultimatums.[1]

"As soon as the Cabinet was over, we got on again to the French," wrote Lord Halifax, "and Daladier eventually agreed upon a statement being made in both Houses at 7.30, in which we should restate our position, but in deference to French no time limit."[2]

This arrangement was very nearly the undoing of Chamberlain. For his statement to the House of Commons at 7.30 p.m. fell far short of the expectations of that tense assembly. It began by stating that there had been no reply to the warning message delivered by Sir Nevile Henderson, but ascribed this delay possibly to an Italian proposal for a Five Power Conference being considered in Berlin. It rejected the idea of a conference while Poland was being invaded and Danzig subjected to "a unilateral settlement by force". The statement continued that "His Majesty's Government will be bound to take action, as stated yesterday, unless the German forces are withdrawn from Polish territory", and mentioned that a time limit was under discussion with France. In paragraph 4, however, the Prime Minister misjudged his footwork. "If the German Government should agree to withdraw their forces, then His Majesty's Government would be willing to regard the position as being the same as it was before the German forces crossed the Polish frontier, that is to say, the way would be open to discussion between the German and Polish Governments of the matters at issue between them, on the understanding that the settlement arrived at was one that safeguarded the vital interests of Poland and was secured by an international guarantee."[3]

When the Prime Minister had finished this statement there was a short but furious debate, after which he retired to his

[1] Churchill, *The Gathering Storm*   [2] F.O. 800. 317
[3] Documents on British Foreign Policy, Third Series, Vol. VII, p. 521

room in the House of Commons to consider his position. "The general feeling was that the French were trying to run out of their engagement to Poland and were taking us with them," wrote Halifax. "I could not acquit some members of the Cabinet of having fed the flames of suspicion." His own statement in the House of Lords had not gone badly, but as he was changing for dinner, the Foreign Secretary was called away from Eaton Square to Downing Street by the Prime Minister, telling him that "the statement went very badly in the House of Commons, people misinterpreting the inability to give a time limit to be the result of half-heartedness and hesitation on our part.". . . "There had been a very unpleasant scene in which much feeling had been shown. I never heard the Prime Minister so disturbed. He told me the statement infuriated the House. . . . He did not believe, unless we clear the situation, that the Government would be able to maintain itself when it met Parliament next day." Sir Alexander Cadogan and Sir Horace Wilson were drawn in. On the telephone to Paris, Halifax exhorted the French to agree to a time limit expiring at 11 a.m. on the 3rd. "The French said they must act rather later."[1] The French General Staff sought in fact to make a condition that R.A.F. Bomber Forces would at once be available to them to make good their own deficiency in that arm, as the price of an early declaration of war.

The Chamberlain Cabinet, as distinct from the first War Cabinet, met for the last time at 11.30 p.m. on September 2nd, when the Prime Minister reported an earlier meeting of Ministers in his room in Parliament to consider their difficult position in the Commons. "He recognised the strength of feeling, he said, even among the most loyal supporters of the Government. He had taken immediate action. He had himself spoken to M. Daladier on the telephone and explained that there had been a painful scene in the House of Commons and that we could not hold the position on an ultimatum expiring at 8 p.m. or 9 p.m. on the Sunday. After some argument with the French, the Chiefs of Staff had been asked for their advice and he now sought that of the Cabinet. Sir John Simon thought it essential that when the Prime Minister met the House of Commons at noon on Sunday September 3rd, he should be

[1] F.O. 800. 317

able to state the result of the delivery of the ultimatum. He suggested therefore that the ultimatum should expire at 11 a.m., since it was essential that the Prime Minister should be able to show that action had been taken."

Upon this course the Cabinet expressed general agreement. It was finally decided, after several alternative hours had been discussed, to instruct Sir Nevile Henderson to present the British ultimatum at 9 a.m. on the 3rd September, to expire at 11 a.m. Unless it was accepted, a state of war would exist from that hour. Next morning Herr von Ribbentrop refused to receive the ultimatum and Sir Nevile was obliged to hand it to Paul Schmidt, the German Foreign Ministry interpreter. There was little doubt from the dismay shown in Hitler's entourage that the determination of the British to honour their obligation was not fully expected. The courteous and reasoned style of such Memoranda as that presented by Sir Nevile on August 28th, which had left openings to Germany for negotiation, had been misread.[1] There was an anticlimax on the morning of September 3rd for Lord Halifax, who went to the Foreign Office, but found "nothing to do", except to tell the persistent Mr Dahlerus, who telephoned from Berlin, that "I did not see that there was any good in Goering coming here".

Mr Chamberlain broadcast to the nation at 11.15 a.m., announcing that Great Britain was already at war. In a speech followed by the wailing of sirens in a test alert, the Prime Minister said: "You can imagine what a bitter blow it is for me that all my long struggle to win peace has failed. . . . Yet I cannot believe that there is anything more or anything different that I could have done and that would have been more successful. Up to the very last it would have been quite possible to have arranged a peaceful and honourable settlement between Germany and Poland. . . . But Hitler would not have it. He had evidently made up his mind to attack

---

[1] General Halder noted thus the German reaction to this British document: "Chamb's letter conciliatory. Endeavour to find a *modus vivendi*. (Opinion in Cabinet divided.) Dignified tone. It is clear that (they) cannot refrain from rendering assistance. Concept of vital interests and integrity elastic. England to participate in definition. Face must be saved. England gives assurance that Poland will come to conference. . . . General impression, England 'soft' on the issue of a major war." Documents on German Foreign Policy, Series D, Vol. VII, p. 568.

Poland whatever happened. Although now he says he put forward reasonable proposals which were rejected by the Poles, that is not a true statement. The proposals were never shown to the Poles nor to us. . . ."

"We have a clear conscience", said Mr Chamberlain and he exhorted all to do their duty, fighting against brute force and bad faith. . . . "I am certain the right will prevail." In the House of Commons, the scene of recent criticism, he struck a note of pathos that would ordinarily have accorded with resignation from office—"Everything that I have worked for, everything that I had hoped for, everything that I have believed in during my public life, has crashed in ruins. . . ." Yet he hoped "to live to see the day when Hitlerism has been destroyed". It was not his intention to resign.

The War Cabinet met for the first time in the fifth hour of war. They were now comparatively few in the Cabinet Room. Chamberlain had at last accepted his powerful rival and critic in the Conservative Party, Mr Winston Churchill, to be First Lord of the Admiralty. The Prime Minister had retained Sir John Simon in the Treasury, with a seat in the War Cabinet, and had made Sir Samuel Hoare Lord Privy Seal for the purpose of keeping him there too, while Sir John Anderson became Home Secretary and would attend only as required. Sir Kingsley Wood and Mr Hore-Belisha were members, and Lord Chatfield as Minister for Co-ordination of Defence. Lord Hankey, their former Secretary, was brought back in managing capacity as Minister Without Portfolio. At their first session the War Cabinet decided on daily meetings at 11.30 a.m., with other Ministers, the Chiefs of Staff and Officials attending, according to the matters under discussion.[1] In this way Mr Chamberlain remained until May 10th 1940 at the Head of Government, his ability for debate and chairmanship still evident, until defeat in Norway and the impact of the massive German offensive in Western Europe brought about demands for a Coalition, loss of confidence in Chamberlain, and his enforced resignation.

The German Documents show that Hitler and Ribbentrop were angered at a sharp rebuff from Chamberlain to German peace overtures in October 1939. He had been stiff in his attitude after September 3rd, but one ingredient of war he

[1] Cab. 65. 1, p. 16

seemed unable to supply. A new fire is evident in a letter which Mr Churchill, fresh in the Cabinet, wrote to Lord Halifax on September 10th while Sir Percy Loraine was still conveying peace ideas from Ciano.

> My dear Edward,
> From his latest telegram, Loraine does not seem to understand our resolve. Surely he could be rallied to a more robust mood. It would make no difference to our action if Poland were forced into a defeated peace. Surely he ought, as the occasion arises, to make it clear that we intend to see the war through to a victorious end, whatever happens to Poland.[1]

Neville Chamberlain received late in September 1939 a letter from President Roosevelt, written on the day that Britain declared war and sent by Atlantic Convoy.

> My dear Mr Chamberlain,
> I need not tell you that you have been much in my thoughts in these difficult days. I hope and believe that we shall repeal the (Arms) Embargo within the next month.

The Prime Minister replied to the President that:

> I retain full confidence that we shall come out successfully in the end. My own belief is that we shall win not by a complete and spectacular military victory . . . but by convincing the Germans that they cannot win. Once they have arrived at that conclusion, I do not believe that they can stand our relentless pressures.

This optimism that the war could somehow be won without a major decision in the field is evident in letters to his family and in speeches, though such illusions no longer find place in the terse Minutes of the War Cabinet. "I have a hunch that the war will be over by the spring", he wrote in November 1939 to his sister Ida in the United States. . . . "It won't be by defeat in the field, but by German realisation that they can't win and that it isn't worth their while to go on getting thinner and poorer." These hopes may have been nourished by certain false moves in the Intelligence field, such as that which ended

[1] F.O. 800

about this time in the Venloo Incident, in November 1939 when agents of Himmler were discovered to have been masquerading as German Opposition men seeking contact with Britain. However that may be, this optimism was still distressingly apparent on April 5th 1940, when shortly before the German invasion of Norway Mr Chamberlain told the Conservative Central Council in a speech that "Hitler has missed the 'bus". Such lapses of language and thinking contrast with the documents of the War Cabinet, in which pessimism and caution have their place. One costly R.A.F. raid on Wilhelmshaven sufficed to show that British air strength could not yet play a decisive role in Europe and that Britain, in view of her retarded aircraft production and personnel training programmes in 1937 and 1938, would, as Lord Swinton had in 1938 forecast, require to be at war for six months before she could exert her air power at all.

The pattern of the war, at any rate as much of it as Mr Chamberlain was destined to see as Prime Minister, was laid out in a meeting of the War Cabinet on September 14th, which communicated its views and policy through the Marquis of Lothian, British Ambassador in Washington, to President Roosevelt in a Most Secret telegram.[1]

> The course of the war now in progress was, of course, carefully considered by the Staffs before the war, and in fact the present military situation was foretold with considerable accuracy. Two important conclusions were arrived at.
>
> The time factor will work in favour of the Allies and against Germany; consequently Anglo-French strategy should be adapted to a long war, beginning with a phase of defensive strategy, while building up resources and imposing the greatest measure of economic pressure.
>
> The fate of Poland will depend on the ultimate outcome of the war; i.e. on our ability to defeat Germany, and not on our ability to relieve pressure on Poland at the outset. It was laid down that this should be the overriding consideration which should determine our course of action.
>
> On the 22nd August, before the receipt of President Roosevelt's message, we had issued the most stringent instructions to our Commanders that only purely military objectives in the narrowest

[1] F.O. No. 538, September 16th 1939

sense of the word were to be bombarded from the air or from the sea. It was, of course, understood that in the event of the enemy not observing any of the restrictions which the Governments of the United Kingdom and France had thus imposed on the operations of their armed forces, these Governments reserved the right to take all such action as they might consider appropriate.[1]

After a week of war the War Cabinet reviewed the position with a view to deciding whether these instructions should be relaxed or adhered to. The relevant factors were as follows:

Up to the 12th September we had no reliable proof that the Germans had, in fact, departed from their understanding to restrict air action to military objectives.

As long as we adhered to the bombing instructions there was no way in which we could really effectively damage Germany. It is obviously important that our limited forces should not be frittered away on uneconomical and ineffective tasks.

The only effective alternative would be to adopt plans under which it would be necessary to attack a range of objectives which, while unquestionably legitimate, would be such as to involve loss of civilian life.

The advisability of adopting this course was conditioned by the following factors:

Would it, in fact, relieve pressure on Poland?

In the opinion of the War Cabinet it would not.

Its repercussions in France.

For the past week the French have been engaged in the concentration and mobilisation of their Reserve Army which is, in fact, not yet complete. General Gamelin has consistently restrained us for obvious reasons from taking any action which might bring retaliation upon his mobilisation centres and his communications to the frontier.

An extension of land operations on the Western Front is probable subsequent to the French concentration, and it is considered desirable not to do anything that would prejudice the capacity of our Air Force to exploit this opportunity for combined allied air operations that might well relieve pressure on Poland.

As far as this country is concerned, contrary to expectation, no air attack has yet taken place. This gives us most valuable breathing space to complete our preparations. The blockade has started,

[1] This was restated on September 3rd in an Anglo-French declaration which made plain that Allied action at sea and in the air would be confined to military targets.

I

the Germans are already expending considerable effort, and the time factor has started to come into play. Therefore some further extension of the interval before we embark on intensive air operations is in our interest.

In particular, every week is of value to us in increasing our reserves in aircraft, anti-aircraft guns, etc., and generally improving the security of the base from which our offensive operations will ultimately be launched.

A delay in the inception of the air war is all to the advantage of the defence of this country and of our sea-borne trade.

There are, of course, substantial arguments in favour of an early initiation of air operations on an intensive scale.

On balance, however, it was considered unlikely that the early initiation of intensive air action would materially improve our chances of winning a short war, while the possession of an Air Striking Force relatively intact and with increased reserves will go far to ensure that the Germans for their part cannot win it. . . . On purely military grounds it was concluded that we should therefore adhere for the present to our existing policy.

The choice, if indeed a choice existed in the conditions of unpreparedness accepted in the past three years of the Chamberlain Cabinet, was calculated and correct, though it implied a belief that Germany could be contained in the West.[1] The War Cabinet of September 14th fixed a broad strategy for the years to come, which would be operated despite setbacks and mistakes, one of which mistakes was the assumption in the mind of Chamberlain that the Germans would give up, because they would see that they could not win. President Roosevelt in a long interview with Lord Lothian on September 17th "expressed entire satisfaction with British air policy". He forebore to point out, and the British forebore to inquire of him concerning, the unrestricted German bombing of Polish towns, lest a dangerous duty be argued under the Anglo-Polish guarantee to retaliate upon strongly guarded German targets. "It seems pretty clear from the War Cabinet Minutes," commented Sir Alexander Cadogan on September 21st, when public indignation in Britain was growing at the lack of support for Poland and the reports of unrestricted German bombing, "that the

[1] Upon this, as Chamberlain admitted to Sir Samuel Hoare, his own latter optimism had been built.

message that it was decided not to transmit to the President was one asking him to investigate German air action in Poland." For the telegram of September 16th had already tacitly admitted knowledge of excesses, while ruling out reprisals for reasons of long-term strategy.

Over by the spring! It was the 'phoney' war that was over by the spring, to be followed by the Blitz war, for which Chamberlain liked to believe the moment might already have passed. Denmark was overrun early in April 1940 and then Norway, despite the Royal Navy and British and French landing parties. On May 7th and 8th, with evacuation of the British forces from Norway proceeding, Mr Chamberlain conceded to an angry House of Commons a debate on the war situation, a debate in which the fate overtook him that he had nearly suffered on September 2nd 1939.

Mr Leo Amery in the course of debate quoted at him the words of Cromwell to the Long Parliament: "You have sat here too long for any good you have been doing. . . . In the name of God, go!" Lloyd George, himself not blameless of credulity towards Hitler, demanded that Chamberlain relinquish the seals of office. Although Chamberlain survived a vote of censure, he had lost face and was so shaken that he spoke afterwards to Churchill of a National Government, in which he might relinquish the leadership. On May 10th the German Blitz broke upon Belgium and Holland. This news at first prompted Chamberlain to consider remaining at his post, as he confided to Sir Kingsley Wood; but Sir Kingsley dissuaded him from the idea. On that day Chamberlain and his Cabinet resigned and the same night Winston Churchill became Prime Minister.

CHAPTER XXI

Conclusions

IT IS FITTING to break with the main stream of events at this stage and to review what the released papers reveal about the Chamberlain Cabinet. They throw more light both on the character of Chamberlain, a powerful Prime Minister, and on the working of the Cabinet system. No assessment of the personality of Chamberlain can be complete without recourse to the Birmingham University collection of his family papers, which I have studied through the published extracts only,[1] but his essential qualities, traits and failings are clearly brought out in the Cabinet papers.

His style of leadership and his method of seeing and working are certainly further illuminated. At times when I have compared the Cabinet record with Professor Keith Feiling's standard biography of Neville Chamberlain, I have found myself at variance with the Academy style portraiture of his subject.

But I do not discover a significant difference between the public and the private Chamberlain; he was not a sort of Jekyll in Parliament and Hyde in 10 Downing Street, at least not in the Cabinet Room. His optimism and his caution were fairly evenly spread in both places. There is rather more frequent optimism after Munich in his Cabinet assessments and in private than he ventured in public, and though never so absolute as his 'peace in our time' declaration, frequent enough to dispose of the idea propagated since in some Conservative Party circles that the sole aim of his diplomacy was to win time for rearmament. The Cabinet papers do not reveal a superior logic or what were his most confidential thoughts, though they do show how he laid bare his main argument and how he managed his team. He appears never to have written for the Cabinet a complete account of the considerations that decided him in the period of the Berchtesgaden–Munich talks. His

---

[1] Feiling, Iain MacLeod, Templewood. It should be noted that not all the Neville Chamberlain papers have yet been deposited with the main collection in the care of the Library of Birmingham University.

ascendancy over his colleagues seems to have made any such procedure superfluous.

As to his style of leadership, the Cabinet narrative confirms that he was unfortunate in his dealings with younger men. He parted company in a cold and deliberate fashion with Eden, Duff Cooper and Hore-Belisha, as well as with the older Swinton. Of Eden he wrote that "I have gradually arrived at the conclusion that at bottom Anthony did not want to talk with Hitler or Mussolini, and as I did, he was right to go."[1] Chamberlain, unlike Sulla with Pompeius Sextus, did not gladly allow a young man his triumph. When it came to conscription, he snatched the subject away from Hore-Belisha and introduced it to the Cabinet himself. When it came to mobilising the Fleet after the continuous entreaties of Duff Cooper in September 1938, it was Chamberlain himself who gave the instructions to the First Sea Lord, leaving the First Lord of the Admiralty to be informed subsequently. Enough has been quoted of the repeated demands of Lord Swinton for accelerated and expanded air strength to make it seem ungrateful to have dismissed him at the time of criticism in Parliament. Others did not fare well for similar reasons that fall into this pattern. Earl Winterton, we have seen, was sharp about an increase of air strength after the Munich crisis and compared the attack on Czechoslovakia in 1938 in its effect on Britain with an attack on the Isle of Wight. Earl De La Warr, the first, Chamberlain noted in his tablets, actually to state his preference for war to appeasement in September 1938, was shifted from the high post of Lord Privy Seal to the humble Ministry of Education. When his mind was made up on policy, and that already appears to have been the case early in 1937, Chamberlain could be as hard in pursuit of his aims as any dictator.

The Cabinet composition in May 1937 contained a wider range of minds than the Cabinet that faced the war crisis of 1939. After the Munich Agreement, he hailed back Runciman, brought in Anderson, degraded De La Warr and let Duff Cooper resign. In his January 1939 reshuffle, he brought in Chatfield, but kept Inskip and shelved Winterton. Of the twenty-three Ministers whose opinions and responsibility were necessary to the decisions on war and peace in August 1939,

[1] Templewood, *Nine Troubled Years*

eighteen Ministers were so like-minded with the Prime Minister
as to preclude a real sifting of policy. Only MacDonald, Elliott,
Oliver Stanley, Hore-Belisha provided a little leaven to the
debate. This had become a Cabinet of nonentities, presided
by one magisterial personality.

In this personality an unsuspected trait emerges which is
compatible with the tendency in the Prime Minister to arrogate
all action to himself, a sudden appetite for popularity. "I did
not go there to get popularity," he explained about Munich
in his Birmingham speech of March 17th 1939, a remark that is
curious since nobody had accused him of such a motive, but it
betrayed an underlying foible. He had once lectured Hore-
Belisha against that vice and on his return from Munich had
remarked to Halifax that "all this (the public excitement) will
be over in three months". However, the Cabinet records
show that he digressed upon the applause of the German
public and upon the impression that he had himself made upon
Hitler. He is conscious of the temptation "to sit back and bask
in this popularity while it lasted", but wrote on October 16th
that he was "differently constituted" and already a little
impatient with it".[1] Nevertheless, on November 6th 1938,
he felt it "the right thing for many reasons" to go to Paris on
November 23rd, "to give French people an opportunity of
pouring out their pent-up feelings of gratitude and affection, to
strengthen Daladier". . . . This vein is not exhausted in January
1939, when the Prime Minister described Mussolini as showing
"not the slightest sign of jealousy at the great reception given
to the Foreign Secretary and the Prime Minister". Considering
the strain under which he had put himself—he confessed to
being very close to a nervous breakdown on October 2nd
1938, and to have "lost all sense of time and recollection of
days"[2]—the need for popular reassurance is comprehensible.

He was at the time of Munich on the threshold of seventy, the
period of life in which King Lear was ready to give much away
in exchange for a show of affection. The strain is evident, not
only in his language, but in that of Halifax and Henderson,
the principal exponents of his policy and men who resembled
him in physique and intellect. There is a tendency to lapse

[1] Feiling, *The Life of Neville Chamberlain*
[2] Letter to Ida Chamberlain, October 4th 1938

from official language into the colloquial—Mussolini becomes
Musso in correspondence, and when the mind becomes
untaut in his family letters, the superficial view prevails. In
Cabinet, too, the hedged and provisoed talk of men dealing
with the unknown must also have lapsed sometimes into what
may be termed Cabinet colloquial, and must have required
tidying action by the secretaries.

Our sense of futility in re-reading some of the Cabinet
record does not perhaps take into account that this was at best
a policy being improvised after the initiative had passed to
Germany. Sir Samuel Hoare described it as "the double line",[1]
borrowing the phrase from Chamberlain. "The double policy
of peace and rearmament", he wrote, "needed not only very
skilful handling, but also a very subtle presentation. In a sense
the two aims were contradictory, difficult and sometimes almost
impossible to reconcile . . . Chamberlain certainly possessed
sufficient quickness of hand. If his touch lacked anything, it was
the sensitive feeling that gave the exact measure of strength to
each of his efforts." Sir Samuel refreshed his memory from the
Cabinet papers before writing his own autobiography, but
conforming to the convention of Cabinet responsibility he did
not bring out some of his own arguments in Committee
against Chamberlain on foreign policy.

It is in some respects not agreeable but necessary to exhume
the character of a dominating personality in a recent historical
period. As I have said, Chamberlain was rising seventy when
these strains came upon him. He was known to all his colleagues
as a reserved man and silence may increase prestige, but when
his reserve was discarded, as in his family letters, we discover
a certain simplicity of thinking, naïve at times, as if he had
discovered a remedy for international difficulties in a personal
diplomacy of his own, difficulties that he thought capable of
definition in few words. His was very much the English approach
to foreign politics, one of sustained astonishment that some
formula could not be found to suit all parties, as if some deep-
rooted dispute had never existed.

His method of working over a subject consisted of revolving
it in his own mind, deciding on the direction in which he was
going, fortifying his opinion with those of chosen associates

[1] Templewood, *Nine Troubled Years*

and then proceeding to demolish any opposition that these views might encounter along the way. His half-brother, Austen, had detected something that could be described as a tone deafness in foreign affairs and told him over the dinner table in the presence of Eden that "of course, Neville, you know nothing about foreign affairs". In fact Chamberlain had gathered enough about foreign affairs to have acted well on expert advice, but advice was what on essentials of policy he was unwilling to take, except from like-minded people to himself. The attendance sheets on Policy Committee records show how seldom he availed himself of the presence of his Chief Diplomatic Adviser, Sir Robert Vansittart.[1] As to Austen's stricture, Neville had not the classic cast of mind of Curzon or Eden in statecraft and brought an eager and homely approach to problems. "His decision once reached was hard to shake",[2] and therefore it would have been important that it should be well informed. It was formative of his own political background that he accepted in March 1930 the Chairmanship of the Conservative Research Department—"through my new department I shall have my fingers on the springs of policy . . . we shall be at once an information bureau and a long range research body". This close connection never ceased, and we find the Research Department acting for him when Prime Minister as a Foreign Intelligence Bureau, with Sir Joseph Ball at its head assisting his personal policy moves with Signor Dino Grandi, the Italian Ambassador. We find him writing of affairs of State through the open post to Ivy Chamberlain in Rome, and fastening upon the Swedish intermediary, Birger Dahlerus. Such intermediaries sometimes bewildered or reduced the Foreign Office to momentary impotence, filtered as they often were through Sir Horace Wilson in 10 Downing Street. Sir Horace as Chief Industrial Adviser had no real status or experience in foreign politics and the consequence of his presence was, if

[1] Chamberlain was readily suspicious of attempts to undermine his policy and his doubts upon Vansittart were sufficient for him to have initiated some surveillance of his social contacts, discovering thus that he was in touch with Winston Churchill. An awkwardness between the Prime Minister and his Chief Diplomatic Adviser, amounting to a personal dislike, seems to have inhibited Chamberlain from a frank discussion of this relationship, the result being a lack of confidence and a gap in the system of advice.

[2] Feiling, *The Life of Neville Chamberlain*

anything, to emphasise the preconceptions of his Master. Friends like Lord Brocket, a Conservative Party Peer with friends in the Nazi Party, running mesasages to and fro; other "friends of mine" are mentioned as coming back from Czechoslovakia early in 1938 with reports that all Sudeten Germans wanted territorial union with the Reich; bankers and business men with an eye open to politics as they travelled—all these offered opinions that were not at variance with his own, and were apt to oversimplify the issues.

Iain MacLeod in his *Neville Chamberlain* defends Sir Joseph Ball of reproaches about underhand dealings with the Italian Embassy at the time of Eden's resignation, asserting that "it was not true that Chamberlain interfered more with Foreign Office business than is natural for a Prime Minister". This misses the point that Chamberlain, by reason of his own very marked preferences in foreign policy and his impatience with the Foreign Office, was in particular need of responsible orthodox advice to balance his own impulses. The role of Sir Joseph Ball, a former Special Branch officer turned Party politician in the back room, is anyway likely to remain obscure, as after much hesitation on the question of writing memoirs, Sir Joseph burned a large part of his private papers shortly before his death.

It appears to me a futile exercise to seek to except Neville Chamberlain from what were plainly his own qualities and characteristic methods. He was not what MacLeod has sought to make him out, though a formidable and respectable party leader. Although Sir Samuel Hoare seeks also to deny these attributes, Chamberlain was a shy autocrat and made his own policy in silence before he made it Cabinet policy. If appeasement began as a common Cabinet policy, it was he who gave it such an emphasis as to add a pejorative sense to the word. I can, moreover, find no example in two and a half years of Cabinet meetings in which the discussions in Cabinet altered his mind on a subject, though he was known to alter it between Cabinets. In forming our view of him, we must read his own evidence about the decision to go to Berchtesgaden when confronted with intelligence reports from Germany—"on Tuesday night I saw that the moment had come and must be taken if I was not to be too late. So I sent the fateful telegram and told the Cabinet next morning what I had done."[1] There has been absolutely no evidence since that such haste was necessary or indeed that he was so advised at the time. Subsequent events illustrated the wisdom of not evading Cabinet responsibility.

Had Chamberlain been successful, had he not been obliged to resign in May 1940 for lack of parliamentary confidence at the time when his country had been put in the very position that his policy had sought to avoid, he would have deserved a place in history as a great Prime Minister. He would have been forgiven for relying at a critical moment on his own vision and his own powers of decision. As it was, we must accept that his vision may have been distorted in a field where every error is grave and that his timing was probably wrong. To embrace a Cabinet policy of no risks of war in 1938 may have been necessary, but to convert that into a policy of no risks of risks was to carry it beyond strict necessity.

This criticism may be illustrated by the remarks of Chamberlain to Daladier on April 29th 1938, when a policy of declared Anglo-French resistance to Germany over Czechoslovakia was put forward as practicable: "even if the chances against war after such a declaration might be 100–1, as long as that one chance existed they must consider carefully what their attitude must be". Certainty of victory was the only condition on which he would have consented to move. However, it must be said that this was not his view alone, and that the case against any new commitment to France was strongly put in the Cabinet of April 27th by Simon and Kingsley Wood.

The three broad issues upon which the Chamberlain Cabinet stands at the bar of history are that with a large Parliamentary majority it failed to rearm in time; that it surrendered over Czechoslovakia in 1938, when it need not so have done; and that it failed in 1939 to achieve an alliance with Russia, thus entering war with less effective allies than could have been found in 1938.

As to the first of these charges, we have seen how often since May 1937 the Treasury was to remind the Cabinet that the first aim must be to conserve the economic strength of Britain.

---

[1] Letter to Ida Chamberlain, September 19th 1938, Feiling, *The Life of Neville Chamberlain*

We have seen the Inskip Memorandum proposing to limit rearmament to a fixed level of resources. We must also recall that in the Baldwin Cabinet, Mr Chamberlain was Chancellor of the Exchequer, which associates him for a long period with national unpreparedness. In October 1940 three weeks before dying, he wrote of his stewardship to Baldwin that "I also introduced Conscription, but I had to fight for every one of these things. . . . in Sept. '38 we had only 60 fire pumps in London. . . . Some day these things will be known."[1] He was forgetful of his own resistance to conscription, forgetful of the cry from the Director-General of Munitions in January 1937 for decisions on military equipment. In his severe torment, he cannot be blamed for fortifying his conscience, but history has also to be served. They were the same minds in Cabinet which on March 14th 1938 decided against Scheme K for the R.A.F. and decided on March 22nd that policy must be one of no risks of war because of military unpreparedness. "He thought armaments were a wasteful form of expenditure", was one explanation by Sir Horace Wilson.[2] A key to the thinking of the Prime Minister in 1937, 1938 and most of 1939 was that war by his double policy could be avoided altogether. This brings us from the record on material provisionment to the second two charges, relating to the years 1938 and 1939.

The year of Czechoslovakia was that in which he read Professor Temperley's *Foreign Policy of Canning* . . . ("you should never menace unless you are in a position to carry out your threats".) He admitted in September 1938 that this fortified his view "that we should be wrong to allow the most vital decision . . . as to peace or war . . . to pass out of our hands. . . ." He may earlier have been impressed by Mr Strang's Minute written before the fall of Austria also invoking Canning's advice against threats without backing. He was less impressed by the dictum of Sir Edward Grey about diplomacy without backing, quoted in a Cabinet paper,[3] that "the risk of an atttack on the United Kingdom . . . is not one to be settled by diplomacy". Every man tends to draw on his own reading of books, to be selective of his literary food in forming political opinion. I am tempted to wonder what book the Prime Minister had been reading about

[1] Letter to Lord Baldwin, October 17th 1940.   [2] To the author
[3] Memorandum "The Requisite Standard of Air Strength"

the Jacobites in the Court of France that prompted him "largely to discount" the advice from the German Opposition in August 1938 when they warned him that Hitler had made up his mind for military action against Czechoslovakia in late September.[1]

On these narrow reckonings we step into the twilight fields of intelligence, seen only darkly, since many documents are excluded from public scrutiny. It is to be noted that Mr Chamberlain did not offer to circulate these to his Cabinet colleagues at the critical time of his visits to Germany and defends himself for not so doing. His main sources would have been Sir Alexander Cadogan, who as Head of the Foreign Office was also in charge of its Foreign Intelligence Service, Sir Stuart Menzies of M.I.6 and Sir Robert Vansittart, who handled many sources of his own. We know now that Hitler was about three weeks from the climax of his military preparations when he received the signal from Mr Chamberlain that he wished for talks. We do not know on what intelligence Mr Chamberlain made up his mind, other than the Memorandum on Herr von Kleist from Vansittart published in Documents of British Foreign Policy,[2] the Boothby Report and the Henderson dispatches. It is evident from Lord Halifax's descriptions and other personal recollections[3] that there was more than the solitary testimony of Herr von Kleist that showed some cracks in the edifice of the Third Reich. We know of none that described Hitler as both bent on war and sure of absolute support.

The assumption grows among British historians that the British attitude of ultimate caution in 1938 was due to inner knowledge that France was divided and unlikely actively to honour her obligations; that France could not attack in the West and had achieved no kind of aircraft production. Yet this cannot be the sole or even the main explanation. If we recall the Chautemps–Delbos visit to London in November 1937, we find the two French Ministers firm enough about the French pledge to military action in aid of Czechoslovakia "whatever the nature of the aggression". When Daladier and Bonnet visited in April 1938, they were equally affirmative that an Anglo-French Entente would be efficacious. Although

[1] Documents on British Foreign Policy, Third Series, Vol. II, Appendix.
[2] Third Series Vol. II, Appendix.
[3] Kordt and Weizsaecker Memoirs

the timidity of Bonnet later became a byword, had not the ebb of French confidence in the summer of 1938 something to do with the absolute refusal of the British to accept a new commitment, or even to say that in no circumstances would they take action? The assumption by Halifax that the French would welcome a release from their treaty engagement was spoken in advance of any such official French attitude. Furthermore, the Chiefs of Staff report on relative strength of Certain Nations at January 1st 1938 assessed that no European power was able then to conduct a successful offensive war on land. It assessed the French Army as numerically still equal to that of Germany. The position of France in 1938 was not otherwise than it proved to be in 1939, when the French were equally not prepared to do more than hold the Maginot Line, though in 1938 with more prospect of holding it successfully for a longer period. Since British strategy then envisaged in any case a long war, in which a blockade rather than a land offensive against Germany would be decisive, the inference is strong that Austria should have been the storm signal and Czechoslovakia the *casus belli*. The policy of acceleration on deficiencies and expansion of armaments should then have started in December 1937 at latest and not in October 1938 and March 1939. We may have in memory Hore-Belisha's statement to the Cabinet that the Germans at the latter date had acquired the equipment of thirty-eight Czech divisions. There is some weakness evident in Cabinet assessments of the position of Hitler. In the critical days of September 1938, when four British Ministers were seeking to manage the crisis over Czechoslovakia, Mr Chamberlain seems to have assumed that it was possible for Hitler to order an attack on Czechoslovakia at any moment, whereas the German Wehrmacht was working to a fixed timetable. Chamberlain accepted further that the use of British deterrent action, such as mobilisation of the Fleet which had been contemplated in mid August, would not be positive.

The British Ambassador in Berlin advised strenuously against timely warnings, alleging that they could not be delivered, because Hitler had not made up his mind for war—an opinion that differed from that later expressed by his own principal informant. For the definitive view of Sir Ivone Kirkpatrick,

Head of the Embassy Chancery in 1938, as recorded in after years was that Hitler was bent on war in 1938 and was only stopped with difficulty. The likelihood of preventive action by the German Generals, who were then still far from accepting Hitler's authority in military matters, was also discounted at the time, though a remark by the Marquis of Zetland in Cabinet suggests that the attitude of General Ludwig Beck, Chief of the German Army General Staff, may have been known to a few. For Zetland "wondered what sort of regime would exist in Germany after a world war. Might it not be even more dangerous to us than the Nazi Regime?" Lord Halifax, the minutes show, thought of a revolt against Hitler as a possibility but rejected it as something on which to build or alter policy, saying also that criticism afterwards for having failed to stand firmer would leave him entirely unmoved. With the strength of Hitler's internal authority the Cabinet does not appear to have concerned itself, and this subject is also unrecorded in Policy Committee and Inner Cabinet Minutes. The Vansittart Memorandum, the letter of Mr Robert Boothby, M.P., and a remark by Mr Duff Cooper are the sole British allusions to the subject. Sir John Wheeler-Bennett, a respectable authority, in his *Nemesis of Power*, asserts that the British and French Prime Ministers and their Foreign Ministers went thoroughly into the contingency that Hitler might be overthrown in a prolonged confrontation of wills over Czechoslovakia with the Allied powers. In the form of a series of questions, similar to the re- marks of Lord Zetland, he postulates that any German Govern- ment succeeding that of Hitler, including a monarchy, would, according to their reasoning, be hardly less a problem to Britain and France than that of Hitler. Sir John asserts further that "these considerations undoubtedly played a part in the formu- lation of policy in London and Paris".[1] I have been unable to discover either in the Cabinet or Foreign Office papers any memorandum or meeting at which these alternatives were set forth or discussed formally and my conclusion is that the rejection in August 1938 of conspiracy as a factor in the equation was instinctive rather than the product of settled discussion. Instinctive also are the objections enumerated by Lord Zetland and Sir John and seen to be hollow in the light

[1] Sir John Wheeler-Bennett, *Nemesis of Power*

of history. They may also have been secondary considerations; for to have tested the strength of Hitler's authority would have meant embarking into the area of risks which Mr Chamberlain held to be precluded by previous Cabinet decisions not to go to war over Czechoslovakia, not to risk a war occurring and therefore not to prolong the tension—"so I sent the fateful telegram". In his last months and weeks the idea must have infested his mind that he might have acted differently when certain options still remained open, such as not putting the brake on the French, and not discouraging the Czechs from offering resistance. "Never one instant have I doubted the rightness of what I did at Munich. . . . Whatever the outcome it is clear as daylight that, if we had had to fight in 1938, the results would have been far worse".[1]

As to the negotiations with Russia, Keith Feiling seeks to clear Chamberlain of "any trace of an ideological motive",[2] finding no evidence of it in his letters, though one of them seems to me to come near ideology: "I must confess to a profound distrust of Russia . . . and her motives, which seem to have little connection with our ideas of liberty and only concerned with getting everyone else by the ears."[3]

It is also clear that the high Anglican conscience of Lord Halifax made him a bad adviser in the Cabinet when it came to overcoming certain legalistic and moral scruples in getting to terms with Russia. We find him in the critical debate on the Chiefs of Staff plea for a rapid alliance with Russia ranged on the side of those who quibbled and played for time. The imprint of Munich had made him determined to acquiesce no longer to blackmail, a determination which fastened almost equally upon Germany and Russia.

Those were natural sentiments, but it does now seem axiomatic that even a bloodstained ally had the right to stipulate that there should be no separate peace, and to this demand Mr Chamberlain was resistant. It may also be doubted whether Sir Thomas Inskip in his April 1939 interview with the High Commissioners of the Dominions did more than invite opinions on the desirability of a Russian alliance without offering persuasive reasons for it.

Whereas the Prime Minister accepted the advice of the Chiefs

[1] Feiling, 456, 446   [2] *Ibid.*, 407   [3] *Ibid.*, 403

of Staff in 1938 on avoiding the risk of war, and again in April 1939 on the small military value of Russia as an ally, he subsequently resisted their plea that a full alliance with Russia should be quickly concluded to prevent a Russo–German agreement. He did not really believe in this possibility and his advice from Berlin was that such an alliance would drive Hitler to make war immediately.

As a Chairman Neville Chamberlain did not, I find, really share his long-term vision with his Cabinet. He laid the bricks and let others do the pointing. He allowed them to assist in the drafting of a letter, but never threw open the question whether it ought to be sent at all. To the end he seems to have believed in the efficacy of personal letters in diplomacy signed by himself, parallel to Foreign Office notes, the effect of which they often mollified. He never lost his belief in the importance of his personal diplomacy, until it became an obsession to maintain links of an incongruous kind in hopeless conditions for the sake of not losing touch altogether. If these activities belonged to the double policy of playing for time, they were also counter-productive to British influence.

Nowhere do I find Mr Chamberlain as Prime Minister leave a Cabinet meeting with a conclusion different to the proposition which he first tabled in the agenda. His moments of doubt and deliberation were reserved to such places as his Room in the House of Commons, to City friends, or the Informal Meetings of Ministers in 1938. In that period, Cabinet usage was least observed, but in 1939 the issues appeared less acute and the outcome more inevitable and the Cabinet appears to have been more regularly informed and the Foreign Policy Committee more regularly used. The Cabinet papers show that Chamberlain pursued his double policy with singular perseverance, afforded a protective diplomacy at certain vulnerable moments at heavy cost to the balance of power, and was an unconscionable time in rearming.

SELECT BIBLIOGRAPHY

The Cabinet Minutes and Memoranda, 1937–9
The Cadogan Diary (Extracts)
Documents on British Foreign Policy, Second and Third
Series, H.M.S.O.
Documents on German Foreign Policy, 1919–39, H.M.S.O.
Foreign Office Archives, 1937–9
Minutes of the Foreign Policy Committee of the Cabinet and
Memoranda, 1937–9
Papers of the Prime Minister's Office, 1937–9
Records of the Committee of Imperial Defence
The Vansittart Papers

Avon, the Earl of: *Facing the Dictators*, Cassell, 1962
Beck, Colonel Joszef: *Dernier Rapport*, Editions de la Baconière,
1951
Birkenhead, the Earl of: *The Life of Lord Halifax*, Hamish
Hamilton, 1965
Churchill, W. S.: *The Gathering Storm*, Cassell, 1948
Colvin, Ian: *Vansittart in Office*, Gollancz, 1965
Duff Cooper, Alfred, Viscount Norwich: *Old Men Forget*,
Hart-Davis, 1953
The Duff Cooper Diary, unpublished
Feiling, Keith: *The Life of Neville Chamberlain*, Macmillan, 1946
Gilbert, Martin and Gott, Richard: *The Appeasers*, Weidenfeld
and Nicolson, 1963
Harvey, Oliver: *The Diplomatic Diaries of Oliver Harvey*, 1937–40,
Collins, 1970
Halifax, the Earl of: *Fulness of Days*, Collins, 1957
Henderson, Sir Nevile: *Failure of a Mission*, Hodder and
Stoughton, 1940
Hoare, Samuel, Viscount Templewood: *Nine Troubled Years*,
Collins, 1954
The Ironside Diaries, Constable, 1963

Kordt, Erich: *Nicht Aus Den Akten*, Union Deutsch, Stuttgart, 1950

MacLeod, Iain: *Neville Chamberlain*, Muller, 1961

Maisky, Ivan: *Who Helped Hitler?*, Hutchinson, 1964

Margach, James and Swinton, Earl of: *Sixty Years of Power*, Hutchinson, 1968

Minney, R. J.: *The Private Papers of Hore-Belisha*, Collins, 1960

Mosley, Leonard: *On Borrowed Time*, Weidenfeld and Nicolson, 1969

Namier, Sir Lewis: *In the Nazi Era*, Macmillan, 1952

Schacht, Dr H.: *Account Settled*, Weidenfeld and Nicolson, 1949

Simon, Viscount: *Retrospect*, Hutchinson, 1952

Swinton, Earl of: *I Remember*, Hutchinson, 1952

Vansittart, Lord: *The Mist Procession*, Hutchinson, 1958

Memoirs of Ernst von Weizsaecker, Gollancz, 1951

Wheeler-Bennett, Sir John: *Munich, Prologue to Tragedy*, Macmillan, 1948

Wheeler-Bennett, Sir John: *Nemesis of Power*, Macmillan, 1953

Index

France—*cont.*
 invades Czechoslovakia, 149,
  165; and the front against
  German aggression, 193; and
  Poland, 197; proposes tripartite agreement, 204–5; Staff
  talks with U.K., 225; delays
  ultimatum to Germany, 247–8,
  251–2; divided and weak, 268–9
Franco, General Francisco (Spanish
  insurgent leader), 43, 50
Franco-Soviet Pact, 38
French Cameroons, 43
Fritsch, General Baron von (Commander-in-Chief of German
  Army), 91*n.*
Funk, Dr Walther (German Minister
  of Economics), 184

Gafencu, Gregori (Roumanian
  Foreign Minister), 188
Gambia, 42
Gamelin, General (French Com-
  mander-in-Chief), 165
George VI, King, 23, 91, 135, 185,
  241
Germany: colonial restitution issue,
  36–7, 39–40, 42–3, 53–4, 87–8,
  90; declines to deal with
  U.S.S.R., 38; air parity with
  Britain, and *Luftwaffe* strength
  in 1938, 46–7; outside the
  League of Nations, 55; military strength (Jan. 1938), 60–1;
  aircraft production, 69, 119;
  February (1938) crisis, 91,
  93; opposition groups in, 138,
  268; the Generals' plot against
  Hitler, 167; pogrom against
  Jews after Munich, 175; boundary agreements with Czechoslovakia, 175–6; rearmament
  after Munich, 176; anti-Comintern pact with Italy and
  Japan, 180; and Roumania,
  188; aggressive designs on
  Poland, 194–7, 228–9, 237–8;
  proposed secret visit by Goering to London, 234–5; Non-
  Aggression Pact with U.S.S.R.,
  235–8; and the British guarantee to Poland, 238–44; in-

vades Poland, 244–5; ultim-
  atum to, 247–54; peace over-
  tures rebuffed, 254
 See also Austria; Czechoslovakia;
  Hitler
Gestapo, 138
Gibraltar, 221
Goebbels, Dr Josef (German Propa-
  ganda Minister), 51
Goering, Hermann (Reich Marshal,
  C.–in–C. *Luftwaffe*), 50-1, 135,
  153, 184–5, 234–5, 239, 241–4,
  253
Gort, General Lord (C.I.G.S.), 93,
  171, 206, 219, 221
Grandi, Dino (Italian Ambassador
  in London), 264
Greece, 199
Greenwood, Arthur, M.P., 197, 204
Grey, Sir Edward (Foreign Secret-
  ary), 69–70, 267

Hacha, Emil (President of Czechoslovakia), 185
Hailsham, Viscount (Lord President
  of the Council), 108, 111, 140,
  153–4, 157
Halder, General Franz (Chief of
  German Army General Staff),
  167, 248*n.*, 253*n.*
Hale, E., 133
Halifax, Viscount (Lord Privy Seal,
  later Lord President of the
  Council, later Foreign Secretary), 28, 35, 97, 108, 139,
  146–7, 162, 232, 254–5, 262, 268
 alliances, 190–1
 Austria, 94–5, 100–1
 Chamberlain rebuked by H., 185
 conscription, 219
 Czechoslovakia, 109–11, 113–14,
  135, 149–50, 157–9; May crisis,
  129–31; Runciman mission, 134,
  137; question of military intervention, 140–2, 144; H. begins
  to differ from Chamberlain
  after Bad Godesberg rupture,
  163–4; Munich Agreement,
  168, 170–1; Hitler's anger at
  restraints of Munich agreement, 179–81; German protectorate and end of British
  obligation, 186

Poland—*cont.*
against German aggression which includes U.S.S.R., 191–2, 200, 203; desires secret arrangement with U.K., 193–4; German aggressive designs on, 194–7, 228–9, 237–8; defensive alliance with U.K., 197, 202, 227, 236–7, 247; Beck refuses guarantee to Roumania, 199; Danzig question, 228–9, 231–2, 236, 238, 240–1, 244, 251; requests financial assistance, but denied, 231–3; refuses U.S.S.R. right of military passage, 235–6; Anglo-German negotiations, 234–44; invaded, 244; requests fulfilment of British pledge, 250; lack of support for, 258–9
Portugal, 192
Pound sterling. *See* Currency depletion
Prague, German entry into, 184–5, 189

Racyksnki, Count Edward (Polish Ambassador in London), 242, 245
Reichenau, General von, 128
Rhineland, German entry into, 19–20, 23
Ribbentrop, Joachim von (German Foreign Minister), 17, 37, 89–90, 91, 93, 101, 103–5, 129, 136, 148–9, 152, 184–5, 235, 248, 253–4
Roosevelt, F. D., 72, 243; rebuffed by Chamberlain; letter to Chamberlain on outbreak of war, and the reply, 255–9
Roumania, 194*n.*, 195, 214–15, German pressure on, 188; objects to front against German aggression, 192; Poland refuses guarantee to, 199; British guarantee to, 199, 202
Royal Air Force, 23, 32, 73, 175. *See also* Air Ministry
Royal Navy, 138, 149, 259
Runciman, Walter (later Viscount Runciman; President of the Board of Trade; later Lord

President of the Council), 32–3, 148, 153, 223, 261; mission to Czechoslovakia, 134*n.*, 137, 142, 149, 189; and the ultimatum to Germany, 247

St Germain, Treaty of, 100
Sargent, Sir Orme (Assistant Under-Secretary of State in the Foreign Office), 60, 92, 98–101
Sassoon, Sir Philip (Minister of Works), 17
Savage, M. J. (Prime Minister of New Zealand), 44
Schacht, Dr Hjalmar (President of Reichsbank), 28, 39–40, 51, 180
Schmidt, Dr Guido (Austrian Under-Secretary for Foreign Affairs), 94, 95*n.*
Schmidt, Dr Paul (German Foreign Ministry interpreter), 102, 154–5, 253
Schuschnigg, Dr Kurt von (Chancellor of Austria), 54, 56, 93*n.*, 94, 98, 100, 102, 104–5
Schwerin-Krosigk, Count von (German Finance Minister), 180
Seeds, Sir William (British Ambassador in Moscow), 199, 208, 210, 226
Seyss-Inquart, Dr (Austrian Minister of the Interior), 94
Shadow Factories, 116
Shipping, 247
Simon, Sir John (Home Secretary, later Chancellor of the Exchequer), 32, 35, 38, 46, 108, 146, 162, 191, 207, 211, 216, 241–2, 254, 266
Control of Expenditure memorandum, 222–3
currency depletion, 178–9, 236
Czechoslovakia, 110, 154; S. meets Daladier and Gamelin, 165; Munich Agreement, 169–70; question of guarantee after Munich, 171
foreign credits, 227
France, 121–2
Germany, 38, 131–2; colonial restitution, 87; ultimatum to, 252–3
Lanark speech, 139–40